Mine Enemy

Mine Enemy

Amalia and Aharon Barnea

Translated from the Hebrew
by
Chaya Amir

GROVE PRESS
New York

Copyright © 1986 by Amalia Argaman and Aharon Barnea
Original Hebrew edition published by Edanim Publishers, Ltd.
Translation © 1988 by Grove Press, a division of Wheatland Corporation

Published by Grove Press
a division of Wheatland Corporation
841 Broadway
New York, N.Y. 10003

Library of Congress Cataloging-in-Publication Data

Barnea, Amalia, 1950–
    Mine enemy.

    Translation of: La-lekhet shevi.
    1. Ta'mari, Salah, 1942–   .   2. Palestinian
Arabs—Biography.   3. Jewish-Arab relations—1973–   .
4. Lebanon—History—Israeli intervention, 1982–   —.
Biography.   I. Barnea, A. (Aharon)   II. Title.
DS119.7.B27813   1988   956.92'044'0924   88–6957
ISBN 0-8021-1006-1

Manufactured in the United States of America

Designed by Irving Perkins Associates

First Edition 1988
        10   9   8   7   6   5   4   3   2   1

To our children

Contents

Preface

The birth of this book was accompanied by difficulties and a great deal of soul-searching. We knew that a book written by two Israelis about a Palestinian who is a prominent member of the PLO (Palestinian Liberation Organization)would not be readily accepted, and might even inspire opposition. Up to the last moment, we were plagued by doubts and hesitations. But this book, one that raises many questions and provides far fewer answers, has turned out to be a true best seller in Israel, among readers both of its Hebrew and, more recently, Arabic editions.

This book is not an account of a political confrontation. It is a story of a personal, human encounter. We try to describe not only events and facts but also to convey the sense of this experience: a story of personal contact which takes place on the narrow fringe of sanity that still exists at the edge of hatred and violence. It is neither objective nor balanced, and does not mean to be. The story of Salah Ta'mari is the story of a Palestinian who does not fit the commonly perceived image of a PLO member. In many cases we made it possible for Ta'mari to speak for himself and shatter this negative stereotype.

The facts presented in this book were derived from a variety of sources. Everything described by Ta'mari regarding his relationships with various Israeli authorities while he was a prisoner of war was independently verified. But as far as Ta'mari's relationship with us is concerned, we tried to be faithful only to our own feelings, even if those were sometimes contradictory.

In some parts of the book the unknown is greater than what is revealed. Due to various restraints, particularly those imposed by the Israeli military censorship, we were compelled to change the names of certain people and places and to camouflage certain events. Some other events have not been included at all out of concern for the safety and security of the individuals involved. We hope the day will come when this danger will disappear and these untold stories can be told.

The book, the fruit of our joint labors, is written as though it is told by Aharon, except for the epilogue, which is Amalia's. Salah Ta'mari and Dina Abd el-Hamid helped as much as they could to fill the gaps in our knowledge, doing so with great open-mindedness and friendship. Without their assistance we could not have embarked upon this venture. Nevertheless, everything in these pages is solely our responsibility.

Many other people deserve our gratitude. First and foremost among them is Amalia's father, the writer Menahem Barash-Roi; Edanim Publishers, which first published the book in Hebrew; and the staff at Grove Press in New York. A long list of close friends assisted and encouraged us, read the manuscript, offered their comments, and helped with friendly advice. Each one of them knows his part and his contribution. To all of them our thanks.

Finally, we hope and pray that our two children, Reyout and Or, grow up in peace, not war, surrounded by love, not hatred.

AMALIA (ARGAMAN) AND AHARON BARNEA
1988

Mine Enemy

1

"If there is a next time . . ."

"Listen, Areleh, I've got a story for you."

The spokesman for the IDF (Israel Defense Forces) was at the other end of the line. I pricked up my ears.

"We've got the commander of the RPG [rocket-propelled grenade] kids. Want to interview him?"

"What's his story?"

"Well, for one, he gave himself up in Sidon."

"And . . .?" I wanted a little more substance.

"He's willing to talk to the media."

I thought that over for a minute. "Will it keep for a couple of days?" I asked. "I'm really swamped here."

Major Danny laughed. "Sure. He's not going anywhere for a while."

The call had reached me at the studios of the Israel Broadcasting Authority, where I worked as the correspondent for Arab affairs. It was more than two weeks into the war in Lebanon and the IDF had thrown up a thick smokescreen around everything. We were dependent for news on the Arab stations, on foreign broadcasts, and on the grapevine, and I had practically bunked down at the studios for the duration. I had to cull the news, verify it, translate it into Hebrew, and then prepare my newscasts— and we were running them twenty-four hours a day. Time was the one thing I had very little of.

And to tell the truth the story itself wasn't that tantalizing. First of all, Sidon was almost ancient history. The IDF had entered Lebanon on June 6, 1982, with the declared aim of making war for peace, in "Operation Peace for Galilee": pushing the enemy back to the environs of Sidon, twenty-five miles to the north, in order to put the Galilee settlements out of the range of artillery fire. Now, two weeks later, the IDF was already in East Beirut, almost fifty miles to the north. Sidon had fallen eight days after the fighting began and the Israeli public was split down the middle in an unprecedented and highly vociferous controversy for and against the extended war.

So much for Sidon. As for the RPG kids—named after their weapons, the only ones the Fatah manufactured by itself—they were already old hat and I, personally, had had my fill of PLO (Palestinian Liberation Organization) prisoners. They all told you the same story—each with his own brand of excuses. When faced with a microphone, they didn't know what national pride was and usually ended their "interviews" by calling down the wrath of God on their leaders.

I had had my first taste of this brand of "terrorist," as we had begun to call them then, in an interview some fifteen years before, right after the Six Day War. The interview took place at the police station in Hebron where the Israeli Military Administration had set up headquarters. The prisoner was brought to me in a dingy little room. He was a man of about thirty and shaking like a leaf. I thought I'd calm him down with a cigarette but his nervousness was so intense he could hardly smoke. "*Shukran, shukran,*" he kept repeating—thank you, thank you. The situation made me extremely uncomfortable. As far as he was concerned I represented absolute power. For the first time I realized what it must mean to be in the position of an utterly helpless prisoner. I kept telling myself that he was nothing but a lousy little killer and there was no reason for *me* to feel upset. But throughout his litany, I remained in acute distress. He said he was only a poor guy earning ten dinars a month. Two weeks before, a man by the name of Abu Ali had offered him two hundred fifty dinars to explode two grenades. He knew it was wrong but how could he refuse, he had a wife and four children, etc. etc. etc. Finally, he was ready to tell the whole world just where this Abu Ali was hiding. If this was an example of the Palestinian freedom fighter, I figured we didn't have too much to worry about.

He never saw his money, of course, and got twelve years for his troubles.

Abu Ali, head of the Fatah in the Hebron and Gaza area, was caught a few days later and sentenced to eighteen years. As a result, for me at least, PLO prisoners were hardly the stuff that scoops were made of.

Yet Major Danny had succeeded in arousing my interest on one point: the man was willing to talk to the media and this in itself distinguished him from the common run of PLO prisoners. They had always been panic-stricken at the idea of an interview. Still, my time at the moment was not my own. I made a mental note to check on the story as soon as the pressure let up.

That letup materialized about a week later. Philip Habib came to Beirut to mediate an agreement on the evacuation of the PLO and took center stage. I called Major Danny and asked him if the interview he had promised could be arranged for that afternoon. He assured me that there was no problem and that if I got to the prison by four, the section warden would be waiting for me. I called my wife and told her she could expect me home early for dinner. She was somewhat skeptical. I had been less than a model husband and father during those weeks.

"Don't tell me you're finished for the day?" she asked. It was about one o'clock.

"Practically," I answered. "Nothing but the one o'clock news magazine, a meeting with a BBC correspondent, and a short interview with a PLO prisoner."

Amalia, herself a reporter, remained skeptical. "I won't plan a soufflé," she joked.

As it turned out, she could have skipped the whole dinner.

I drove up to the gates of the military prison, going over what the army spokesman had told me. In fact, I had only two starters: one, the man had turned himself in and two, he was willing to talk to the media. Ah, yes. He was the commander of the RPG kids. Demerit. How can you send twelve-year-old kids to their deaths, shouldering weapons that were bigger than they were?

The section warden was waiting for me in his office. He introduced himself as Zuri Ben-Nun. He was a redhead, about forty, heavyset and orthodox. His crocheted skullcap marked him as belonging to the more westernized generation of observant Jews, while the exposed fringes hanging out from under his shirt emphasized the militancy of his religious-nationalist beliefs. If these were not sufficient evidence of his spiritual leanings, there was a parchment hanging over his desk engraved with a line from Psalms 3:8: "For thou dost smite all my enemies on the cheek."

He pointed me into a comfortable chair and buzzed for one of the guards. "Bring in 129," he told him. Then he picked up the phone and ordered some light refreshments. Meanwhile, I took out my tape recorder and put it on the floor.

A few minutes later the guard came in with the prisoner. No. 129 was tall, badly dressed, and unshaven. He kept blinking as if the lights were too strong for him. I stood up. That was *de rigueur* in the Arab code of good manners. Ben-Nun introduced us in Arabic: "Mr. Barnea, from Israel Radio—Salah Ta'mari."

"Aharon," I added, and gave him my hand. Ta'mari took it in a rather perfunctory manner. He didn't look at me. His eyes were busy examining the room.

Ben-Nun left with the guard. "He's all yours," he said before closing the door. "For as long as you like."

I took a hard look at Ta'mari. He was a handsome man, well built, with light skin, green eyes, and dark brown hair. His eyes were red—from lack of sleep, no doubt—and they darted restlessly around the room. I indicated the second chair: "*Tfadal* [please]." He sat down. There was a low coffee table between us.

Suddenly, an involuntary twitch crossed his face and he began to rub his wrists. Apparently the handcuffs had just been removed. He still hadn't looked directly at me.

"Still hurts?" I asked in Arabic, in the Palestinian dialect I was used to.

"A little," he answered, somewhat dryly. "But there are things that hurt even more."

I sat back prepared to hear him out—bad treatment, bad food, humiliation. I'd heard it all before. "Such as?"

A note of anger crept into his voice: "Such as the way you treat your prisoners-of-war. I thought you Jews would be a little more sensitive—after all you'd been through in the holocaust."

This was the last thing I had expected and I reacted with some heat: "Prisoners-of-war!! What army are you in? Regular armies aren't supposed to kill civilians indiscriminately—children, women, athletes—like you people do."

He took a deep breath and then let go with: "When it comes to indiscriminate killing, your pilots don't do such a bad job either! A couple of napalm bombs dropped on a refugee camp hit pretty randomly, don't you think? But of course, the murders you commit are sacred. You Jews have a monopoly on justice!"

In the course of two minutes, he had succeeded in putting me on the defensive. All tensed up, I didn't reply. I hadn't come here to get into a futile shouting match over the rights and wrongs of the Middle East conflict. Forcing myself back into a more comfortable position, I began to fish around in my pocket for a pack of cigarettes.

"Want to smoke?" I offered him my pack of Time.

He took a cigarette and rolled it between his fingers.

"Jewish-made, right?" He had switched to English and loaded the three words with contempt. Then he flicked the cigarette onto the table. "You know what? Next time—if there is a next time—I would rather have you bring me Marlboros, if you don't mind." For the first time, he looked me straight in the eye.

I couldn't contain my surprise. First of all, his unexpected switch to English—and to a fluent English at that—caught me unawares. But, even more, I was struck, and annoyed, by his arrogance. I retorted immediately: "What makes you think I might come again?" Then I added: "And what makes you think I speak English?"

He answered promptly: "You look intelligent, like all of you chosen people, so I assumed you must know English." Without waiting for any comment, he continued: "Whether or not you'll come again, I really have no way of knowing. I just have a hunch that you will."

He was really getting my goat with his "prisoners-of-war," "holocaust," "chosen people," and now his "hunch." What exactly was he after, I wondered, and as I asked myself the question, I realized that whether I liked it or not he had succeeded in arousing my curiosity. I wanted to know more about him. Where had he gotten his good English? Where had he picked up his aristocratic manner? What was at the back of his "Jewish" barbs? Why did I suddenly feel a grudging respect for him?

He was watching me closely now and I had the feeling that he saw himself as a boxer who had taken the first round on points. Okay, I said to myself, keeping score—but remember, it's only the first round.

Aloud, I simply changed the subject. "Sorry I don't have a pack of Marlboros, but these Israeli cigarettes aren't bad. Try one."

He leaned across the table and picked up the cigarette. I lit it for him and he inhaled deeply. For all his arrogance, I could see that he was dying to smoke. But he didn't indulge himself for long. Instead, he began to ask *me* questions.

"How can I be sure you're from the radio?"

I pointed to the tape machine on the floor.

He wasn't satisfied.

I pulled out my membership card in the journalists' union and offered it to him. "I assume you can read English." I tried to inject a little sarcasm into my voice but he seemed to ignore it. He just examined the card and returned it to me.

"Ask away," he said. "I'll answer all your questions."

"I'm sure you have a stock answer for every question," I said, trying sarcasm again to regain my advantage.

But if it worked, I'll never know. At that moment there was a knock on the door and one of the guards came in with a tray and put it on the table. On it was a pot of coffee, cups and saucers, a plate of cookies, and two Cokes.

As the guard walked out, Ta'mari called after him in Hebrew, "*Toda* [thanks]."

"I see you know Hebrew too," I said.

"I picked some up from the guards," he said, and proceeded to demonstrate: " 'thank you,' 'good morning,' 'good night,' 'cigarette.' "

I poured the coffee and pushed one of the cups over to him.

"No thanks," he said, "I'd rather have a Coke."

We drank in silence and then I said: "Before I tape you, I want to ask you a couple of questions. That's what I usually do in interviews." This was generally true. Except at the moment it wasn't the whole truth. I simply wanted to know more about Salah Ta'mari than was necessary for any interview. I wanted to know more than I was prepared to admit even to myself.

"You've been introduced to me as Salah Ta'mari. What's your full name?" I was speaking Arabic again. An Arab name is customarily composed of a first name, the father's name, the grandfather's name, and the family name.

"Salah Ta'mari has been my full name ever since I joined the Fatah."

"You mean it's your underground alias?"

"No," he said emphatically, "it's not an underground alias and the Fatah isn't an underground. The Fatah is the Palestinian liberation movement— the Zionist movement of the Palestinians."

I made up my mind to ignore his provocations.

"Let's drop the comparisons," I said. "People in your organization have assumed names—like Abu Amar, or Abu Jihad. What Abu are you?"

"I'm no Abu at all," he insisted, "just Salah Ta'mari."

"You're from the Bethlehem area, aren't you?" I pulled out my first rabbit.

"I'm not from the Bethlehem *area,* I'm from *Bethlehem.* How'd you guess?" His surprise was evident.

"Well, I belong to the chosen people, so I should know."

He smiled and then laughed. The ice was broken and he conceded the second round.

"Really, how did you know?" He didn't try to conceal his curiosity.

The fact is that I wasn't absolutely sure that he was from Bethlehem. What I did know was that there was a Bedouin tribe called Ta'mara which had settled in the vicinity of Bethlehem and I guessed that that was where he took his name from. But I had also noticed distinct Bedouin phonemes in his Arabic pronunciation, such as the hard "g" in place of the "q" sound. During graduate studies at the University of California at Berkeley, I majored in linguistics, in the dialects of spoken Arabic. (My dissertation was "A Socio-Linguistic Analysis of the Spoken Dialect of the City of Gaza" and I had spent half a year there doing my field research.)

In any case, I told him what I knew of the Ta'mara tribe and he followed my remarks with more than polite interest. Then he reached out for another cigarette and lit it himself. This act was not in keeping with formal Arab host-guest behavior, which is highly coded. It was, rather, the careless gesture of a man completely at ease. Something perceptible had changed in our relationship.

I returned to my question about his real name. It hadn't escaped me that he insisted on calling the Fatah a "movement" and not an "organization." Most of the Palestinian prisoners I had encountered used the word *munazama,* which connotes the military or operative aspect of "organization." The full name of the Fatah is Harakat Tahrir Falastin, the Movement for the Liberation of Palestine, and Ta'mari's insistence on calling it a movement indicated that he laid greater stress on the ideology behind it.

"My real name is As'ad Suleiman Hasan," he said, satisfying the Arabist in me.

"And where did you pick up such good English?"

"My English isn't really that good. My wife's English is better."

"So, where . . .?" I didn't pursue the reference to his wife.

"I studied English at the university in Cairo."

"Cairo University?" I asked. "Or Ein Shams?" Rabbit Number Two.

He raised an eyebrow. "I see you also know Cairo."

"Yeah. I lived there for almost a year, three years ago. I was the press attaché at the Israeli embassy." Without giving it too much thought, I noticed that I was letting him interview me as well. I got back on track. "What did you study?"

"I got my M.A. in English literature, on T. S. Eliot."

We were soon involved, in English again, in a discussion of Eliot's poetry. We had stopped fencing and were just talking now. Since my familiarity with English poetry in general and Eliot in particular was limited, he did most of the talking and I did most of the listening. I noticed that whenever I asked a question, he would answer in a slightly didactic manner. I wondered if he had been a teacher.

Every now and then I caught myself thinking in some remote, strangely detached corner of my mind that this interview could provide a terrific headline for a story: "PLO Terrorist Gives Zionist Enemy Insights into Eliot's Imagery." And I began to wonder why I required the labels. My defense mechanisms were, apparently, hard at work against my natural sympathies. Goddamn it! I could really get to like this guy!

I decided to steer the interview back to more conventional lines. "How old are you?" I asked.

"Forty," he answered; "that is, I'll be forty in October."

"That makes us practically the same age." I found myself giving him information again. I was, in fact, two years younger. "When did you study in Cairo?"

"In 1962."

"And when did you join the Fatah?"

"Eighteen years ago, when I was still a student."

"In Cairo?"

"Yeah, in 1965 I became active, with all the others. It was the beginning of the movement."

Suddenly these bits of information integrated into a significant frame: it dawned on me that the man sitting opposite me joined the Fatah together with Yasir Arafat (Abu Amar), Khalil el-Wazir (Abu Jihad), Salah Khalaf (Abu Ayyad), and Farouk Kadoumi (Abu Loutuf), the founders of the

Fatah and its leaders today. He was, it appeared, a member of that group—although he was about ten years younger than the others.

In other words, Salah Ta'mari belonged to the Fatah leadership, and if so, he was the seniormost Fatah member ever to have fallen into Israeli hands. Why had I wasted time on T. S. Eliot? My subject was Arab affairs, particularly Palestinian affairs. I was a journalist by profession and here was my golden opportunity—information from a reliable inside source. I took another long, hard look at Salah Ta'mari. I had to make a new assessment. But I was distracted again for a moment. He hadn't yet touched his coffee. Maybe he was afraid there was something in it.

The recorder was still on the floor, in its case. I'd get around to that too, in due time. Now I wanted to concentrate on the man in front of me.

"What did you do after you finished your studies?"

"Well, I wanted to go back to Bethlehem. I wanted to be an English teacher. But it was 1967 and I couldn't go back. You people had already occupied the West Bank."

At this point, I didn't have to ask specific questions. Ta'mari began relating the story of those years in a logically articulated narrative.

Instead of returning home he went to Jordan, to the Jordanian side of the Jordan Valley, to be precise. At that time, the end of 1967, the beginning of 1968, Palestinian activists were concentrated in that area. It was from there that they crossed the river for their raids into the occupied territories.

"The central command was in Karameh," he continued, "and . . ."

"Karameh?" I blurted out. A tiny explosion had gone off in my head. "What were you doing on March 21, 1968?" I asked. That was the day of the battle of Karameh, which is indelibly inscribed in the history of the Fatah. After a series of incidents perpetrated by the Fatah against Israeli targets, Israel decided to take retaliatory action against Fatah bases in the Jordan Valley, first and foremost Karameh. The PLO had received intelligence about the impending attack, but decided that instead of retreating in the face of the superior army, they would remain and fight.

He didn't follow my train of thought and just shrugged. "What do you mean? I was the commander of the Fatah in Karameh."

"You were the commander in Karameh? Oh my God!" I hit my forehead with my hand.

Ta'mari watched me for a minute without saying anything. Then he

11

leaned back and half closed his eyes, turning something over in his mind. When he finally surfaced, it was to say softly: "Goddamn it, in the back of my mind I remember your bloody voice."

On March 21, 1968, I was covering the Israeli attack on Karameh for the radio. Right after we entered the village, one of the officers came over to me and said: "You speak Arabic, right? Look, we want you to help us." He handed me a microphone and told me to climb on top of the jeep. He gave me a list of all the Fatah people in Karameh. I was to read off the names, one by one, tell them to lay down their arms and walk to the schoolyard. It was IDF policy to try and forestall unnecessary bloodshed on both sides by offering the Fatah their lives in return for surrender.

The first name on the list was Salah. I now remembered what was written there: "Salah, commander (of Bedouin origin)." Only the first name. But next to the name was a description of his house and a note to the effect that he liked animals and kept chickens.

That day I must have read out that list dozens of times, maybe a hundred. And each time I started with "Salah." A lot of people on the list eventually came out, their hands raised over their heads. Salah never materialized. Toward evening we left Karameh with our prisoners, our dead, and our wounded.

Now, Salah and I looked at each other in disbelief. My "bloody voice" had called out his name all day long fourteen years ago. I wondered how he had survived, because in the end we had blown up the entire village.

"I spent the whole day running around from one position to another, dodging bullets and artillery fire. When I saw your tanks closing in, I took shelter in one of the houses. Then I realized that your sappers were mining all the houses. I just sat under a table and hoped for the best. Sure enough, the blast went off and the whole house went flying. That was about 5:30 in the afternoon. Your people finished off the village in about an hour and left. Believe it or not, I survived—without a scratch."

The interview had taken a strange turn. Our "previous meeting" added a new dimension to our relationship. We were "war buddies" now. Well, not quite, but almost. In any case, Salah Ta'mari took his first gulp of by-now lukewarm coffee. Whatever suspicions he might have had were gone.

He continued the narrative, filling in details of his work in the Fatah, his stay in Jordan, his move to Lebanon. He gave me a precise account of everything that had happened to him between the outbreak of the war and his surrender to the Israelis. In retrospect he gave me the material for much of this book, but at the time, in the office of the section warden, I wasn't thinking about books. I had forgotten the tape recorder. I had forgotten what time it was. All I knew was that the man had captivated me and I hung on his every word.

Ta'mari was entirely unpredictable. Not only was he open-minded and generally knowledgeable but he was particularly well informed on Jewish subjects—Jewish history, Zionist history, the holocaust, the State of Israel. I noticed that he referred to the 1973 war not as the "October War"—as most Arabs do—but as the "Yom Kippur War," and he knew the significance of the holiday. "You should've seen my library in Sidon," he said at one point. "I had every book on Jewish history that came out in English."

Ta'mari spoke but he wanted to listen, too. I found myself offering him information about various periods in my life. He was fascinated by my knowledge of Arabic and Palestinian history, just as I was fascinated by his knowledge of the "Jewish problem." He couldn't compliment me enough on my mastery of Arabic. "Where did you get such good Arabic?" he kept asking.

"You know," I said, "Anwar Sadat once asked me the same question."

At the time of Sadat's first visit to Jerusalem and his speech in the Knesset, my life was progressing along two parallel tracks: I was broadcasting and editing the news magazines for Israel Radio, and I was completing my academic studies in Arabic, Arab culture, and the history of the Middle East. When I returned from the United States in 1976, after completing my formal studies, I had been offered the post of lecturer in Arabic by Tel Aviv University. I just might have turned fully to an academic career. But Sadat's first visit to Jerusalem and his speech in the Knesset changed not only the history of Israeli-Egyptian relations, they changed my whole life. The hope of peace with an Arab country seemed to open possibilities for me that made any cloistered university career look dull by comparison.

I covered Sadat's visit and every subsequent event connected with the peace process. Whatever I knew as a student of Arabic and Arab history, I planned to apply exclusively to my work as a journalist. And I had the opportunity to do so as press attaché in Cairo and as the radio correspondent for Arab affairs.

In 1979 Sadat paid a short visit to Haifa to meet with Prime Minister Menahem Begin. After their meeting, Sadat held a press conference in the garden of the Dan Hotel. We were sitting in lawn chairs in a semicircle around Sadat, plying him with questions. I asked my questions in Arabic. Sadat was relaxed the whole time, puffing away on his pipe. When it was over, we approached him one by one to thank him and say goodbye.

As I extended my hand, Sadat took his beloved pipe out of his mouth and asked me: "*Siyadtak bititkalam arabi kwayes awi—min feyn?* [The gentleman speaks Arabic very well—how come?]"

"Mr. President," I answered, "there are two explanations." Sadat was interested.

"First of all," I said, as seriously as possible, "my father comes from Poland." Sadat chuckled. "But the second reason is because . . ."—and now I paused for dramatic effect—"my mother also comes from Poland." Sadat burst out laughing.

Ta'mari was in stitches when I told him the story. Had anyone been eavesdropping on this "interview," he would have been convinced that we were two schoolmates who hadn't seen each other for twenty years and were now making up for lost time. I don't mean to imply that by now we were in agreement on anything—we were still on opposite sides of an abyss, politically and ideologically. He was still a prisoner and I a representative of his jailer. He was a Palestinian, I an Israeli. There was no way of getting around that.

I could not forget for a moment that he was a senior officer in the Fatah and a member of the PLO, an organization—or movement—most of whose members not only refused to recognize the right of Israel to exist but who wanted to wipe us off the face of the earth. For many Israelis, the PLO was Public Enemy Number One, the incarnation of all evil.

Nor had I changed for Ta'mari. I was from the Israeli-Zionist establishment, of which Israel Radio was a propaganda tool. I was part of the occupying power that prevented him from returning home. We remained on opposite sides of the battlefield and all the mutual sympathy that had been generated that afternoon, all the "chemistry," couldn't change this.

Nonetheless, the natural rapport between us enabled us to joke, to discuss certain issues openly and even with a certain objectivity. I was particularly interested in hearing his views on terrorism. This was, for me, perhaps the most crucial issue of all.

Ta'mari tried to place his views on the issue in what he considered a proper perspective.

"I'm neither a psychologist nor a psychiatrist," he began, "but fundamentally I don't believe that anyone really likes to kill—unless of course he is mentally ill. And the mentally ill are usually a small percentage in any society, not a category you can refer to as a distinct class or sector of public. You can't judge a resistance movement by the acts of terror perpetrated by a small group."

I believed him and I believed that he himself had never killed gratuitously. From his stories I was able to gather that he had even endangered himself to save human life. There was an incident in which he prevented an enraged mob of Palestinians—and the civil war in Lebanon had given the Palestinians good reason for rage—from slaughtering eighty Christians who had taken refuge in a church in Damour.

At seven o'clock I chanced to look at my watch (the intuition of a newshound) and was appalled. I had spent three hours with Salah Ta'mari without having taped a single word. Moreover, I hadn't heard the news since noon. Who knows what had happened meanwhile, in Beirut, in the war, in the world. I pulled out a small transistor radio and turned on Kol Yisrael. "It is reported from Beirut," went the opening headline, "that the American mediator, Philip Habib, now in Damascus, is about to wind up details of the PLO evacuation from Beirut." The second headline was "The IDF continued to bomb terrorist positions in West Beirut all afternoon."

I automatically switched to Radio Monte Carlo. It was a common enough occupational instinct but I also wanted Ta'mari to hear the news. We listened in silence. When the news was over I asked him what he would do now if he were Arafat.

"I don't know what the exact situation is in West Beirut," he answered, "but I suppose I would try to reach an agreement which would allow our men to leave Beirut—but on one condition: without humiliating them as soldiers."

It was time to tape the interview—if I wanted to get home that night. Ta'mari indicated that he was ready. I cleared off the table and put the recorder in the middle. I began with a few questions about his childhood and youth, his studies, joining the Fatah, and what he had done in 1967. Then I asked: "What did it mean to be a member of the Fatah then and now?"

"It meant and still means to believe in the principles of the Fatah, to give up any personal ambitions you might have and devote yourself exclusively to the Palestinian people."

15

"What have been your particular fields of activity since 1967?"

"For a while I was military commander in Karameh. Afterward I was a 'commissar' in a military unit. I was also in charge of certain educational activities within the Fatah. I guess I'm a jack-of-all-trades."

"What's your rank?"

"Lieutenant Colonel."

"Do officers advance in the Fatah from one rank to the next as in most armies?"

"Sure, but I don't think rank is all that important. Sometimes I think my rank was forced on me. War may or may not be an art, but if it is, it's . . . it's the poorest of all the arts. So I really can't get excited about having a high rank."

"Do you wear a uniform with your rank on it?"

"No, never. I never did, not even in the best of times. I just don't like the idea of rank."

"But there are people who do, aren't there?"

"Of course there are and they have a perfect right to do so."

"How would you rank yourself in the Fatah leadership?"

"I report directly to Abu Amar [Arafat]."

"You get your orders from him directly too?"

"For the most part." For the first time, he hesitated. "In fact, though, I usually take my own initiatives. . . ." Again he paused. "But he's my boss, he's my leader."

"I want to understand," I persisted. "If you want to take an initiative, do you have to get authorization first?"

"Sometimes I get authorization after the fact." He was smiling. "Sometimes in the middle."

"There's always a direct line between you and Arafat? There's no intermediary—like Abu Jihad, for instance, the head of the military arm of the Fatah?"

Ta'mari answered diplomatically: "I was appointed to my last job by Abu Amar. I reported to him—down to the smallest details. And that was fine with me."

"What was your last job?"

"I was commander of the Fatah youth organization and a member of the executive committee of the Fatah in Lebanon. I also went on a few missions abroad—lecturing, making speeches, holding seminars, and the like."

"What do you mean by 'abroad'?"

"Abroad is abroad, all over the world. Wherever my passport could take me."

"Why did you give yourself up?"

Ta'mari hesitated again, weighing his words carefully. "For a number of reasons," he began. "First of all, one particular stage in developments had been brought to an end—by the so-called Operation Peace for Galilee. There were new realities—and one more dead man, Palestinian or Israeli, was not going to make any difference. On the contrary, it would just have made one more family miserable. A new situation forces you to take a new look at things. Secondly, I didn't want to become a burden on the people who were hiding me, who had turned their kids into lookouts to alert me every time an Israeli patrol approached. They never told me outright that they were scared but I could feel it."

"Before we began to tape this interview we talked, and you told me about what you did in Al-Jiyya and in Damour—with regard to the Christian community. Would you like to give us some details?"

"I hope you'll excuse me but I have no intention of repeating those stories. If I did something, I did it out of conviction, out of the principles that I acquired in the Fatah. I just did my duty or what I thought was my duty. The people there can talk about it, if they like. I'd prefer to skip it."

"Okay, but at least say something general on the subject."

"Well, in general I think that war is ugly and inhuman—even if you believe you're fighting for a good cause. And it's particularly cruel for people who enjoy life, who would prefer peace but who find themselves pinned in on all sides. I don't enjoy war and I think that there is a nobility in trying to lessen the suffering of ordinary people. It doesn't sound realistic. Maybe it's crazy: the laws of war are probably diametrically opposed to the laws of human life. Sometimes you are forced to screw up a whole operation in order to save a wounded man or a child or a woman, and then get into a fight with your own people whether or not it's worth it. Still, that's what I believe. War could be less ugly if we all stuck to a more generous, more noble moral code. In any event, I've tried to live by some such code. Whether or not I succeeded it's hard to know, but the fact that I tried gives me some satisfaction."

He spoke with conviction. But now the questions were going to get harder. "Do you think that the murder of the athletes in Munich, the murder of the children in Ma'alot, or the blasting of the Savoy Hotel in Tel

17

Aviv by members of an organization of which you are a proud member are compatible with the 'generous and noble moral code' of which you spoke?"

Ta'mari fidgeted a little in the chair.

"You don't have to answer that if you don't want to," I said.

"I'll answer. There's no question that I won't answer. There's no question that I'm ashamed to answer. Everything has an explanation and it also depends on who does the asking—and why, and if he really wants to hear my answers or whether he likes the answers he already has."

"The microphone is yours," I said.

"Basically, as I told you before, wanton killing is despicable. Killing innocent men, women, and children is monstrous. So why don't we condemn people according to the scale on which they carry out their murders—that is, according to the number of people they kill. Children were also killed in the school in Bahr el-Bakr in Egypt, in the raid on Deir Yassin, in Beirut. In Beirut I saw them torn to shreds by shrapnel. So why don't we begin by condemning *all* these acts and, at the same time, condemn the injustice which generated them.

"You know, people react to injustice differently, according to their psychological makeup. If you slap me, I might just slap you back—then we'd be even. But maybe I'd kill you. Maybe I'd just burst out crying. Maybe I'd run for my life. Maybe I would just ask you why you did it. There are Palestinians—just like there are Jews—who try to rationalize retaliation or revenge. There are others who attempt to find a more original answer to the challenge. You can find young Palestinians who answer fire with fire—that's retaliation, revenge. I, personally, think that the pilot, the king of the skies, who dropped the bomb on the school, killing all the kids inside, deserves harsher condemnation than the frightened and frustrated young man you call a 'terrorist.'

"The fact that you are exceptionally competent propagandists doesn't mean you're right. Even if you can paint every ugly act in rose colors, it still doesn't change the facts. We didn't carry out the raid on Deir Yassin, we were its victims. At Bahr el-Bakr, we were the victims. In Beirut, we were the victims."

"Didn't you ever ask yourself why?" I cut in.

"Naturally. I'm always asking why. I have no home. The Israelis want to destroy my existence as a Palestinian. I can't think of any other reason. That's my explanation for terrorism, whether you agree or not.

"Maybe it's the old story of the white man and the Indian. When the

18

white man is killed, it's blamed on the fact that the Indian is primitive and naturally cruel. When the Indian is killed, it's because the white man is brave. That's the way it is with us. You can bomb schools without suffering any guilt feelings. But we're the scum of the earth because some of our young people commit atrocious crimes. That's not what I'd call a fair or objective view."

"You told me before," I said, moving to another subject, "that if you were the commander of the Fatah in Beirut, you would try to reach an agreement on evacuation provided your soldiers weren't humiliated. Where would you go?"

"That's another question altogether. You know, I have the impression that nobody really wants us. It's impossible to build another level of the world between the sky and the earth. We can't rent an island at the North Pole and there's a dispute over the South Pole anyway. As for outer space, the big powers are already dividing it up between them. So that's a real problem that we're supposed to solve by ourselves. But, you know, there is a simple solution: let us go home, to Palestine."

"Practically speaking, do you have any suggestions to make to Yasir Arafat?"

"I think I can leave it to him. I trust his judgment. When he makes a mistake, it's often because of the influence of other people on him or the circumstances. That doesn't mean I'd follow him blindly. But I think that in really crucial matters, he's right. I hope he goes where he wants to."

"And what should he do there?"

"Keep up the fight, naturally. We've already made some significant gains politically speaking, and diplomatically. We have friends all over. There are even lots of Israelis who sympathize with our aims. It's not the end yet, by God. It's just the end of an era. We really believe—not only hope and pray—we really believe that in the end we'll achieve our rights."

"Do you think or feel or believe that the period of armed struggle is over?"

"Practically speaking—yes, at least for the next few years. By the way, we never claimed that the Fatah alone would be able to crush the Israeli military machine or even come close to it. We always thought that we constituted a core around which the Arab countries would unite. But since 1973, for all intents and purposes, we have been fighting Israel alone. In any case, should the military struggle be resumed, I don't think it will be by the central forces in the PLO."

19

"In other words, you think the political struggle is more important now?"

"It was always a political struggle. There is no such thing as armed struggle for its own sake. All wars are fought for political ends but if it's possible to achieve your aims in some other way, why fight? The balance of forces between us isn't equal: you're armed to the teeth, we're not. You have a broad and sturdy base, we don't. Armed struggle may continue in some other form but it's bound to be to our disadvantage. That's why I favor political action and political struggle.

"Our generation did what it had to do. I gave eighteen years of my life to the struggle. And I'll go on, though I am sure any sensible combat soldier would retire after so long. I'm not retiring, just switching channels. I'm sure it will be just as efficient once we get the hang of it. I think we can learn the lesson. Some of us already have."

That was a good place to end the interview and I pressed "stop." We taped the interview twice, once in Arabic for Israel Radio's Arabic station, and once in English with a Hebrew translation for station Kol Yisrael. The whole thing took about an hour. Ta'mari looked exhausted. He had been concentrating on every word he said: he knew that lots of people in the Arab countries listened to Israel's Arabic broadcasts and he was also anxious to make the right impression on the Israelis. He asked me to replay the whole thing. I was also bushed. It had been a long day for me too. But I replayed it and we both listened in silence.

When it was over I could see that he was satisfied. "You know," I pointed out, "it will all be edited before it's broadcast."

He nodded. "Will you let me hear the edited version?"

What he meant was, would I come again?

I said yes. I would have come even if he hadn't asked. His hunch had been right.

It was after nine when I got up to leave. And I had promised Amalia that I'd be home for dinner. Ta'mari got up and I gave him my hand. He held it for a little longer than was necessary—as if he had something further to say.

"Could you do me a favor," he finally asked, in English. "I would really be grateful if you would call my wife and tell her that I'm alive."

"No problem," I answered and took out a pen. "Where can I find her?"

"Try this number in Cairo," he said, and while I was writing it on the back of a pack of cigarettes, he added: "Ask for Princess Dina."

20

I did a double take.

He laughed: "Yes, she's a queen and I'm the son of a cook."

For a minute I thought he was joking. But he made it clear that he wasn't: "My wife was the former queen of Jordan, King Hussein's first wife."

He had given me my chance, now remembered, when he first mentioned that his wife spoke better English than he, but I had let it pass. Still, to sit for five hours on his little bombshell and then to let it go off when I had one foot out the door . . . "Okay," I said, sitting down again, "let's have the story."

For more than an hour he filled me in on the details of his meeting with Dina and their marriage. His last sentence was: "And tell her that everything happened because we forgot the piece of paper. She'll know what I mean."

This time, when I got up to leave, I half jokingly asked: "Are you sure there's nothing else you want me to do for you?"

Salah Ta'mari smiled: "Well, now that you mention it, there is. If you could find my friend David Cornwall, tell him I'm sorry I didn't have time to read the manuscript."

I didn't know at the time that David Cornwall was better known as John le Carré. Nor did I know that the manuscript in question was *The Little Drummer Girl*. There were many things I didn't know at that stage.

I arrived home after midnight. Amalia was waiting up for me, worried sick that something had happened. I assured her that everything was fine and began to tell her about Salah Ta'mari. "Can you believe . . ." I began, six hours of impressions spilling out, but Amalia cut me short: "I am not interested in your terrorist." She was emphatic. "I don't want to hear a word about him or about any other murderer in this house!"

Two weeks later, she was serving him coffee in our living room.

2

"In order to fight, I've got to stay alive."

Salah Ta'mari looked up from the dinner table at the sound of the approaching planes. Israeli Phantoms. The roar of the engines was unmistakable. Half a minute later, everything in the refugee camp of Shalita in West Beirut was vibrating under the impact of the explosions.

He rushed outside. The noise became unbearable as the Phantoms dove in over the nearby stadium, raining devastation on the apparently harmless sportsground. His first thought was how to get the children out of danger. He ran back into his friends' house and grabbed the two smallest children, shouting, "Get them all out of here." Half dragging, half carrying the children, with the others following, Ta'mari led the way down into the nearest shelter.

The bombing of the stadium in West Beirut was the opening gambit of Operation Peace for Galilee. As the grandstands collapsed, the munitions depots underneath began to explode. The stadium was the site of the PLO's central arsenal.

Yasir Arafat wasn't in Beirut that day. He was off to Saudi Arabia on a mission for the Organization of Moslem States. His aim: to mediate a peace settlement between Iraq and Iran. Taking his place at the emergency meeting of the PLO's High Command, now assembled in the bunker of that same apartment house, was his deputy, Abu Jihad.

For a year now, a truce between Israel and the PLO had been in effect.

There had been some minor infringements, but on the whole both sides had observed the agreement. Nonetheless, it was the opinion of Ta'mari and others from the PLO leadership that the IDF would eventually mount a massive invasion of Lebanon. Additional proof was piling up all the time. Whenever the subject was discussed, Arafat, Brig. Gen. Abu el-Walid, head of military operations, and Col. Abu Zaim, head of intelligence, were of the opinion that the invasion was only a matter of time.

They differed, however, over the probable scope of the invasion. Arafat was convinced that the Israelis would stop at the Zaharani River, south of Sidon, although they would bomb PLO headquarters in Beirut and Tripoli. Abu Musa (Sa'id Meghari), on the other hand—recently appointed deputy to el-Walid—believed that Israel would try to reach Beirut and the Bekaa Valley to the east, in a broader operation: "It will give them the chance to hit the Syrians as well."

Ta'mari was later to say that from the moment Ariel (Arik) Sharon became minister of defense in Begin's government, he was sure that Abu Musa was right. The specter of Arik Sharon had been haunting the Palestinians ever since Kibya, in 1953. (The raid on the Jordanian village of Kibya was the first important rung up the ladder in Sharon's military career: he had led a paratroop unit in a reprisal action for the murder of an Israeli family. Almost the entire village was razed and sixty-nine people killed, half of them women and children. Although the scope of the action was sharply criticized, Sharon won the retroactive support of then prime minister, Ben-Gurion.)

At the meeting in the bunker Abu Jihad proposed that the PLO retaliate for the bombing by a massive shelling of Israeli settlements along the Lebanese border. The proposal was accepted unanimously and within two hours orders went to PLO artillery units in southern Lebanon. That evening, Friday, June 4, 1982, at 5:30, Safed was hit by Grad missiles and Nahariya by Katyushas. The kibbutzim of the Huleh Valley and the Naftali Range in the north were pounded by artillery and mortar fire.

Fire continued from both sides of the border all night long. Ta'mari followed developments from the bunker of the High Command. During the night, the apartment house next door was hit: the Israeli Air Force had missed the PLO's supreme operations command by a few yards.

Ta'mari was fairly confident at first. He knew exactly what the field strength of the PLO forces was. Only three weeks earlier he had participated in an emergency meeting of the command of the Kastel Brigade in southern Lebanon, where its six battalions were deployed as far north as Sidon. The commander of the brigade, Haj Ismail, had reported that the recently acquired 130 mm. artillery had been moved farther south, in the direction of the Israeli border. PLO artillery strength had been increased in the course of twelve months from eighty to two hundred launchers. In the last few weeks, units had also been equipped with personal land-to-air Strela (Sam-9 antiaircraft) missiles. Ta'mari himself had ordered the mobilization of members of the Ashbal youth movement, aged twelve and up, into units where older members of their families were serving. He knew that all leaves had been canceled and that an emergency call-up of all the militias in the south had gone into effect.

By Sunday night, he was less optimistic.

Saturday night and all day Sunday, Israeli planes had bombed southern Lebanon, particularly in areas where there were underground munitions dumps. Ta'mari himself had helped plan these subterranean arsenals on the mountainsides and he realized full well that the IDF was making them inaccessible by strewing the slopes with delayed-action bombs.

Sunday morning, when news came through that an Israeli tank force had crossed the border and was advancing north in the direction of Tyre, Ta'mari left for Sidon in his Volkswagen Beetle. He had vowed to himself that he would be with his men if—when—fighting broke out. He wanted to make sure that his militias, together with the Ashbal, put up a good fight. He wanted to prove to the Israelis that the invasion into Lebanon was not going to be a walkover.

At noon on June 6, Ta'mari ate lunch in Sidon with Dina. It was their last meal together. He knew that the Israelis were headed for Sidon, maybe even Beirut, and he wanted Dina out of the country.

It wasn't a happy occasion. Ta'mari was on edge. He described the situation in the area and explained to Dina that he wanted her to get to Beirut as fast as possible and get on a plane to Cairo. Dina tried to calm him down and get him to eat. She wasn't anxious to leave and tried to make Ta'mari understand her point of view. But he was adamant.

"I *have* to be here. I have a duty to perform. But this whole business has nothing to do with you. There is no reason whatsoever for you to get involved in it. You won't be helping anybody. Please." Then he tried another tack: "Your mother is in Cairo. She'll be very happy to see you. You know she's not well. She'll go crazy if she can't keep in touch. Who knows what's going to happen here."

Dina was not convinced. She wouldn't get in the way. She wouldn't keep him from his responsibilities. But she was, after all, his wife. Her place was at his side.

Just then the doorbell rang and Ta'mari went to answer. It was Abdallah, his driver. From the hall Dina could overhear him: the Jews had already crossed the Kasemiya Bridge over the Litani, north of Tyre.

It was 2:30 in the afternoon. Sidon was about fifteen miles from Tyre. It was, then, only a matter of hours before the IDF would be entering Sidon. Ta'mari looked for Dina. By now she was in the kitchen making coffee. "Go and pack," he said. "I insist, right now!" This time Dina realized she had no alternative.

To Abdallah he said: "Take Dina to the airport in Khalde and get her on any plane going out. I don't care where to." Khalde was a few miles south of Beirut. Then he went into the kitchen and poured three cups of coffee. He gave one to Abdallah and took the other two to the bedroom.

Dina was packing a small suitcase. Unlike her usual practice, she appeared to be taking very little with her. Usually, she would just sweep up everything in sight into as many suitcases as were needed. Today, her packing was considered. Except for a few clothes, she took only a photograph of Salah with her and a small drawing he had recently made of a horse.

Ta'mari gave her the coffee. Dina took a sip, put the cup down, and continued to pack. Just then they heard the deafening whistle of a shell. Everything in the room shook. They could hear the tinkle of broken glass downstairs. Ta'mari shoved everything in sight into the suitcase, jammed it closed, and took it downstairs. Dina followed. Abdallah was waiting outside. "Just pray that you get through the shelling in one piece."

At the door of the Beetle Ta'mari grabbed her by the shoulders—half in embrace, half in an attempt to get her into the car faster. "God be with you," he said.

"Salah!" Dina suddenly cried out through the half-open window, as if she had just remembered something important, but Salah was already shouting at Abdallah: "Go ahead, get moving!"

A little later he remembered her plaintive cry.

Dina had always been a great believer in omens and good-luck charms. Ta'mari, the rationalist, had scoffed at them secretly but had gone along with her nonetheless. Before every trip, she would tear a piece of paper in two and give him half. When they met again, she would "redeem" his half.

Ta'mari had always managed to keep it. Now, for the first time in twelve years of marriage, they had forgotten their little ritual.

The only one of the family left in the house in Sidon now was Ta'mari's seventeen-year-old sister, Rim. Mahmoud Faris of the UNRWA (United Nations Refugee Welfare Agency), his wife, and her mother shared the upstairs of the house with them. With Dina's departure and the outbreak of hostilities Rim took over more of the household duties, which included feeding the pets—most notably among them Markhaba, Ta'mari's parrot. *Markhaba* means "hello" in Arabic and it was the parrot's greatest (and only) linguistic achievement. Before he left, Ta'mari told Rim not to leave the house. "If you need anything or if anything happens, talk to Mahmoud."

A few hours later, as darkness fell over Sidon, Ta'mari left in a jeep for the Joint Operation Headquarters of the Palestinian organizations, the nerve center of the PLO in the south. It was located in a bunker near Sidon's one and only hotel, the Tanus. Haj Ismail, as commander of the Kastel Brigade, was first in command.

The main street of Sidon was jam-packed with cars, trucks, pickups, wagons—anything on wheels. Thousands of families were trying to make their way north, out of the way of the approaching war. Their belongings were strapped to the tops of their cars and as many people as possible were crammed into all available space. The boulevard had been forcibly turned into a one-way thoroughfare. Ta'mari's jeep, which was headed in the "wrong" direction—south—had to maneuver its way against the swelling current.

Late that night, he reached headquarters. It was reported that an advance force of Israeli tanks had reached the town of Sarafand, about twelve miles south of Sidon. It wasn't clear whether Tyre and the refugee camps in the area had been occupied. What was clear was that the road through Tyre had been breached and the Israelis were moving north without stopping.

Ismail ordered his officers to deploy their troops defensively at the southern entrance to Sidon and Ta'mari left for Ein Hilweh, the refugee camp which blocked the southern access to the city. His militia was there and he knew the setup as well as he knew the palm of his hand: the commanders, the munitions dumps, the underground passageways, the communications lines, the bunkers, the antitank defenses. He was absolutely sure that the IDF would not only try to push through the camp to the city, but that they would attempt to occupy this strategically located point as well.

Orders from Beirut were crystal clear: the IDF was to be held back by a delaying action. The Americans had given Israel the green light for a short, limited operation. The PLO was convinced that a cease-fire would be put into effect within hours. The IDF had to be prevented at all costs from reaching Beirut.

That night information reached Ismail's Joint Headquarters that Israeli commando units had landed from the sea and were taking up positions not far from the mouth of the Awali River, *north* of Sidon. He immediately dispatched a reconnaissance force to check it out and when they returned they reported that armored units were landing from dozens of tank carriers offshore. It was clear to everyone that Sidon had been encircled in a pincer movement, to everyone, that is, but Haj Ismail. In any event, at the moment he refused to set store by the report. Despite repeated communiqués on the disintegration of his forces all over the south, he kept faith with Arafat's prognostication—that the Israelis would *not* cross the Zaharani.

Ta'mari tried to calm everyone down, to arrest the growing panic: "We don't have to worry about the armored force. They won't be going *into* Sidon: they'll be moving north." He was sure the IDF was intent on reaching Beirut. "We have to stop them in the south."

On one matter, he was calm and collected. He was sure that Dina had managed to reach Beirut in time and get on a plane to Cairo. What he didn't know was that she had missed the last plane, that by the time they reached the international airport at Khalde, it was closed. And he wasn't to know the truth until months later, when he was already a prisoner in Israel.

At dawn the next morning, Haj Ismail notified his commanders that he was leaving to check the situation in the Awali area. Some of them were suspicious when they saw him get into an ambulance. Later that day, headquarters lost touch with the ambulance. A reconnaissance unit dispatched to check on what happened returned empty-handed: the ambulance was nowhere in the area. The first-in-command of the Kastel Brigade had deserted.

Ismail later claimed that when radio contact with the ambulance had been broken off, he decided to move general headquarters to Shtura in the

Bekaa Valley, an area controlled by the Syrian army. Military observers believe that Ismail's sudden departure was the most significant factor in the total disintegration of his brigade. Ta'mari merely comments: "When a soldier is exceptionally brave, you decorate him. If he is frightened, you don't have to punish him."

In the history of the war in Lebanon, the battle of Ein Hilweh was the toughest. On this point, Israel and the PLO are in accord. The Palestinians saw it as their Masada. Many Palestinian fighters were prepared to go to their deaths rather than surrender, even if this meant taking with them women and children. They succeeded in delaying the advance of the Israelis up the coastal road for two full days. The stubborn resistance of the Palestinian militias in the refugee camp—at a time when PLO units in the south were in total disarray—took the Israelis completely by surprise.

The resistance at Ein Hilweh was based primarily on small neighborhood defense units and on civilian fighters. It was the battle of Ein Hilweh, in fact, which prevented the IDF from making an unimpeded triumphal march into Beirut. After "softening-up" the camp from the air, tank-borne Israeli soldiers were forced to dismount and enter the camp on foot: the tanks were practically sitting ducks for the RPGs and antitank missiles. In the battle of Ein Hilweh the tanks had to *follow* in the wake of the infantry. The camp was ultimately subdued, house after house, neighborhood after neighborhood, in a battle of attrition which finally terminated Palestinian resistance in southern Lebanon. After the smoke cleared, most of Ein Hilweh was a mound of rubble.

A few hours before Israeli paratroopers breached the main road through Sidon, Ta'mari managed to make his way out of the camp in a jeep. He needed a few hours' sleep. He also wanted to see Rim and Abdallah. Driving up the main boulevard, he saw that most of the apartment houses on both sides had collapsed. When he reached his street, he noticed a black hole where the tower of the mosque had been. For a moment he was afraid that his house had suffered a similar fate. He was relieved to see that only the outer wall of the library had been destroyed.

Rim was in the kitchen with Faris, his wife, and his mother. Faris showed him a circular that had been dropped by Israeli planes over the city: "The IDF will occupy Sidon in a short time," it read. "All civilians are requested to walk down to the beach, north of the port. Arms must be left behind. Anyone found bearing weapons will be shot on sight. The IDF will not harm civilians. Terrorists who turn themselves in will not be harmed." At the bottom of the circular the message was repeated: *"Kulkum al-bakhr* [Everyone to the beach]."

"Nobody is going to any beach," Ta'mari ordered. "You're all staying here, at home. Nobody's moving."

There was a look of desperation on Rim's face.

"Don't worry," he said, "I'm spending the night here."

Rim filled the kettle with water.

"Where's Abdallah?" Ta'mari asked.

Faris's wife and mother looked at Ta'mari's grime-covered face and then lowered their eyes. It was Faris's uncomfortable duty to break the bad news: "He left your car in the garage and went to Ein Hilweh to fight."

That night and the next few nights, Ta'mari slept on the porch—with a Kalashnikov. Before retiring, he would put Markhaba's cage behind the easy chair in the living room, covered with a blanket. The parrot liked to sleep in the dark.

Until the final fall of Sidon, Ta'mari spent his waking hours moving from one position in the city to another, from bunker to bunker, from one apartment house to the next, from one narrow alley in the casbah to another. These positions were partially manned by members of the Ashbal youth movement, in Ta'mari's charge. He spent a good deal of his time with these youngsters, watching them unpack crates of ammunition at a frenzied pace in the biggest bunker of all, located underneath the Christian hospital, and later sniping at the commanders of the Israeli tanks standing upright in their turrets. Ta'mari marveled at their dedication, at their stubborn refusal to give up, although they knew how heavily the odds were stacked against them. Their courage, he later told me, was consolation of a sort for the calamity of defeat.

At dawn on the fourth day, he was awakened by a loud knocking on the door. He leapt out of bed and hid behind the door to the porch. Rim went barefoot to open the front door.

An Israeli officer and three soldiers stood there. Ta'mari could hear every word.

"*Markhaba,*" one of them said in Arabic. "Is Salah Ta'mari your father or husband?"

"My brother."

"We have information to the effect that he has returned from Beirut. We would like to search the house. We won't hurt you."

Rim stammered: "I don't know anything. I haven't seen him or heard from him for a long time."

Two of the soldiers went into the kitchen while the third entered the living room. The officer remained with Rim. All of a sudden a shrill voice called out: "*Markhaba, markhaba,*" from behind the chair. The soldier jumped in the direction of the voice as the other three came running. He saw the blanket and pulled it off. The parrot was doing its set piece. Ta'mari couldn't see their faces from where he stood but he could hardly keep from laughing. Clutching his Kalashnikov, he realized at the same time that he could easily prevent the four men from ever walking into an Arab house again.

When they had recovered their composure, they left. "Tell your brother, if you see him, that the best thing he can do now is turn himself in. His 'kids' tell us he's a smart guy."

When he heard the command car pull away, Ta'mari came back to Rim, who was white as a sheet. "I'll make some coffee," he said, and went into the kitchen. Rim heard him say "*khalas*" under his breath, a word meaning "that's it," or "that's the end."

Ta'mari didn't want to frighten his upstairs neighbors by waking them so early. He waited instead until they came down by themselves. He told them he wanted Rim to sleep with them from then on. For Rim he had another request. "Meet me tonight at exactly eight o'clock at the gate of Abu Majdi's orange grove." Then he left. He didn't take his Kalashnikov with him.

For ten days Ta'mari went underground, hiding in orange and banana groves and going from house to house trying to discover who of the Fatah people were still alive, who had been caught, who was wounded. Every evening at eight Rim would appear, bringing him food. At first he toyed with the idea of rounding up whoever was left and organizing local resistance to the occupation. But there were, in fact, very few men left. Most of them were crowded together in a temporary compound on the beach. Furthermore, the whole city was under a strict curfew. There were only frightened women in the houses, gathered in the innermost rooms, and children wandering around in pajamas all day. Here and there, he came across refugees who had returned home only to find their houses gone, destroyed. Sidon had become a city of people whose major concern now was where to find drinking water.

On Friday, Rim failed to appear at the appointed time. Ta'mari had overslept a little—on the roof of a shed in one of the orange groves—and was a little late, but not enough to explain her absence. She had always been punctual, waiting patiently for him if he were late. Now he was overcome with feelings of remorse. He had endangered her unnecessarily.

She finally appeared, breathing heavily. "I wasn't careful," she apologized. She had been caught in barbed wire in the court of the mosque and her knee was bleeding. Ta'mari tore off his shirt and bound her leg.

"Let's go home," he said, and then again he mumbled, more audibly this time: *"Khalas*—that's it."

They made their way haltingly through the orange groves, dodging spotlights and flares. Ta'mari had to support Rim: it was hard for her to walk by herself. When they reached the house, they sat in the darkened kitchen and Ta'mari gave her a piece of paper: "If anything happens to me, make sure this gets to Dina."

Rim wanted to know what it was.

"My will."

"When did you write it?"

"Yesterday," he told her. "For a while I thought it was the end. I was on my way to Saruji's house." Saruji was the principal of the local school. "But suddenly an Israeli half-track rolled up, blocking the way, and in a matter of seconds the place was surrounded by soldiers. I stayed put in the orange grove for the night, and while I was sitting there I scribbled my last will and testament."

For the first time, Ta'mari saw his sister crying.

"There's only one important thing in the will," he continued. "I want this house to be sold and I want the money to be used to buy ten thousand musical instruments for ten thousand Palestinian children. Dina will know how to handle it."

Rim seemed a little ashamed of herself and she wiped her eyes. "What's going to happen now? Where will you go?"

"I'm not sure. It's almost impossible to get out of Sidon. The Israelis and the Christian Phalange are blocking all the roads. And if that's not bad enough, they're also out looking for me."

Suddenly, Rim saw her older brother in a different light. His buoyancy, his perennial optimism, were gone. He was troubled, deeply troubled.

"Let's see if we can make it to Ibrahim el-Hilou. He'll be able to help us, to hide us. At least we'll be able to rest there. I've got to get some sleep." El-Hilou, a friend, was the Maronite archbishop of Sidon.

The last ten days had not only depleted Ta'mari's physical resources, they

31

had destroyed something at the core of his consciousness. His faith in the PLO's military potency, built up in blood, sweat, and tears during ten years in Lebanon, had been eroded. No, not merely eroded but entirely dissolved in the flow of events. The Palestinians had been defeated in the field of battle by a superior force. Armed struggle was not the answer. There had to be other ways.

"I was in shock," he told me later. "And I began to feel guilty although I don't really think I was guilty of anything. My whole life I've tried to keep the fight clean, aboveboard—during those ten years in Lebanon, too. My feelings of guilt were generated by the fact that I saw with my own eyes how four hundred thousand Palestinians in southern Lebanon were turned into scapegoats for a hundred million Arabs all over the world. I have a sense of responsibility for them and it gives me no rest. I know we made mistakes and now those miserable people are paying for them. I can't say that their misery doesn't affect me. That's why I didn't leave Sidon at the beginning of the war. I could have. I wanted to encourage them, raise their morale, convince them that not everything was lost, try and help them keep faith. But the reality was different. And the ring around me was getting tighter. I never thought I would turn myself in voluntarily. I wanted to live, to finish my task. That's how I found myself on the way to el-Hilou."

Under cover of darkness, Rim and Ta'mari made their way to the Maronite Church. Their friend the archbishop wasn't there. They were met by his deputy, a man known in Sidon as *Abuna* Hanna, "our Father" Hanna.

Ta'mari was ill at ease. "I'd like to sleep here for a day or two, until they let up on the searches."

Hanna was amenable at first. "Why not? *Tfadal.* You're a friend. You've done a lot for us. After all, we do owe you something." He brought them into the reception room and gave orders to prepare coffee.

Ta'mari began to explain his view of the present situation. He felt the need to convince Father Hanna of certain things which el-Hilou would have understood intuitively. Hanna became uneasy.

"You know," he said, finally, "it's dangerous to keep you here. We might get hurt. Not only by Israelis, or Palestinians, but also by certain groups of Lebanese who are hostile to the Maronites. They certainly won't let us off if they find out that we're harboring you."

"What do you propose then?" asked Ta'mari.

"That you turn yourself in to the Israelis. To tell you the truth, if you don't, I will." He was resolute. "If you don't go, I'll bring them here."

"Okay. You be my guarantee. Go to the Israelis—I'm sure you know where to find them—and tell them I want to turn myself in. But on one condition—that they don't humiliate me." It was bad enough being humiliated by a local priest.

To his frightened sister he said: "My war is just beginning. In order to fight, I've got to stay alive. You understand." He was trying desperately to explain his position.

The priest brought them coffee and then left for the offices of the Israeli administration at the Shab Hospital.

In less than an hour he was back. As he entered, Ta'mari stood up. Father Hanna had come with a major and two soldiers.

The major first turned to Rim: "You can go home. Nothing will happen to you." Then he walked over to Ta'mari and introduced himself: "My name is Major Yitzhak Rabin. I'm from the civil administration in Sidon."

Ta'mari blanched. He didn't think it was an appropriate time for jokes, although the man certainly bore a strong resemblance to Rabin. This was his first face-to-face meeting with an Israeli and—as he was to do in subsequent meetings—he was the first to attack.

"Your treatment of civilians and children is brutal, major," he said in English. "Some day you'll have to account for it. Don't be surprised if all the Jewish values you allegedly represent lose all meaning."

The officer was astonished. He hardly expected this kind of behavior from a terrorist who had this minute given himself up. But he kept his cool. "Please give me your personal particulars."

But Ta'mari wasn't ready yet. "I'm not turning myself in unless you promise to abide by the promises made by Ariel Sharon."

"What exactly did Sharon promise?" asked the major. "Something personal?"

"Nothing personal. But who knows, maybe his promises aren't worth any more than all the promises made by your leaders, including your prime minister. They're all pretty worthless. Begin announced an operation of thirty miles or less and you're already besieging Beirut. No, I refer to what I heard on the radio and read in your leaflets, that any Palestinian fighter who turns himself in will not be humiliated. That's all I insist upon."

"No one will show you disrespect. We promised Father Hanna that you would be treated with dignity and that's precisely what we're doing."

It was after midnight when the jeep reached the gates of Al-Safa, a warehouse at the eastern end of Sidon's main street. Surrounded by a wall of cinder blocks, the warehouse was serving as a temporary compound for prisoners. An MP opened the heavy iron gates. The jeep entered a court-yard and parked in front of a clearing that had been turned into headquar-ters. Through the window Ta'mari could see a sea of prisoners sitting on the ground.

The officer brought him over to the man in charge. "This guy claims to hold the rank of lieutenant colonel in the PLO. He's turning himself in."

Ta'mari noticed that the senior officer had the same rank.

"Your name," the officer asked.

"Lt. Col. Salah Ta'mari. I would like to be together with the rest of the men."

Lt. Col. Yehuda Shatz examined the new prisoner. He noticed that Ta'mari was trembling. "Get yourself a blanket," he said, "and you can join the others."

Ta'mari wrapped himself in a blanket he took from a pile and walked over to the prisoners. It was hard to estimate the exact number of people there—hundreds, maybe thousands. Most of them were handcuffed and all were sitting with their heads between their knees. Only when he sat down did the bad smell hit him with force. Apparently the men were not allowed to move—for anything. Some of them were crying softly, others groaning, others mumbling prayers. Israeli soldiers were moving among them, writing numbers on the backs of their shirts with felt-tip pens. Ta'mari got up and went back to Shatz.

"You're treating these men like animals," he said, "and even animals are usually treated better."

Shatz listened. "What exactly do you want?"

"I want you to give orders to stop that kind of treatment. Besides, I'm cold, and if I'm cold, so are they."

"Sorry," Shatz answered, trying to be patient. "There's nothing I can do. Those are the conditions. We're all out here in the cold. If you want to, you can sleep in the car," and he jerked his head in the direction of a large vehicle.

Ta'mari looked at the car, which was parked nearby. "I couldn't stand the sight of those miserable people, moaning and groaning," he later told me. "I was afraid I might lose control and lose my head."

He entered the car but a few minutes later told the guard to call Shatz. "I can't sit here inside while they're all freezing out there and I can't sit out there because I might do something desperate."

Shatz realized he had a strange customer on his hands. But Ta'mari's human weakness and his attempt to conceal it moved him. "You know what," he said, "go home, get whatever you need, and come back here tomorrow morning."

Ta'mari was astounded.

"And what if I run away?"

"You won't run away."

With measured steps, Ta'mari returned to the car. He didn't know quite how to digest Shatz's proposal. And he pondered it all night. The next morning, he went over to Shatz and asked him if the offer was still good.

"Why not?" he answered. "What made you change your mind?"

"I see it's going to be a long story. I'll need some clothes and some books."

He also wanted to see Rim, to make sure she'd gotten home all right and to see, perhaps, if there was any message from Dina.

"Okay," Shatz said. "I'll take you in my jeep." And soon two lieutenant colonels—one from the IDF driving, the other from the Fatah giving directions—made their way through the streets of the ghost town.

"*Iftah tarik* [you go in]," Shatz said as they stood at the door. He seemed familiar with Arab customs. Ta'mari stood frozen to the ground. "Go on in," he repeated, "and please, get rid of the women."

Ta'mari had suddenly panicked. He had been struck by the idea that the Phalange, hearing of his surrender, might have taken over the house. He turned to Shatz: "Come in with me."

"You go in first," said Shatz. "Send the women out and then I'll join you."

At that moment, Ta'mari chose to tease Shatz rather than reveal his fears. "You're really not afraid that I'll run away?"

"Try it," said Shatz. "I'm the fastest draw in the East."

Ta'mari went in and Shatz followed. Rim and Mrs. Faris were sitting in the living room. Ta'mari invited Shatz to sit down and asked Rim, who didn't understand what was happening, to make some coffee. Shatz sat down with Mrs. Faris. Ta'mari went to another room and returned a few minutes later with a suitcase.

"I'm ready," he announced to Shatz. Then in a loud voice, intended for Shatz's ears, he said to Rim: "It's a hellhole there in the compound," and the two men left.

When they returned to the warehouse, Shatz suggested to Ta'mari that he leave the suitcase in the office. Ta'mari left it there and went to join the other prisoners on the ground.

In the daylight he was able to see the prisoners clearly. He knew many of them and recognized a lot of civilians who had nothing to do with the PLO. He also discovered that most of Sidon's community leaders were there: people from the schools and hospitals, from the municipality, and from public institutions. The soldiers were still trying to finish the count, identify all the prisoners, and get their papers in order. The morning sun was already beating down fiercely. Everyone was thirsty.

Ta'mari didn't spend too long among the prisoners—or, as they had recently been dubbed, "the rounded up." After about an hour he heard his name booming out of the loudspeaker. Shatz wanted to see him.

"I have orders to transfer you out of here."

"Where to?"

"To Israel."

"Why?"

Shatz didn't reply. He just reminded Ta'mari that his suitcase was still in the office.

Ta'mari was taken by pickup. In accordance with standard practice, he was handcuffed. He sat in the back between two soldiers. Colonel Shatz rode next to the driver.

All the way down to the border checkpoint at Rosh Hanikra, Ta'mari saw a countryside in ruins: burned-out orange groves and orchards, destroyed bridges, crumbling houses, and abandoned villages. When they crossed the border, Shatz stopped the car and told Ta'mari to come sit up front. "I want you to see the State of Israel."

In Nahariya they stopped at a café for breakfast. "Nahariya on that summer morning reminded me of Paris," Ta'mari told me months later.

A few miles before they arrived at the Israeli prison, Ta'mari was blindfolded. His fatigue together with the monotonous jerking of the vehicle made him doze off. When he awoke, the blindfold was removed, and he found himself facing another Israeli—a somewhat corpulent redhead of about forty, wearing a crocheted skullcap over his red hair, Zuri Ben-Nun.

36

3

"What in the world made me bring him here?"

That entire summer of 1982, Israel's war in Lebanon was beginning to deteriorate into a political and military quagmire. Meanwhile, Salah Ta'mari sat on the sidelines, most of the time in isolation, in his cell.

Since I could freely come and go, I didn't find the cell particularly depressing. True, the entrance was a heavily reinforced door; the small hatch could only be opened from the outside; and the two barred windows faced out onto blank walls. But the cell itself was spacious and boasted a small separate lavatory. There were books and writing materials on a small table and both a chair and a stool. Ta'mari was also allowed an electric kettle, coffee and sugar, and an unlimited supply of cigarettes. Furthermore, he was allowed a visitor—not on any regular basis but without too much red tape. The second time I visited him it was to let him hear the edited interview. The third time, less than a week later, I had no particular reason to come other than my natural curiosity and the strange chemistry that seemed to flow between us.

Ta'mari had been installed in his quarters a few days after arriving and from then on was allowed to spend some time each day outside in a small screen-covered inner courtyard. But during the first few days he had been confined to a small, airless cell whose only convenience was a pail and cover. It was of those first days that he spoke to me on this visit, days that

37

comprised the first chapter of what he was later to refer to as "his battle for sanity."

The pail, he told me, was his first symbol of struggle.

"I used to sit looking at it, swearing I would never use it. That would be my way of resisting degradation. But it wasn't easy. It meant that I had to stop eating. So I did. I fasted for the first day. I didn't touch any of the food they gave me. The result was that I began to feel weak. The second day I realized that if I became weak I wouldn't have the strength to carry on any kind of a struggle. I would break down—which is what the enemy wanted. So I made a compromise. I licked a little bit of jam every day.

"I finally found the strength I needed in a strange place—in a dream I had about my mother. You know, I was rather weak and it was stifling in the cell and I fell asleep. Apparently, the bruises on my wrists from the handcuffs were bothering me considerably because they played a part in this dream.

"I was in Bethlehem, walking down the *a'qba* for the first time by myself. The *a'qba* was 'the street of a thousand steps' leading up from the wadi to the market in town, and our house was located along the way. My mother was leaning against a neighbor's house, watching me.

"I kept turning to her and complaining: 'Look, mother, look what they're doing to me. Look at these bruises from the handcuffs.' And she kept answering: 'I don't see a thing. It's all in your imagination.'

"She began to move away but then turned back. 'Even if your bruises are real, so what? Do you remember Ibrahim A'nan? He lost both legs and never complained. He worked as an artist creating wonderful things and you complain about a little pain in your wrists.'

"She again began to move out of my line of vision, her back toward me. But I could hear her last words as she disappeared: '*Avda'tak l'allah* [I am leaving you in the hands of God].' This is what Palestinian parents say to their sons when they are about to leave home for good. What they really mean is: 'Son, you're on your own.'

"When I woke up I felt strangely refreshed—as if I could break down the walls of the prison with my bare hands. My feelings of weakness and desperation had vanished."

Ta'mari was elated telling me the story. "After the dream," he went on, "I looked at the pail differently. I suddenly began to think of what interesting uses I could make of it other than what it was intended for. I could turn it over and sit on it or stand on it. I could dance with it. I could use it as a tom-tom. The first thing I actually did was turn it over and sit on it. But because of my long legs I ended up in the pose of Rodin's *Thinker.* I found that very funny and couldn't keep from laughing. The guards thought I had gone off my rocker. Maybe I had a little, but it was good for me."

From then on, even after he was moved to his new cell, Ta'mari became enterprising. Every small thing proved a challenge to his ingenuity. If, for example, he wanted to read after "lights out," he had to find some sort of independent lighting system, and he did: he saved the oil from his ration of sardines, and with a fuse made of wool from his blanket, and a tin can, he "invented" a combination burner–night light.

"The problem is not merely survival," he wrote in his diary during the first few weeks in prison. "Merely to survive is rather easy. The question is how. You can break down, or become permanently embittered, or try and forget everything. You can turn yourself into a heap of rags without any effort. The problem is how to survive while maintaining your own identity, remaining effective as a human being, reaching the right conclusions, and engaging in positive action. You have to learn how to interiorize your anger, make it constructive, and make it a perpetual lever against whatever injustices, serious or trivial, are perpetrated against you. You cannot allow anything to gain ascendancy over you. You have only yourself to count on."

He took his meals in his cell. From the very beginning he began saving olive pits, which he fashioned into prayer beads using the most primitive of means: the floor was his sanding machine, a piece of wire from the window screen his drill, and threads from his blanket his lacing cord.

He found another "project" for the olives, of which he was apparently given large rations. I usually brought him a couple of cartons of Marlboros whenever I came. Once he greeted me with *"I've* got a present for *you* this time." He went over to the windowsill and took down two jars of cucumbers and olives which he himself had pickled. It was very touching, and surprising. I knew that his rations were not large. He had simply creamed off a little every day, added the salt and sugar, and placed the jars in the sun. He was justifiably proud of himself. "They're for your wife," he said.

Amalia had not yet met Salah. For her he was still "that terrorist." She didn't know quite how to accept his gift.

During the first few months of his imprisonment in Israel proper, Ta'mari managed to make the best of things. He made friends with the guards, who often agreed to make small purchases for him at the prison canteen. He was particularly fond of sweets and fresh and dried fruits, and on my visits I always loaned him small sums of money.

There was one guard—and Ta'mari continued to ask after him long after he was released and we would meet in distant places—who would bring him samples of his mother's cooking every time he came back from his day off, baked goods and various spicy dishes from her Moroccan-style cuisine. Ta'mari enjoyed being spoiled.

One thing the guards paid little attention to was his indefatigable singing. For long periods during the day he would raise his voice in song, and was usually joined soon after by some of the other prisoners. In fact, the singing was only a cover for communication among them. This way Ta'mari introduced himself to his fellow prisoners, made their acquaintance, and exchanged information and small talk with them. When he learned that the prisoner in a neighboring cell was an old man in bad health, he made it his business to get some dried fruit to him every day— either through the good offices of sympathetic guards or through a crack under the door.

Zuri Ben-Nun, the section warden, was the one who made my visits to Ta'mari possible—after getting the approval of the higher-ups, naturally. He would pass my requests on with alacrity and always await my arrival in person. He never put a limit on the duration of my visits. He also agreed without reserve to pass on my most unusual request of all: to allow Ta'mari out for a day, for a look around the country.

It was clear to everyone that Ta'mari was not simply a run-of-the-mill prisoner. He was the highest-ranking PLO officer ever to fall into Israeli hands. It was also fairly evident that he would not remain in an Israeli prison forever. And when he did finally leave he would report to the top people in the PLO. That was why, in my opinion—and it was this I tried to explain to the authorities when I asked for permission to take him on a tour of the country—it was important for *us* to show him another side of Israel. Perhaps, always perhaps, he would realize that Israel was not what poisonous Palestinian propaganda made it out to be, what he himself was so thoroughly convinced of.

Aside from the fact that he was a top-ranking officer, he had managed to impress whomever he met with his decency and personal integrity. In his radio interview he had spoken of the need to put emphasis on political struggle, which upped his credentials with the Israeli establishment. He had also revealed a serious interest in and familiarity with Jewish history and tradition and the history of Israel and Zionism. Even if his knowledge had been acquired in order to "know the enemy," it was highly impressive.

All this was taken into consideration by the authorities when I made my rather outlandish request. But four weeks after his surrender and just two weeks after my first interview with him, I was granted permission to take him out for the day. I would be his "guide" and two guards would accompany us.

When I came into his cell to pass on the good news, I was elated: I deeply believed in the efficacy of what I was doing. I told him the news. His only reaction was to ask dryly: "Where are we going?"

"Where would you like to go?" I asked.

He didn't answer immediately. He was apparently weighing the various possibilities very carefully. I had a suspicion that he had thought about such a possibility even before it had materialized. His answer surprised me: he wanted to visit Yad Vashem, the memorial to the six million victims of the holocaust.

There was no cunning in his choice. I was already able to "read" the man. That was really what he wanted. But before I had a chance to digest this proposal, he was making another.

"I'd also like to meet with some Israeli writer, like Amos Oz or Amos Kenan. I know they're both peaceniks. Do you think Oz would be ready to talk to someone like me?"

I told him I would try and arrange it, all for the next day. Before I left he grabbed my arm: "There's someone else I'd like to meet."

I looked at him. What now? I wondered.

"Your wife."

The next day Amalia joined us.

Somewhere along the line, he had become a person with a name and an individual history, no longer just another anonymous terrorist—so much easier to hate. For Amalia this was a major revolution: she had grown up in a religious home in Jerusalem and her parents had been members of Menahem Begin's nationalist Betar organization. Maybe the pickled cucumbers had something to do with it, or maybe my endless stories about him. Once, at the beginning, Amalia had said to me: "You've become the captive of a captive." In Hebrew the pun is better: the same verb is used for both "to capture" and "to captivate." But she hadn't said it lightly.

Amalia is no different from most Israelis who grow up under the shadow of Palestinian terrorism. From the first day of school, when they are taught to report the presence of any suspicious object to the nearest adult lest it turn out to be a time bomb, until the time they themselves become parents and do guard duty in kindergartens and schools, Israelis live with a palpable threat: explosions in buses, stabbings in Old Jerusalem, commando raids on border towns and kibbutzim. It is difficult, after almost forty years of hostility between Jews and Arabs, for either to accept the other with equanimity.

Amalia was prepared to accept the fact that I saw things differently, although she found it hard to agree with me. "The Arabs are your daily bread," she would say. "You know their language and their history and you can recognize the differences between them. It's even important for you to make those distinctions. I can't."

But she did eventually. Stereotype and generalization began to crumble. She began to differentiate between the Palestinian organizations and what they advocated, and she began to apply a human yardstick to Salah Ta'mari. It was important to her that he had made the effort to study Jewish history and Zionism, and although she would—in the heat of an argument—accuse me of "being on his side," she was sensitive to the fact that Ta'mari had become extremely important to me. Burdened by so many mixed feelings, Amalia came face to face with Ta'mari. The rest seemed to happen naturally.

The actual meeting between them that morning was, I believe, more difficult for him than for her, although under the circumstances each was in an awkward position.

The day had been planned very carefully, down to the last detail. We were to visit Amos Oz at his kibbutz, Hulda, in the morning, and Yad Vashem in the afternoon. In the evening we would have dinner together at our house in Ramat Hasharon. I would pick up Ta'mari and the guards at the prison while Amalia waited for us in a nearby gas station.

Even before we pulled into the station, the mood of my passenger was not particularly cheerful. Ta'mari was sitting in the back seat, squeezed in between the two guards, who were armed with submachine guns. They were complete strangers and were probably wondering what in hell I was doing taking a lousy terrorist out for a spin around the country. Amalia was waiting nervously near the road. From where I was sitting, in the driver's seat, I could see Ta'mari in the mirror: he was breathing heavily, his face was as white as a sheet, and he was blindfolded.

I stopped the car and opened the front door for Amalia. The pleasant odor of scent filled the car. Salah could not see her but he smelled the perfume. We drove in an oppressive silence for a few miles at which point the guards removed the blindfold.

"Meet my wife," I said in English, awkwardly. "This is Amalia."

"Nice to meet you," he answered coldly. "I wish I could have met you under more pleasant circumstances." No doubt he was mortified, as a man and as an Arab, being introduced to a strange woman in such a humiliating position.

Amos Oz opened the door of his study and invited us to come in and sit down. The two guards remained outside. Oz went into the small kitchen, where he had prepared coffee. Meanwhile we looked around. The walls were covered with bookcases from the floor to the ceiling. His desk, which looked out on a fig tree, was also covered with books and newspapers. As he returned with a small tray, he explained to Ta'mari that this room was where he worked, that he lived in another apartment with his family.

The coffee and cookies helped break the ice and Oz proved to be an enthusiastic host. He knew all about Ta'mari and had heard the interview on the radio. Ta'mari asked what Oz was working on. Oz answered that he was writing an article about the war in Lebanon.

Ta'mari nosed in on the answer and moved directly into politics without another reference to literature. He told Oz he thought the war was immoral. He said that Ariel Sharon's promise that PLO fighters who surrendered voluntarily would not be humiliated was not being kept. He added that it was like Begin's promise that the war would not exceed thirty miles, that all of Israel's politics were immoral.

Amos Oz, whose negative position on the war was well known, soon moved on to another subject. "Tell me about yourself, Salah"—he addressed him by his first name—"and then I'll tell you about myself."

Ta'mari began. "I'm a Palestinian from Bethlehem. And I'm trying my utmost to return to Bethlehem, in order to live there in dignity as a human being." He spoke of his Bedouin origins, of his childhood, of his uncle who would take him on horseback to Herodium, the ancient Jewish fortress south of Jerusalem, where he, Ta'mari, always dreamt of building his home.

Oz replied in kind, telling him of his childhood in Jerusalem, of his friendship with Arab children from the neighborhood, and of joining the kibbutz as a young man.

Oz has a certain magic with words, and his speech is gentle but impressive. Yet Ta'mari, with his almost total lack of diffidence, was the dominant presence in the room.

He spoke of the artificiality of borders. "We tend to think of borders as something absolute, as if God himself drew them. But any person with an open mind and a modicum of moral courage knows that borders are a human fabrication. Human beings remain human beings regardless of which side of the border they live on.

"Nonetheless," he continued, "people want to *belong*. They need to belong. You can belong to your street or village, or race, or continent, or you can belong to the *human race* in general. When my ideas began to take shape after 1967, I arrived at the conclusion that perhaps my ultimate aim was to become a citizen of the world."

Ta'mari was very intense, as if the presence of a writer whom he admired required an extra effort of articulation.

"But there is still something else that determines belonging," he went on. "Danger."

Oz interrupted. "Are you saying that common danger is what makes you belong to the organization of which you are a member?"

"Absolutely," Ta'mari replied. "And I'll tell you something else. Someday all of mankind will unite in the face of a common danger—from outer space, or maybe from a deadly epidemic. But since, at present, we're part of the game and we cannot allow ourselves to be disconnected from those who have control over our society, they have a dictatorial hold over us. In every society, it's important to be popular. That's why I have to fight for my right to belong, changing my tactics from time to time."

He didn't mention the Fatah. He preferred to keep the conversation on a general, philosophical level. "I have been fighting for my right to belong all my life for the simple reason that I have been deprived of that right. The danger is there and I have to face it together with those who share the same fate. We have to employ various stratagems—not necessarily to achieve happiness but in order to suffer less."

The discussion went on until Oz suggested that we take a break for lunch. He brought us to the communal dining room and Ta'mari stood on line, cafeteria-style, with everyone else. When his turn came, he chose a vegetarian dish. The members of the kibbutz paid little attention to the stranger. Only one of them exchanged a few whispered words with Oz.

Ta'mari and Amalia were the first to sit down and were soon engaged in a lively discussion about Dina. Their original mutual reserve had evaporated. I noticed that Ta'mari had a way with women—when not hemmed in by guards with machine guns. I also had a suspicion that Amalia the journalist was making lots of mental notes for future use.

By the time I sat down Ta'mari had already finished eating. He had wiped his platter clean, so to speak, and I realized, with a pang, that he must have been very, very hungry.

After lunch Oz took us on a tour of the kibbutz. We began with the library, where his wife worked and where we enjoyed another cup of coffee. After that we made our way around the various agricultural buildings—the dairy barns, the chicken runs, the tractor shed. Ta'mari was all eyes and every now and then he would tear a leaf off some shrub, roll it between his fingers, and then inhale its scent. We ended up in the members' club, and this time Amos Oz dominated the conversation. He related the history of the kibbutz up to the 1948 war, pausing to recount the story of the friendly relations that had existed between the kibbutz and the nearby Arab village before the war. Nothing remained of the village today. (Six hundred thousand Palestinian Arabs had fled Israel during the war, some voluntarily, some in panic, and some at the "urging" of the Israeli forces.)

Our last stop was the children's house.

We went in on tiptoe since the children were having their afternoon nap. They were sprawled on their small cots in the sweet slumber of the innocent. Ta'mari seemed to go cold.

Many months later, in another country, he confessed to me that the visit to the children's house was excruciatingly difficult for him. "For the first time in my life, I realized how guilty I felt—although it was in fact guilt for a crime I didn't commit. I felt all your eyes staring at me, trying to see how I measured up to the stereotyped image you have of the Palestinian: child murderer.

"It was awful," he recalled. "My feelings of guilt, and your feelings toward me, and all those sleeping children. I didn't know what to do with myself. I started looking at the drawings on the walls. I understand how little kids draw. I often worked with them in the refugee camps, doing arts and crafts. I was in a fluster and I began to touch all sorts of objects—towels, drinking cups, flower vases. Anything that came to hand. And all the time it was as if Amos Oz were telling me that these were the people my comrades chose to kill. Even if he himself wasn't thinking that, I was convinced that he was."

When it was time to leave, Oz shook hands with Ta'mari. "You know," he said, "I never go to cocktail parties, even though I'm often invited. But I promise you that when the day comes and you are your country's ambassador to Israel and you invite me to your first diplomatic reception—I'll be there."

All the way up to Jerusalem, Ta'mari was quiet, absorbed in his own thoughts—as we all were. When we got to Yad Vashem, he became even more remote. He walked through the museum as if he were hermetically sealed in a bubble, as if he had programmed himself not to see anything, not to react. At first I tried being a guide, explaining the exhibits, but his total withdrawal put me off. Most visitors walk around the museum slowly, stopping reflectively at each exhibit. Ta'mari walked around rapidly, from one scene of horror to the next without so much as a pause between them. Amalia was watching his face all the time, trying to read his mind. There was a moment when I asked myself: What in the world made me bring him here?

What went through his mind on that trip, I also discovered when we were far removed, in time and place, from Jerusalem.

"As we walked through Yad Vashem," he told me, "I realized how much you and I have in common, you and I personally, and your people and mine. I saw what the Nazis had done. They were anti-Semitic murderers. As anti-Semites, they would have eventually reached us, my parents and my family. It was only a question of time. You and I are both Semites— maybe we are even more so. The things I saw there were not new to me. I know what a holocaust is. I know what killing means. That wasn't the first time I saw piles of dead bodies. I've seen too many severed limbs and crushed bodies among my own people. Only"—and here he paused significantly—"only we don't have a museum."

I didn't want to answer him. It was beyond me how a man of his intelligence and open-mindedness could compare the Nazi holocaust with the tragedy of the Palestinians—regardless of what share of the responsibility belongs to Israel. I knew that he had personally experienced the profound suffering of his people, but the equation seemed to me pure propaganda.

The trip back to Tel Aviv was uneventful. We were all rather uncommunicative. Amalia and I didn't even talk, although it is doubtful if anything we might have said would have penetrated Ta'mari's bubble. When we reached the outskirts of the city, I announced that we were in Tel Aviv. Apparently this was enough to shake him out of his woolgathering, because he immediately asked if we could stop for a moment. He wanted to bring some small gift to our daughter.

I stopped at a kiosk and bought a bag of balloons for him.

When we came into the house, the guards following behind, Ta'mari refused to act like an ordinary guest. He didn't admire the pictures on the walls or sit patiently on the couch, waiting for his hosts to give him some cue. He walked from one room to the next, into the nursery and the kitchen, out into the backyard and then back into the living room. He picked up the telephone and listened to the dial tone, and then replaced the receiver. It was as if he were trying to assure himself that he was in the real world.

We were also unsure how to treat our guest during those first few minutes. Guest? Acquaintance? Prisoner? And so we just sat there and let him make the first move. Soon we were all laughing. Ta'mari had taken out the bag of balloons and was blowing them up, one after the other, until the living room was full of colored balloons. Our twenty-two-month-old daughter, Reyout—her name means friendship—couldn't take her eyes off him.

When he finished with the balloons, Salah picked up Reyout and started rocking her on his knee. Amalia looked at me and her glance told me everything that was going through her mind: *our daughter* was sitting on the knee of a Fatah commander!! And having the time of her life!!

"She's very pretty," he said. "And her blue eyes are sensational. She's almost as pretty as my sister's child, who also has great big blue eyes. Her name is Dina."

Then he went into the kitchen, opened the refrigerator, closed it, and began to look in the pots on the stove.

"What are you making?"

"Macaroni," Amalia answered.

"On the stove?" he asked, disbelieving. "Macaroni should be made in the oven. Someday I'll teach you."

I gave him dishes and glasses to carry out to the garden, where the table was set. The guards were not sure whether they should join us at the table. One of them compromised, took some food, and ate it sitting on the lawn. The other remained in the house, half asleep on the living-room couch.

Two neighbors passed by, wheeling baby carriages, and stopped to say hello. We introduced them to Ta'mari. They were stunned. They knew exactly who he was. Salah was enjoying every minute. He liked the idea of having people around and our two neighbors soon joined us at the table. We spoke English—though none of us spoke it as well as he did.

One of the women whispered to me in Hebrew: "He's really cute!"

"Be careful," I warned her. "If he's cute, he might also turn out to be a human being." It was fascinating to watch them relate to Ta'mari, all of their tried-and-true notions about terrorists being turned upside down by their first face-to-face encounter with a live Palestinian officer.

We sat around for another hour or so, fighting off the mosquitoes and drinking coffee, until Ta'mari decided it was time to go. "They're liable to think back at the prison that I've hijacked all of you."

The drive back was exceptionally pleasant. The awkwardness of the morning and the strain of the afternoon were gone. We were at ease with each other, and the ups and downs of that day had brought us close together. We talked about this and that and I told Ta'mari I was glad that he and Amalia had gotten along so well. We spoke about our wives and marriage and family and . . . women in general.

When we had almost arrived back at the prison, he turned to me and said: "Being at your home was pretty tough for me. It was not easy but it was pleasant. If I forgot to say 'thank you,' it was because I was preoccupied, trying to overcome my longing for home."

4

"Penelope is waiting and hoping . . ."

"El Al Flight 338 from London, landing now."

It was close to 9:00 P.M. Outside, the humid August evening hung heavily over the airport. I was inside, in the air-conditioned VIP lounge, decked out in a suit and tie, and chain-smoking like a nervous bride. Although everything appeared to be progressing according to schedule, there was a perceptible tension in the air, born of uncertainty: would she arrive or wouldn't she?

The Ministry of Foreign Affairs had sent one of its most experienced people, Dalia Ne'eman, to serve as the visitor's personal escort. Dalia confided to me that she was "wild with curiosity." So was I. I had never seen a queen in person in my life.

The announcement brought us to our feet. I stubbed out my umpteenth cigarette and Dalia gulped down the rest of her coffee. Together we walked across the tarmac to the plane. A black limousine from the ministry was standing by.

Dina was among the first of the passengers to alight. The blast of hot air ruffled her coiffure and, as she descended, she pushed back some loose strands of hair. She had to do some juggling, as she was carrying a small overnight bag and two packages. I had seen only one picture of Dina—in the Jordanian passport she held jointly with Salah. And though there was very little resemblance between the woman in the faded photograph and the woman now descending the steps, there could be no mistake. I recognized her immediately.

The initiative for the visit to Israel had been Dina's alone.

The night of my interview with Ta'mari, I had tried to locate her by phone. Although it was after midnight, I went straight to the Kol Yisrael radio studios and dialed Cairo from there. I was excited by my meeting with Salah and by the genuine rapport between us, and I wanted to do him that small personal favor. The idea of postponing the call—even for a few hours—never occurred to me.

Ta'mari's sister Jihad answered the phone. When I told her I had a message from Salah, she let out a cry that was joyous and heartrending at once: it was the first sign that her brother was still alive. When she calmed down, she informed me that Dina might be in Belgrade, with another sister, Rihab, the wife of Nur Ali.

The connection between Belgrade and the PLO was logical. PLO commanders often attended courses there and Nur Ali was, apparently, at one of them at the moment. The second call, to the number Jihad had given me, proved another dead end. Again, there were cries of joy and disbelief. I could hear Rihab shouting to her husband: "Nur! Salah's alive. The Jews are holding him prisoner." But still no Dina. Rihab told me that she had just spoken to Dina that morning. "She's been trying to get news of Salah ever since the beginning of the war." No, she didn't know exactly where Dina was but I could find out from a friend of hers who worked in Rome. Would I, please, leave her my telephone number in Tel Aviv?

During the course of that night and the next day, my telephone number in Ramat Hasharon was transcribed in Cairo, Belgrade, Rome, and London. I had the occasion later to meet some of the people with whom I spoke, and they were soon established as my "go-betweens" whenever Dina was in an Arab country and I wanted to get in touch with her.

A few days later, I received a call from Rome. It was Dina's friend, talking to an Israeli for the first time in her life. "Dina is on her way to Cairo. She'll call you directly tomorrow afternoon." It had taken a few days to catch up with Dina, but the minute the news reached her she had left wherever it was she had been, just to make the call.

When the call from Cairo came through it was Amalia who answered. Her initial response was formal, even cold, but she was unable to withstand the swell of emotion at the other end. She was soon consoling the distraught stranger. "Don't worry. Your husband is all right. You can believe me."

Amalia called me at the studio a few minutes later. By now, she herself was not only agitated, she was a petitioner. "Dina is waiting for your call in Cairo," she told me. "Call her right away. Don't keep her waiting." Amalia too, I realized, had suddenly become involved in this human drama.

I placed the call through the international exchange. Amnon, the radio engineer who was handling my interview with Ta'mari, had arranged to tape the conversation. He was almost as excited as I was.

The phone hardly rang in Cairo before a voice at the other end was saying: "Hello, hello, finally, thank you so much." Her voice was quavering. "The news caught up with me only late last night. I got here as fast as I could. I'm so grateful. It was so kind of you to look for me. Thank you so much."

I skipped the formalities of telephone politesse. "I understand that you're under great strain. I want to assure you that your husband is well. I spent quite a long time with him."

"When—if I may ask?"

"Well, I last saw him about an hour ago."

"Will you be able to see him again?"

"I hope so. I don't see any reason why not."

I imagine that either Jihad or Rihab had told her that I met Ta'mari in my capacity as a journalist. She tried not to ask things that might compromise me. All her questions were phrased with great tact, in an attempt to discover how he became a prisoner, the conditions of his internment, how he looked, and most important of all how his morale was.

I repeated to her some of his remarks—so typical of his sarcastic humor—and she laughed, but her voice was choked with tears. And then I apologized for the intimate message that I was about to deliver. I was a little embarrassed myself but I was determined to go through with it.

"Your husband asked me to tell you that he loves you. He wants you to know that in his most difficult hours thoughts of you give him the courage to go on." I was quoting Ta'mari exactly. "He asked me to tell you that one day he would compensate you for all the time he has had to be away." And then I remembered something else: "He also asked me to tell you that everything happened apparently because of the piece of paper."

"Did he really say that?" she asked, surprised. "I'm the one who's superstitious, not he."

"Maybe he's changed," I said, able to relax a little.

"I hope that's the only change," she said, and then added: "Tell him that

51

I send my love. Or better still, tell him that Penelope is waiting and hoping . . . and that I am proud of him, no matter what the circumstances, no matter what he did or what he will do. Tell him not to worry about me."

Dina also asked me to inform Ta'mari that her mother had died. Ta'mari had been very close to his mother-in-law, and in the months prior to the Lebanon war, while she was ill with cancer, he had often helped Dina nurse her. "Mother died peacefully," she said. "Tell him that she often mentioned him toward the end. Now Salah and my daughter, Alia, are all that I have. Tell him to take care of himself."

Amnon turned the tape over. The conversation had not yet ended. Dina had something more to say and she said it directly, without ceremony: "Do you think I might be able to visit him? Is it at all possible? It's what I would like more than anything else, even if only for an hour."

Her question took me by surprise. "I don't know," I said. "I'll have to ask. But I will ask, I promise."

I now had to integrate parts of Dina's conversation into the story on Ta'mari, which was slated for broadcast the following morning, and then I had to try and convince the powers-that-be to allow Dina to visit Israel. I figured that before doing this, however, I had better find out exactly what Ta'mari thought of the idea. His responses were definitely not predictable. I also had to straighten out for myself exactly where the dividing line was between my role as journalist and my role as "friend"—if I could use the word—in this human drama.

For the midnight news, I prepared an item that read: "One of Arafat's senior lieutenants gave himself up to the IDF in Sidon and is now being held in Israel. The prisoner, Lt. Col. Salah Ta'mari, is the husband of Dina Abd el-Hamid, the first wife of King Hussein of Jordan. In an interview held with Ta'mari by our correspondent for Arab affairs, the prisoner said that the PLO should evacuate Beirut because the armed struggle had reached a dead end. From now on the organization should concentrate on the political struggle, which cannot possibly be waged from Beirut under siege."

The next morning at seven the entire interview was broadcast and it was rebroadcast on the weekly news magazine.

The day after, I received permission to visit Ta'mari again, in his cell. When I arrived Zuri Ben-Nun was waiting for me.

He greeted me with a big smile. "The media are really indefatigable," he said. "Now the TV wants to get into the act." Ta'mari, he told me, had no objection—provided I was the one to do the interviewing. Before Ben-Nun left (he was going to evening prayers), he told me that the TV station would call the next morning. They wanted Ta'mari to come to the Tel Aviv studios to shoot the interview. "In this case Mohammed has to go to the mountain."

I went to see Ta'mari in his cell and he rose as I entered. This was my third visit in hardly more than a week. He was anxious for my news but first of all—*noblesse oblige*—he wanted to make me coffee. An electric kettle was one of the luxuries allowed him in view of his rank.

I found that I was able to deliver all of Dina's messages without any embarrassment. "She said to tell you that she sends her love—"

"Or," he interrupted, "that Penelope is waiting and hoping." A wry smile crossed his face.

"And that she made an *oumra* [a private pilgrimage] to Mecca," I continued, "to pray for you."

Then I mentioned that it might be possible—just might be—for her to visit him, and how did he feel about it. His reaction was immediate and negative.

"Here? In this stinking hole? Are you out of your mind? Never in your life!"

"You mean to say that you don't want to see her? You're against her coming to visit you?"

"That's right. I am against her coming to visit me."

"Can you tell me why?" I asked.

"Sure," he said. "Because I love her and I don't want to be with her in a place like this." Then he went on. "My memories of her are the only thing that make life here—if you can call this life—bearable. Thinking about her makes this whole place light up. I once promised her that if I ever gave up my country, I would have to give her up too." He must have been overexcited by the idea that she might come because he was soon carried away by his own rhetoric. "She and my homeland are bound together. Whatever I've done up to now, I did because of my love for her and my love of my homeland. But if being in this cell means that I've given up the struggle, there is no place for her here."

"But," I interjected, "you yourself said—and what you said is being broadcast to the whole world tomorrow—that you are not abandoning the struggle, just switching channels. How have you given up the struggle?"

He was silent, and this encouraged me. Maybe his opposition was not that resolute.

"Okay," I said, "let's drop it for the moment. Anyway, permission hasn't yet been granted and I don't think there's much chance that it will be."

"It's the permission," he said. "That's exactly what annoys me."

"So why don't you save your breath until matters are cleared up," I said a little curtly. I had the feeling that the knowledge that Dina was ready to come had confused his priorities. "Anyway," I said, changing the subject, "I'll see you tomorrow. I'm taking you to Tel Aviv to the TV studios."

The following day, Ta'mari repeated in front of the klieg lights the gist of what he had said in the radio interview. When it was over the accompanying officer suggested that we go for coffee to Dizengoff Street, Tel Aviv's lively center. Most of the cafes were jammed—it was lunch hour—but we found a free table at the Café Park. None of the habitués of the Café Park, or the Café Ditza or the Café Cassit, marching in and out and up and down the street, had so much as a glance for our "guest." Only one woman correspondent, who had listened to the radio interview that morning and stopped to say hello, looked at him suspiciously.

When we finished and got up to go, Ta'mari noticed a book store nearby and asked if it was all right to go in for a minute. We went in for more than a minute. After browsing around, Ta'mari borrowed some money from me and bought two books by Amos Oz in English translation, a couple of books on the history of Zionism and the Jewish people, and four on the holocaust.

A few minutes after I returned home, the telephone rang. Dina was on the line. The connection was very bad but we made the best of it.

"I mentioned the idea of the visit to your husband," I said, knowing full well that that was what the phone call was all about. I didn't know exactly how to address her. I wasn't sure I could call her by her first name and "Mrs. Ta'mari" was out of the question. She had never been called Mrs. Ta'mari in her life.

"He's against?" she ventured.

"You're right, but I still have hope."

"So, he's against. What about your authorities?"

Suddenly I had a bright idea. Since Dina was an Egyptian citizen, I thought she could simply go to the Israeli embassy in Cairo, pick up a visa, and come here as a tourist. But the brightness wore off very rapidly. That was no way for a queen to visit her husband, in the enemy's prison.

"I promised you I'd check that out, and I will. Meanwhile," I added, "you can hear your husband tomorrow on Israel's Arabic broadcast. You can also see him tomorrow evening on Israeli television."

She had twenty-four hours to get from Cairo to Amman where the reception of Israeli TV and radio was very good. It didn't take her that long. For me to get permission to bring her to Israel took a little longer.

When I first raised the subject before a senior officer of the IDF, he simply shrugged his shoulders. The idea looked absurd to him: King Hussein's ex-wife visiting a PLO prisoner in the heart of enemy territory. I didn't give up though. I knew the officer personally and counted on the fact that there was a broad-minded man underneath the uniform and stern exterior.

"You know," I said, "she could simply come here as a tourist. She has an Egyptian passport."

The idea amused him and we began to look at all the pros and cons of the situation. Considering the hostility of the international media to Israel in the wake of the Lebanon war, a humane gesture of that sort wouldn't hurt. Even if the visit were kept a closely guarded secret, she, Dina, would know how to get the message through where it counted. In the end, he agreed to pass the idea on to his superiors.

A few days later I was called in by the senior officer. "Okay," he began dryly and a little pompously, "she can come for forty-eight hours as the guest of the Israeli government. Tomorrow morning you're invited to sit with the people from the Ministry of Foreign Affairs to plan the visit, hour by hour. We're casting our bread upon the waters."

"For you will find it after many days," I predicted, completing the biblical phrase.

I phoned Dina in London, telling her to go to the El-Al counter at Heathrow where she would receive a visa on her Egyptian passport. She wanted to know if she could bring her husband a few things. I didn't see why not.

Now, as she descended the steps, I was sure that the two packages contained "a few things" for Ta'mari. And, indeed, one of them did. But the second was for us, for Amalia and me. Both contained cheesecake from the London shop Louis, on Finchley Road. In one of our numerous conversations, I told Dina that Amalia and I had spent our honeymoon in London, and that every time it rained—that is, practically every day—we

55

would dash into Louis and stuff ourselves on cheesecake until the rain let up. I was to discover that these little anecdotes were never lost on Dina. Ta'mari, it turned out, was also a cheesecake lover.

As her foot touched solid ground, Dina looked around, somewhat ill at ease as could be expected. I waved to her and the minute I caught her eye she smiled, relieved. I walked over and she greeted me with "Ahalan [greetings] Aharon," to which I responded "Ahalan wasahalan [greetings and salutations] and welcome to Israel." She responded: "Here I am," and there I was, face to face with the former queen of Jordan.

Dina was fifty-three, more than ten years older than Salah. Although not beautiful in any classical sense, her attractive visage radiated nobility, delicacy, and warmth. Her high forehead and deep brown eyes gave her an open look. Her hair was light brown flecked with gray, and arranged in a chignon. She wore plain silver earrings.

Dina was dressed in a finely tailored black suit, which became her rather full figure, and spike heels (I was never to understand how she managed to move around so quickly and so gracefully on them).

I introduced her to Dalia Ne'eman and explained that Dalia was from Israel's Ministry of Foreign Affairs and would be her official escort during her stay. Dina shook hands with Dalia stiffly, somewhat put off, I think. She became tense and began to cover up her embarrassment with exaggerated expressions of gratitude. It was a habit with her, I learned.

We took her to the limousine. Dalia took her passport and I asked her for her baggage stubs. There were four. Dina smiled: "And I didn't have enough time to get him everything I wanted."

I explained that Dalia would take her to the hotel and I would join her there a little later with Salah, and her bags.

Ta'mari's opposition to the visit didn't change nor did it in fact change anything. After all, we were three—Dina and I and the Israeli authorities—against one.

When I came to pick him up—he had been transferred that morning to a house in the Tel Aviv area—he was sitting in the garden with his guards, eating supper. They had spent the day playing backgammon. The beard he had grown in prison was gone. He was as clean shaven as an ad for razor blades. He was wearing blue jeans, a denim shirt, and sneakers. The leather belt on his pants had been mine—until the previous day, when he'd admired it and then "borrowed" it permanently.

"Dina is on the way to the hotel," I said.

Ta'mari lit a cigarette. "Where is it?"

"On the coast."

"How many stars?" he asked, facetiously.

"Five," I answered, "and the room faces the sea. It's gorgeous."

"You Israelis are suckers for royalty, aren't you?" he continued, trying to annoy me. But he was becoming tense.

"We adore royalty," I answered.

"You're not the only ones. The whole world does."

"The way you look now, you don't seem to be so indifferent either," I said. "Let's go."

We got into the car—Ta'mari and the guards and I. Most of the way he was quiet. He kept changing the position of his long legs, trying to find a comfortable way to sit. Finally he broke the silence.

"There's something wrong with this whole business. Why did you bring her here? You weren't thinking of her, only of yourselves." He raised his voice. "How do you think she's going to feel when it's over? How do you think she's going to feel after seeing me in a fancy hotel when she goes back to where she has to and knows that I'm going back to where I came from? Did anybody think about that?"

"Salah," I said, "she wants to see you. All we did was make it possible."

"So why don't you go whole hog then? Why can't we spend the night together?"

I began to lose patience with him. "Why don't you wait and see what happens. Maybe something will change. I'm not responsible for these arrangements."

"What can change? Why should anything change? Except, maybe, for the worse. Just this morning Ben-Nun told me that he doesn't know how long I'm going to stay in that place."

His approaching meeting with Dina had apparently made the thought of returning to the solitude of his prison cell unbearable.

There were, however, no changes in the plans. Ta'mari and Dina were to spend very little time alone.

We got off the elevator on the eighteenth floor. There were two guards sitting on either side of the door to the hotel room. They rose as we approached. Ta'mari knew them and they shook hands. One knocked on the door and the other opened it. Dina and Dalia were sitting at either end of a small coffee table, waiting. They got up as we entered. Dina did not

rush to her husband, nor he to her. First, the necessary ceremony: Dalia
had to be introduced.

Ta'mari was at least two heads taller than Dina. His first words to her
were: "You shouldn't have come, Dina."

She answered him with: "Why not? I am entitled to see you. I would
have gone to the ends of the earth just to see you alive and well."

"You missed his beard," I put in, hoping to lighten the atmosphere of the
first strained moments.

"Not entirely." She smiled and turned to Ta'mari. "I saw you on television, in Amman. But I must say I prefer you this way."

"You'd prefer me any way you found me," he said, still maintaining his
reserve.

"You're probably right," she returned, looking at him intently.

There was a knock at the door and one of the guards came in carrying
four bags. Ta'mari grinned wholeheartedly for the first time. "Only four?"
he said. "What happened? No time to pack?"

Dina was at the bags immediately, taking things out. But it was as if her
hands were severed from her body. Her glance didn't leave Ta'mari for a
second. "How have you been? Is it very hard for you? Your eyes are so red."

"I'm all right, Dina," he answered softly.

Dalia got up to leave. She addressed Dina: "I'll be here tomorrow at
about nine. Goodnight, everybody."

For a moment, Dina's eyes darted back and forth between Salah and me.
Then she blurted out: "For goodness' sake, you two look alike."

She was not the first person to make that observation.

"How is Sweetie?" Ta'mari asked suddenly. Sweetie was the nickname of
Alia, Dina and Hussein's daughter.

"She is praying for you. So is your mother." His mother lived in Kuwait.
"So is Rihab and everybody else. It was terrible not hearing from you since
the beginning of the war."

The conversation turned to their neighbors in Sidon, and when Dina
informed him that a particular neighbor's son had been killed, he covered
his eyes with his hand. "How do you know?" he asked.

"I know," she answered.

I realized that my presence in the room was becoming oppressive.

"Sweetie was with me during the whole terrible time," she continued. "I
don't know what I would have done without her. Without her—and
without him." She looked at me gratefully.

"Yes," said Ta'mari, following his own train of thought, "I wish I could have been with you when your mother passed away. It must have been so painful." For the first time, she touched him. She took his hand and pressed it warmly in hers.

"You were," she whispered.

Most of the contents of the suitcases were on the bed by now—new clothes, sneakers, underwear, hardcover books, pocket books, a transistor radio, a Walkman, a small battery-operated TV, computer games, mechanical toys. Before I knew what was happening, a small gray mouse with a piece of cheese in its mouth jumped up at me. When I winced, Ta'mari burst out laughing. Dina watched him, her face radiant. I figured this was a good time to go.

"I've also got a daughter at home," I said. "I guess I'd better go now."

"I have something for her," said Dina, and began searching through one of the suitcases.

"It can wait till tomorrow," I said.

Dina came over to me and said: "Thank you for making this happen." We all shook hands and I sensed that her hand stayed in mine a little longer. They were standing very close together as I left, and they followed me with their eyes down the hall.

Not long after I left, Ta'mari was taken back to his lodgings.

The next morning Dalia joined Dina for breakfast. Dina again wore black—this time a light summer dress with a white collar. She was still in mourning for her mother. Before she left the hotel she called me at home, our first "local" telephone conversation. She wanted to thank me again and find out when she could meet Amalia. I told her that we were meeting for lunch, and that I would bring Salah. After that we would all come back to Ramat Hasharon, to our house, for coffee with Amalia.

I made reservations at a fish restaurant on the sea and went to pick up Ta'mari. When I got to the house I found the two guards deep into a game of backgammon. Ta'mari was sitting in a corner, reading.

"How do you feel this morning?" I asked.

"*Elhamdelila* [praise the Lord]," he answered, putting his book aside.

"No complaints this morning?"

He looked at me a little skeptically. One didn't have to have a degree in psychology to notice that Dina's presence had improved his mood considerably.

"How do you feel about fish?" I asked.

"I love fish," he answered, "especially when I cook it myself."

The lunch was not a great success. Neither Dina nor Ta'mari ate very much and Ta'mari was intent on voicing his pejorative opinions about Israeli jails and Israeli guards and the way Israel treated its prisoners in southern Lebanon. He spoke bitterly and loudly. Dina listened in silence.

"When you get back to Europe," he said, and his words were intended for me and Dalia too, "I want you to call a press conference and report on everything I've told you. That's what I'd like you to do."

Dina replied softly. "I will do whatever you think is right but you know that we are not publicity oriented. Besides, I look at this visit as an entirely private affair. I have no intention of making it public."

Ta'mari repeated many of the things that he had said in the interview—particularly about "switching channels," and "a new approach" to the struggle for a Palestinian state. In the middle, Dina turned to me and said: "You know that Yasir Arafat and Farouk Kadoumi think exactly like Salah. But if there's no progress on the political front, don't blame Salah for what happens."

When we took leave of Dalia and got into the car, I suddenly turned to Dina and asked her: "Weren't you afraid of coming here?"

"I can't say that I wasn't frightened at all," she answered. "After all, I was going into *terra incognita*. On the other hand, I wasn't really worried. I was doing what I wanted to, what was important to me. During those weeks when I had no news at all from Salah, I think I would have traveled to the moon to find out what happened to him. You know," she went on, "people sometimes find themselves in totally unexpected situations where they have to make snap judgments. I had no problem deciding. In the last twenty-four hours, I've experienced some strange emotions—sitting in the plane, touching down at your airport, meeting you and Dalia. Even now, I can't say that I'm entirely at ease."

Dina looked me straight in the eye. "I felt instinctively that I could trust you. The fact that your people authorized the visit reinforced my feeling that I was dealing with someone whose motives were humane. You know, I really think that honest relations between people can move mountains. What I did and what you and Amalia did for me can only be for the good." Then she added: "I'm really eager to meet her."

"Count to ten," I said, "and we'll be there." I turned to Ta'mari, who was sitting in the back. "Maybe you count. You've been so quiet the whole way." Dina laughed.

A few yards from the house, Ta'mari asked me to stop the car. A bougainvillea shrub in full purple flower had caught his eye. He got out of the car and broke off a branch. "We have a shrub like this in front of the house in Sidon," he said, and gave the branch to Dina: "I remember how your mother loved it."

Amalia was waiting for us in front of the house. She was holding Reyout in her arms. I could see excitement written all over her face. That morning she had told me how unnerved she was by the very idea of the visit.

Dina got out of the car, walked up to Amalia, and presented her with the bougainvillea. "What a sweet baby," she said, and the two women were almost touching—each excited in her own way, each trying to conceal the excitement as well as she could.

We went through the house and into the garden. Amalia served coffee and Dina sat with the cup and saucer on her lap, her legs crossed, and her back as straight as a ruler. She took no milk or sugar and didn't touch the cake. Ta'mari, meanwhile, was playing hide-and-seek with Reyout, who found him a wonderful playmate. "She's as pretty as Nur Ali's daughters," he said, "but they are prettier."

It wasn't long before I noticed that Dina had tired of playing the perfect guest, of being socially "correct" all the time. All she wanted, in fact, was to talk to her husband or, more precisely, to listen to him.

Every time Amalia went into the kitchen for something she seemed to delay her return a little longer. Finally she called me to come and open a bottle of Coca-Cola. "Stay here a minute," she said a little impatiently. "Can't you see they want to be alone?"

For Amalia it was apparent from the first minute. It took me a little longer to realize that. But it was true: since Dina's arrival in Israel they hadn't been together, alone, for more than a few minutes.

From the kitchen I could see them, leaning toward each other, talking rapidly and in hushed tones. I stalled for a while, first in the kitchen and then on the phone, and when, finally, I returned to the garden, Ta'mari looked at me like a fellow conspirator: "It really took you quite some time to open that bottle. Dina should have bought you a good bottle opener from London."

Dina asked me if I could play the interview for her the way it was broadcast over Kol Yisrael, and I obliged. She listened to his English and the Hebrew translation, entirely engrossed, raising her eyes from time to time to look at her husband. I realized that she hung on his every word.

She seemed to read my thoughts because she turned to me and said: "When he talks it sounds better, more convincing, more dramatic." She admired her husband and didn't really care who knew it. Ta'mari, for his part, considered Dina the judge sitting on high, about to announce the verdict. Her reaction would be an indication of how the others would react—his comrades in the Fatah, his commanders, his family. And he didn't give her much time to think it over. He wanted to know what she thought immediately. Long before I was fully aware of it, Ta'mari had understood that the interview was a milestone in his life, for his future in the PLO. Dina fully understood his sentiments.

Before we brought Dina back to the hotel and Ta'mari back to his guards, we digressed a little from protocol. We gave Dina a small gift, a ceramic vase from one of Jaffa's art galleries. Dina was embarrassed, pleased, and grateful. "I hope you'll agree to accept a few mementos from me, too," she said, and put three small packages on the table. One contained a silver-plated cigarette case for me, one a snake-shaped brooch for Amalia, and the third a turquoise-studded necklace for Reyout.

As Amalia pointed out to me later: "When it comes to gifts, it's hard to compete with a queen." And in the course of time we were to discover this over and over again.

The next evening we came to say goodbye to Dina at the hotel. She would be leaving early the next morning. On the way, Amalia asked me if I thought Ta'mari really appreciated Israel's gesture in letting his wife visit him in the middle of the war.

"Why don't you ask him?" I said.

Dina's room looked as if a whirlwind had just passed through. Nothing had been packed. Everything was lying around in unstudied chaos. Dina and Ta'mari sat on the bed, I sat in a chair, and Amalia sat on the floor, on a rug, near the bed.

Amalia looked up at Salah and Dina: "You know, sometimes people meet and afterward each goes his own way and that's the end of it. Somehow I have the feeling that that's not the case with us four. I have a feeling that nothing will ever be the same again—even if each of us appears to go his or her own way. I see it as a 'fateful encounter.'"

Now she turned to Ta'mari. "I can't get over the feeling that your attitude to this meeting is different from Dina's. I mean, the fact that we are all sitting here in a hotel in Tel Aviv and soon Room Service is going to bring us coffee and sandwiches or something—it just doesn't mean the same thing to you. I know you've been through hell. But despite that—or maybe because of it—I hoped that this visit would be a positive experience for you. I was wrong, wasn't I?"

Ta'mari didn't hesitate. "Yes, you were." He was very candid. "Nobody has promised me that all the evil is behind me. How can I give myself over to the brighter side of things?"

Amalia continued. "The difference between you and Dina is, I guess, greater than I thought. Dina was expecting the worst. She didn't know what had happened to you. She was so worried about you sometimes she wished she were dead. That's what she told me. She decided to take a chance, to throw all her fears and suspicions to the winds—just to see you alive and well. That's what makes her feel obliged to this human gesture. What's happening now to Dina is the best thing that ever happened to her."

Dina nodded in agreement. "Amalia's right," she said.

Amalia kept going, talking to Ta'mari, looking for the right words. "I know it's hard to ask you to see the brighter side of things. But maybe at least you could try and see what's behind the fact that we're sitting here now together."

"We'll never forget what you did." Again Dina replied for Ta'mari.

Now I joined in. "You have to realize that 'you' means the State of Israel. That's what Amalia is trying to explain to Salah—that 'we' are the State of Israel." I sounded like a fanatic Zionist.

"I want to know," Amalia said, still addressing Ta'mari, "whether or not when all this is over, when the war ends and you are a free man again, and you are sitting in the station in London or in the park in Paris and an Israeli or a Jew happens to be sitting next to you—if you'll be able to talk to him too?"

"First of all," he answered, "I'd have to see if I could find in him the Israeli I know. After that, I'd see." That was all. Mr. Caution.

The silence thickened and became oppressive. And then, without warning, Ta'mari was on his feet, walking around the room. "Amalia," he said, "I don't want to talk about gratitude because those are only words. But I will promise you one thing: I will never do anything that will make it possible for someone to come to you with a newspaper and a screaming

63

headline and say 'See what that terrorist friend of yours did!' I will never do anything that will make you or Aharon ashamed of me."

It was a promise made for himself for which he alone would assume responsibility.

His promise was enough for us.

We got up to leave. I had a lump in my throat. It was clear to me that Amalia and Dina were both deeply moved. Nevertheless, they both kept their composure. "You don't have to ask," Amalia said to her. "We'll try to keep in touch and take care of Salah."

I shook hands with Dina and—reading her mind—said: "No, believe me. You can call whenever you like. It's no trouble."

Dina took me at my word and her calls were frequent. She wanted news of her husband. She had left him not knowing when she would see him again, if it were a matter of weeks, or months or years.

I could hardly guess that in a very short time our roles would be reversed—that she would be calling in order to give *me* world-shaking news.

5

"The Black Rose of Jordan"

Dina Abd el-Hamid was twenty-seven years old when King Hussein's private plane landed in Cairo to take her back to Amman for their wedding. She had not been taken out of silver wrappings for the occasion. Dina was a lecturer in English literature at Cairo University. What, precisely, the future held in store for her she didn't know. As a daughter of the Hashemite family, she had met Hussein when she was younger and their friendship had ripened considerably in the past four years. If she had moments of foreboding, they were only natural under the circumstances: her entire life was about to change. But of one thing she was sure: she would do her best to justify the king's choice.

It was evening when the plane landed in Amman. As Dina descended, she was suddenly bathed in spotlights and could hear the crowds crying from all sides: "Long live Dina! Welcome Queen Dina!" It was an exhilarating moment.

Hussein stepped forward to take her hand and the cheering of the crowds grew louder. The king's entourage was all smiles. Yet the king himself, a young, dark, mustachioed man of small stature, was not smiling. Dina's flight had been delayed in Egypt and by the time it reached Amman, darkness had fallen. The Jordanian monarch had been deprived of his opportunity to meet his bride's plane in the air, with him at the controls of the airborne escort, and his people had been deprived of a royal air show.

MINE ENEMY

The story of Dina's life as Hussein's queen seldom came up during the long and frank conversations Amalia and I held with her. At our very first meeting, we discovered her discomfort at our curiosity and peeping into that period of her life—the curiosity of people who seem to view those bearing regal titles as being altogether different from ordinary mortals. Had she agreed to open up and discuss at length that period in which she had endured continuous suffering and received little respect from certain members of the family, we might have come to a closer, more precise picture of life in the palace in Amman and the lifestyle of the English literature lecturer who became a queen. But Dina, despite her share of bitterness, is a person of nobility. She would never turn on her former family. Her position was, and always will be, that of noblesse oblige.

In spite of everything that took place, Dina treats her former husband, King Hussein of Jordan, with the dignity accorded royalty, and is averse to divulging details about the royal family or her own life inside the palace. When the subject comes up she gracefully side-steps it with a humorous remark or simply brushes it off. Her references to Hussein tend to be formal rather than casual—he is always the King or King Hussein.

Dina has never initiated a discussion of those years. Nevertheless, she responded to every question we asked. Noting her sensitivity, we decided not to question her too extensively regarding that period of her life. She seemed to welcome the limits we put on our curiosity.

To complete the picture, we traced her past from other sources: we searched archives for press coverage from the fifties and read various studies of modern Jordanian history and the history of the Hashemites. We quickly learned that Dina had been covered by the media from all angles, much in the same way that Princess Diana of England has been covered in the eighties. There were countless reports, stories, interviews, and photographs, spread throughout hundreds of newspapers and magazines. From the minute the engagement was announced, everything Dina said or did (or was rumored to have said or done), everything she wore, everywhere she went, down to the smallest detail, was grist for the mill. Her photographs ornamented the covers of Arab weeklies and monthlies.

During our repeated meetings we sometimes shared with her information we had independently collected. Occasionally her response was disbelief and she would dismiss the information as nonsense, saying, "I have already seen that movie." Sometimes, however, she laughingly acknowledged an item or was completely surprised that certain information had become public. Once, to her great astonishment and pleasure, we showed her a photograph from our own collection, a photograph she had never seen before of herself, her mother, Fakhriyya, and her daughter, Alia, on one of Alia's birthdays. She was unaware that that photograph had been taken.

Filling in the puzzle of Dina's life was a fascinating project. We found in her past the beginning, the foundation of the Dina whom we had come to know: A humble, pleasant, agreeable woman who establishes warm relationships and is true to her feelings and convictions. It was sometimes difficult to avoid the temptation of making comparisons, or trying to make psychological generalizations. We found out, for example, that the most important men in her life had something in common. The two men whom she married were both younger than she and, at least to the general public, outwardly macho, though inwardly uncalloused.

At any rate, the reconstruction of Dina's life, as told here—her childhood and adolescence, her teaching, and her reign and banishment—was woven from threads of the press, particularly the Jordanian and Egyptian press. Only parts of the story were given or confirmed to us by her. In some newspapers, especially Arab newspapers, there are certainly some unintentional, rather imaginative exaggerations of the pen. But until Dina writes her own story—if she ever does—this is the story of her life.

The Egyptian and Jordanian press contended that the romance between Dina and Hussein had begun in Britain when both of them were studying there. Hussein studied at Harrow and at the Royal Military Academy, Sandhurst. Dina was reading English literature at Cambridge. During that time, they met once in London.

Hussein's mother, Queen Zayn, who kept close tabs on the heir apparent, encouraged the affair. Aside from the fact that Dina was of unblemished Hashemite stock—from that branch of the family living in Egypt—she was known to be an intelligent and thoughtful young woman, a brilliant student, and a perfect lady. The papers also mentioned that Queen Zayn was not indifferent to the fact that Dina came from one of the most prominent and highly respected Egyptian families. Politically speaking, such a match could only prove beneficial.

Dina and Hussein had met for the first time in 1946 in Amman, at a family gathering. Dina was eighteen at the time, Hussein a boy of eleven.

According to one interview, Dina reported that "he was quiet but very alert. Altogether we were rather similar in character and temperament, maybe because of our family ties and our common background."

Another time they met was when her family made a condolence visit to Jordan in 1951, after the assassination of King Abdullah, Hussein's grand-father. The event was traumatic for Hussein, who was very attached to his grandfather and had accompanied him that day to the Mosque of al-Aqsa in Jerusalem. He not only witnessed the shooting but was almost killed himself by a second bullet, which was aimed at him but deflected by a medallion he wore around his neck. The meeting of the two distant cousins under these circumstances helped cement relations between them: "I tried as well as I could," Dina is reported to have said, "to help him overcome his grief."

When Hussein ascended to the throne in 1953, at the age of eighteen, Dina was already the leading candidate "for assisting the king in perpetuating the dynasty," as the papers put it. At this time Queen Zayn, now the queen mother, gave all her time and energy to the subject of a future Hashemite heir. Relations between the two families became closer.

The engagement was made public in 1955, just a few weeks before the wedding. A royal plane brought Hussein and his mother to Cairo, where they attended the bride's family at their home in the Me'adi section of the city. The king shook hands with his thin, silver-haired prospective father-in-law, and the match became official. The king and his mother returned to Amman soon after, leaving Dina to make her farewells and prepare for the big event.

The house was soon inundated with flowers, mostly roses and orchids, and the press began to arrive in hordes to interview the future queen of Jordan. She was bombarded with questions on a variety of subjects. When the subject of fashion was broached and she was asked to expatiate on her bridal gown, the young woman, who generally dressed with elegant simplicity, responded that she didn't think that spending huge sums on a wedding dress made by a couturier was the first priority of the Jordanian people. There were, she insisted, other things that came first. "Such as?" the reporters wanted to know.

"Such as books," answered the future queen.

Shortly before her departure, Dina attended a farewell party in a small club on the banks of the Nile. The party was given by the humanities faculty of Cairo University for their colleague. "Our only consolation,

Dina," said the dean of the faculty, "is that our loss is the Jordanian people's gain." An elderly professor added: "Dina has been a radiant blossom in our midst and her perfumed scent will remain with us forever."

Dina was very moved. "I would have loved to remain here with you, but the will of my beloved Jordanian people calls." Turning to her students, she begged them not to hold her "defection" against her, and with tears in her eyes embraced them one by one.

A few days later the name of the street where she lived was changed to "Princess Dina Street," and it still bears that name.

Dina and Hussein drove from the Amman airport to the palace at Basman in an open white sedan. They were flanked by a motorcycle escort. The streets were dense with cheering people, out to welcome their new queen. Hussein alternately waved and saluted; Dina just tried to keep her white kerchief from blowing off. The crowds were in a frenzy of delight and the police had to force them back bodily, to keep them from blocking the path of the car. Dina found this display of adulation somewhat unnerving, although she was beginning to grasp what it would mean to be a queen.

When she awoke the next morning, the palace was already surrounded by thousands of people, many of whom had spent the entire night there just to pay tribute to their new queen first thing in the morning. She and Hussein went to the balcony to wave to them. Soon after, Hussein got into his sports car and drove at a reckless speed to Jerusalem and back. It was his way of easing tension. Dina would have liked to go with him, but Moslem tradition was against: the bride and groom were not allowed to be alone in each other's company prior to the wedding, not even in a car.

The couple were married on Tuesday, April 19, 1955, at the palace of the queen mother in Zahran. The ceremony was held in the presence of members of the family only. While Dina sat in one room together with her parents and the queen mother, Hussein was in another, signing the marriage contract. There were two witnesses: his cousin, Faisal, the young king of Iraq, and the Qadi (magistrate) of Amman. The invitees were ushered into the crystal-bedecked palace foyer where they imbibed wild strawberry nectar. Moslems are forbidden to drink alcohol, even at weddings.

The proceedings took only a few minutes—and Dina and Hussein were husband and wife. During the entire ceremony, the bride had not seen her groom.

Dina wore a pearl- and crystal-studded white Venetian lace gown, made by an Egyptian designer. The Italian designer Shubert had made a special trip to Cairo to show and suggest another dress, but Dina was particularly insistent that a level of modesty be observed in accordance with Moslem custom. As a result, the dress was made in Cairo, the sleeves were lengthened, and the décolleté raised several inches. Dina's head was covered with a traditional Moslem bride's veil. When Hussein removed the veil after the bride and groom were brought together, he replaced it with a diamond tiara.

The bride and groom left the palace in the same white car that had taken them from the airport and the car again had to plow its way through the throngs to the palace in Amman for the reception. People were dancing in the streets, which had been especially illuminated for the occasion, and continued their uninterrupted celebrations for the traditional seven days of the wedding feast. Farid el-Atrash, the most popular singer in the Arab world at that time, was brought from Egypt to sing a medley of songs especially composed for the occasion.

King Hussein's first marriage was a real national celebration. The genuine and spontaneous outbursts of joy and adulation never reached the same level in his three subsequent marriages. There was something about Queen Dina that strongly appealed to the Jordanian people.

Dina was born on August 28, 1928, in Alexandria. Her father was Sharif Abd el-Hamid Aal-Awn of the House of Hashem. Her mother, Fakhriyya, was Turkish, of Circassian origin. Many Sunni Moslem Circassians had fled their native Caucasus in the nineteenth century, in the wake of Russian persecution, and settled in Turkey, Jordan, the Arabian peninsula, Syria, and Palestine. Their loyalty to the authorities and their well-known bravery brought many of them into the ranks of the palace guards in Jordan. That Sharif Abd el-Hamid chose a wife from among the Circassians is indicative of the fact that they had become accepted in Arab society.

Abd el-Hamid, like Hussein, was a descendant of Hashem, the great-grandfather of the Prophet Mohammed and like all direct descendants bore the title Sharif, which means "offspring of the prophet." The Hashemites are considered by most in the Arab world to be the most authentic Arabs in existence. For centuries the Hashemite dynasty ruled Hejaz, a formerly independent kingdom in western Arabia where the holy cities of Islam, Mecca and Medina, are located. They were also responsible for guarding the Ka'aba, a building containing the most holy black stone relic to which pilgrimages are made. It is believed to have been erected by Abraham the Patriarch. Throughout the Ottoman Empire, the Sharifs were granted autonomy over this area.

During the First World War, when the Ottoman Empire crumbled and fell, the Sharif Hussein Ibn Ali was at the head of the Arab Revolt that broke out in Hejaz. Initiated and supported by the British, through the good offices of the famous Lawrence of Arabia, the revolt brought about a realignment of forces in the Middle East. Britain and France divided the entire region between them, and Hussein Ibn Ali was awarded two kingdoms, Syria and Iraq, for his cooperation in the revolt. His son Abdallah was made king of Iraq, and another son, Faisal, king of Syria. Later, the French government forced Faisal out of Syria and he took over the throne of Iraq from Abdallah, who was then compensated by the British with the creation of the desert kingdom of Transjordan.

Other branches of the family, among them the Aal-Awns, remained in Hejaz. In 1924, however, war broke out between the Hashemites and Ibn Saud of the Wahabi dynasty from Nejd, the eastern part of Arabia, and by the end of the year, Ibn Saud had conquered Mecca. Two years later he was crowned king of the entire Arabian peninsula (Hejaz and Nejd), which now became known as Saudi Arabia.

Among the Hashemites who found sanctuary in Egypt was Dina's father, who had brought considerable wealth with him from the royal coffers of Hejaz. He purchased land, citrus groves, and other property in Alexandria. When Dina was small the family bought a mansion in Cairo. Part of the family property eventually passed into Dina's hands; but in 1952, during the revolution by "The Young Army Officers," it was nationalized. President Nasser and, later, President Sadat tried to assist in having the property restored to her, but the problem has not yet been solved.

From early childhood Dina's mother instilled in her a pride in her Hashemite origins. Although their language of conversation was Turkish, *Anna* (mother), as Dina always called her, began to teach Dina literary Arabic when she was five, during a childhood illness. When the little girl recovered she surprised her father by her ability to read and write Arabic. Dina had a natural talent for languages, and by the time of her marriage was fluent in English, French, and Spanish as well.

She was a quiet child, although the few friends she did have were always lively and mischievous. She was, apparently, attracted to her opposites. Still her mother, until her death, remained Dina's best friend. As a girl and the only child of a wealthy and notable Arab family, her childhood vistas were severely restricted. But if she lacked playmates, she made up for them with books.

Her mother would accompany her to kindergarten in the morning and pick her up at noon, and this pattern remained in force during her school years until—as was the custom among families of her standing—she was sent to boarding school in England. Her Western education, which continued at Girton College, Cambridge, in no way affected her profound attachment to her Arab, Moslem, and Hashemite roots. On special occasions, especially on visits to the more conservative areas in the Arab world, she even covered her face with the traditional veil as a mark of respect to Moslem values.

After her marriage to Hussein, she gave herself up to a study of the history and traditions of the component peoples of Jordan: the Bedouins, the Circassians, the Sunni Moslems, and the Palestinians. Early on she came to the conclusion that the Palestinians were the best element in the country.

Dina and Hussein moved into the palace in Basman, located on a hilltop overlooking Amman. Soon after the wedding they left for Europe, where they met with heads of state and other political figures. When they returned, "official life" at the palace started for Dina. She had a multitude of servants at her beck and call. A private secretary handled her daily schedule. The only thing she lacked was someone to talk to. "Everyone needs a listening ear," she once told us. "But among all the many people who surrounded me at the palace, there wasn't a single soul I could talk to."

Among her queenly duties were receiving women visitors to the country; lending her patronage to various affairs connected with women and children; presiding over afternoon teas and cocktail parties and, at times, balls. The last chore was one of the most difficult for her. "I could never imagine myself dancing in public. That's a Western custom, totally foreign to our mentality," she said in one of her interviews at the time. She was naturally expected to provide the media with some tidbit almost daily, and her interviews were always preceded by a visit from the royal hairdresser. During her "spare" time, she again turned to her favorite companions: books, especially, as always, philosophy and English poetry.

If she hadn't realized it before, it soon became clear to her that all her functions were ceremonial or representative, and would remain as such in the future. She did not play any significant role in state matters. But there was one field in which she hoped that she would be able to make a real contribution: the establishment of a university in Jordan. Jordan was, academically speaking, a wasteland, but Dina believed that it would be possible to find enough lecturers and students to make the project feasible. She had spoken to Hussein about this even before the marriage and he had listened to her with interest, even enthusiasm. Now, however, he dismissed her ideas as being too much of a burden on the budget. "I remember pointing out," she later recalled, "that the budget for the flags and decorations at our wedding alone would have covered a good part of the expenses." She nonetheless pursued the idea in talks with ministers and educators.

These views did not endear Dina to the royal household, and later it was whispered about the palace that her meetings were an attempt to intervene in the management of state affairs. Such were the reports in the Arab press at the time.

The above notwithstanding, Dina was most meticulous in the performance of her representational duties, and the women of Jordan came to love her. Society ladies who frequented royal affairs were impressed by her warmth and modesty and made no secret of their admiration for the queen. But her meteoric rise in the public's estimation was matched by just as meteoric a decline in the good graces of her mother-in-law. Dina was, in the nature of things, infringing upon territory over which Zayn had at one time held full sway. Zayn had the feeling that she was being crowded out.

Zayn's position was easy to understand. Her husband, Talal, came to power after Abdallah's assassination, but because of mental instability was deposed by the Jordanian parliament not long after. Zayn was thus queen of Jordan for only thirteen months. After her husband was committed to an institution in Turkey (where he remained until his death in 1971), Zayn stayed on in the palace with her four children: Hussein, who ascended to the throne, Mohammed, Hasah, and Basma. The new king was only eighteen years old and his mother dominated not only him but palace life and the affairs of state as well.

Although Zayn had approved and encouraged the match with Dina, once her daughter-in-law was ensconced in the palace and began to assume her queenly rights and duties, Zayn felt left out. Not a shrinking violet to begin with, she decided to reassert herself. There was only one way to do this: by eroding Dina's position.

Zayn soon established a network of "private eyes" within the palace.

They kept tabs on all of Dina's moves, inside and out: where she went, with whom she met, to whom she wrote letters, etc., etc. All of Dina's servants became spies for the dowager queen. Zayn openly displayed her malice for the young queen, playing on the seven-year age difference between Dina and Hussein. Zayn was once reported to have called her "that old woman."

It took some time for Dina to sense that a web of jealousy and hatred was being spun around her. She and Hussein still spent all their free time together. True it was very limited, but it was mutually satisfying. They walked in the palace gardens or played tennis or went horseback riding. They discussed politics frequently and found a good deal to laugh over together. Furthermore, Dina was fervently determined to make a success of their marriage.

Yet, as time passed, she sensed that the king was becoming more and more remote. "When I spoke to him, I had the feeling that he was listening out of courtesy rather than interest. I couldn't even be sure that he absorbed what I was telling him. He was becoming alienated from me and soon we seemed to have nothing left in common. His former pronouncements to the effect that he needed me to help him realize his aims now appeared to be empty phrases. I began to wonder why we had married in the first place."

Palace criticism of her mounted. "Everything I did produced negative vibrations. Whenever I went out to attend some affair, it was bruited about that I was undermining royal authority. If I refused invitations and remained at home, it was said that I was a snob, not interested in people."

One day, Queen Dina was invited to an event at the girls' school in Nablus. When she asked the king if he thought she should attend, he said that it was up to her. She decided to go, and left for Nablus in a plane, together with the chief of the royal court, Bahajat a-Talhouni. In Nablus they were given a frenzied welcome. The city elders asked Dina to say a few words to the cheering throngs. Dina apologized, saying she had not prepared a speech. Only after a-Talhouni had contacted the palace in Amman and received permission from Hussein for her to address the crowd did she agree to say a few words. She thanked the people of Nablus for their kind welcome and added: "The enthusiasm you have displayed for me on this visit is an expression of the great enthusiasm and love you bear for your king, Hussein."

When she got back to Amman, she found the king livid with anger. He made no attempt to control his passions and simply poured out his wrath on his wife. A little later she learned the reason for it: Zayn had convinced him that she was competing with him for the love of the Jordanian people, undermining his own popularity. From then on, Dina realized that Hussein was entirely under his mother's influence and that she was considered nothing less than a fifth column in the palace.

Following the Nablus incident, Dina promised the king that she would never again speak in public and Zayn made it her business to inform the Jordanian public that the queen was in disgrace. But that wasn't all. The queen mother began to spread rumors to the effect that relations between the king and his wife were strained and that Hussein was showing interest in other women.

Dina paid little attention to the rumors. She simply clenched her teeth and decided to carry on. She had good reason for doing so: she was pregnant.

"When I told Hussein the news, he was pleased as punch. It had nothing to do with the continuation of the dynasty. He was simply overjoyed at the idea that we were going to have a child. We became close to one another again. He was as warm and loving and considerate as he had been at the beginning."

Alia was born on February 13, 1956. "Anyone who thought that Hussein was disappointed because it wasn't a boy was totally wrong. The king was delighted." Standing by her crib one day, with tears of joy in his eyes, he said he hoped she would grow up to be an aviatrix. Some years later, he named the Jordanian Royal Airlines after her.

"For a short time," Dina told us, "I thought that we had succeeded, with the help of the baby, in overcoming all our troubles. But I was wrong. Soon enough, tongues were wagging again and new plots were afoot. The king surrendered. He made his choice and he didn't choose me."

In the autumn of 1956, when Alia was eight months old, Dina's father was injured in an automobile accident and Dina flew to Cairo to be at his bedside. Hussein refused to let her take the baby along and so Alia was left in the hands of her English nanny, Mrs. Norah Greig, who had been brought from England when the baby was born.

When her father's condition improved and Dina was able to think about returning home, she called Amman to make arrangements. "I think you had better stay where you are," the king told her, "until the situation becomes more propitious." Dina was staggered.

Day after day she repeated the exercise. Day after day she was told "not yet." The king's replies were faltering and evasive, and usually ended with the promise that he was doing his best to expedite her return and there was nothing to worry about. But more than she was worried, Dina was sick with longing for her daughter.

By now Amman was thick with rumors, most of them emanating from the palace in Zahran, the residence of the queen mother. When asked by a reporter if it was true that Hussein was in love with a certain Italian beauty she laughed and replied: "Give him a chance to grow up and become a man." Not long after, she invited the beautiful Flavia Tessio to the palace and introduced her to her circle of friends.

A few weeks later there was a summit of Arab leaders in Cairo, and everyone assumed that Hussein would return from Egypt with Dina. Hussein, in fact, did visit Dina at her father's home in Me'adi, remaining with her until midnight. Dina plied him with questions about Alia. Hussein had brought with him dozens of photographs of the baby and informed Dina that she had already said her first word: "Dada." But little was said about Dina's future.

When Hussein returned to Amman, throngs of Jordanians turned out to welcome back their king and queen. When Hussein descended alone from the plane, the crowds refused to believe their eyes. They remained glued to the ground, refusing to leave the airport. The chief of police was ordered to disperse them after Bahajat a-Talhouni announced that Dina would not return until "greater stability prevailed in the kingdom."

In Cairo, Dina was torn between the conflicting rumors about Hussein's forthcoming marriage to the daughter of the Jordanian ambassador in Syria and her longing for her daughter. She still called the palace every day to get news from Mrs. Greig about Alia.

The axe fell when Alia was nine months old. As the papers of the time reported, Dina was informed by Hussein that a new chapter had begun: "If you think that you and my enemies can use my daughter as a weapon against me," he told her, "you are mistaken." All communication between Dina and the palace was forbidden.

Seven years were to pass before Dina was permanently reunited with her daughter.

Alia's first birthday was celebrated in Amman with due pomp and ceremony. On a platform constructed for the occasion near the Basman palace, Hussein held his small daughter in his arms as he reviewed his army. The entire officers' corps of the Arab Legion stood at attention, in

their resplendent dress, some of them wearing British-style berets and uniforms, others in colorful robes and traditional checkered *kaffiyehs*.

Alia was dressed in a scarlet velvet gown, her head covered with a hand-
embroidered woolen hat to protect her from the zero-degree winter cold.
Mrs. Greig was not on the spot to attend to her charge. Women were not
permitted to participate in military ceremonies and the devoted nanny
waited behind the stage. Alia was the only representative of the female sex
allowed at the celebration in her honor.

Dina was able to follow events from the photographs on the front pages
of the newspapers. She learned that her year-old daughter was already
walking. What she couldn't know was that the Jordanian people had not
forgotten her, that her name was on their lips that day as they celebrated
the royal birthday.

She had sent Alia a birthday present through a relative. She had not yet
been deprived of that privilege. It was a doll's house, complete with five
colorfully dressed "tenants," fully furnished rooms, a "lit" fireplace, gardens, and riding trails.

Many years later, when Alia was already thirty, that same doll's house,
with everything still intact, was sent to another little girl, in Israel.

During the first year of separation Dina fought tenaciously for her right
to see her child, appealing to mutual relatives and to political figures to
soften the king's heart. Finally, when Alia was a year and a half, Hussein
condescended to a single meeting between mother and daughter. It was a
birthday present from Hussein to Dina, on Dina's twenty-eighth birthday.
The Jordanian ambassador to Cairo appeared at Dina's father's house with a
telegram from the king.

"You can go for a visit with Alia tomorrow, Dina," her father told her
after reading the telegram.

"Where?" asked the excited Dina.

"To Istanbul," was the answer.

So it was final. Dina would not be allowed to return to Jordan nor,
apparently, was the king prepared to let Alia visit Egypt. Neighboring
Turkey seemed a suitable compromise.

Zayn was unable to prevent the visit. The king still had some feeling for
his wife. Nonetheless, the queen mother hoped to reduce the repercussions
of the meeting to a minimum. She knew that the newspapers would play up
Dina's birthday and the reunion in Istanbul. A royal order was issued to the
press to refrain from contacting the queen or any member of her family in

Cairo. Furthermore, any mention of the departure of Princess Alia to Istanbul was absolutely forbidden. And to top it off, Zayn notified Hussein that, in addition to Mrs. Greig, a number of servants, and three Circassian bodyguards, she herself would go along to supervise the visit. True she would not be present at the reunion itself, but her proximity to the scene would preclude any untoward happenings. She would occupy a suite in the same hotel on the banks of the Bosphorus and receive complete reports of what was going on. Mrs. Greig, she emphasized, was never to leave Alia alone with her mother.

Dina left Cairo by herself and refused to tell the press the purpose of her trip. The papers were able to report only that Queen Dina, dressed in a simple gray dress and a straw hat, and carrying a book, boarded a regular commercial flight to Turkey. The accompanying photograph shows Dina smiling sadly, her eyes lowered.

The meeting between mother and child was mediated by Mrs. Greig. "This is your mommy," she kept explaining to the confused child who didn't—couldn't—recognize the emotionally traumatized woman who kept pressing her to her breast and weeping into her black curls. Mrs. Greig was no less affected by the meeting, although she knew she had to keep her emotions in check.

The reunion lasted eleven days, at the end of which a messenger from Zayn's suite notified Dina that the visit was over. That same day, her birthday, Dina returned by herself to her father's house. The next day a small item appeared in the Jordanian papers: "Queen Zayn and Princess Alia returned from a short private visit during which the young princess met with her mother, Dina." Astute readers were able to discern the fact that for the first time the title "Her Majesty the Queen" was not appended to Dina's name. It was another of Zayn's royal decrees.

Before the trip to Istanbul, Dina had received the official bill of divorce-ment in a diplomatic pouch from Amman to Cairo. When it arrived, Hussein was in Europe on a spree.

During the next six years, Dina did not meet with her daughter even once. Zayn's cruel vengefulness and Hussein's capitulation to his mother—all of which went under the name of "royal policy"—robbed Dina of the most cherished right of motherhood, the right to be with her child. Yet, despite her bitterness and pain, despite her unending private battle to gain access to her child, she refused to make her troubles public. She avoided the press on the subject, and whenever an enterprising newspaper reporter tried to squeeze a condemnation of Hussein out of her, she would reply: "The king is doing his duty and I am obliged to respect him."

In his biography of King Hussein of Jordan, Peter Snow writes: "His love life after his divorce from Dina in 1957 was no less eventful than his political career. His temperament and his predeliction for adventure and romance brought him into the company of attractive women and girls all over the Middle East and Europe. He could never be persuaded not to speed around in one of his racing cars with a pretty girl at his side. His life was a perpetual race, full of surprises and startling events. His name was linked romantically with those of a number of women, including the German actress Barbara Valentine, the Hashemite princess Hazima, and the Italian beauty Flavia Tessio. But until 1961 there was no talk of a second marriage."

It was only in 1963, two years after Hussein's marriage to Muna, that Dina was allowed to return to Jordan, to stay at the palace and spend time with her daughter, now a schoolgirl. A Jordanian songwriter composed a lovely tango at the time, called "The Black Rose of Jordan," in Dina's honor. People still cheered her when her car passed through the streets of Amman.

Muna was the daughter of a British colonel stationed in the Hashemite kingdom, and her original name was Tony (Antonia) Gardiner. She converted to Islam in order to marry Hussein. Within three years of their marriage she had given birth to four children, Abdallah, Faisal, and twins Zayn and Aisha.

According to the grapevine, it was Muna who pressed Hussein to allow Dina to return to her daughter, at a time when she herself was undergoing the same hardships in her marriage that her predecessor had undergone. Rumors were rife about Hussein's affairs with other women, especially when he was off in Europe. Muna was not able to prevent her own decline in royal favor in favor of her successor—Alia Tokan.

More than twenty years after Dina had been reunited with her daughter, she and Amalia were driving in Dina's Jaguar in London. It was the summer of 1985. Dina stopped the car in front of a stately old building, a hospital.

"This is where it happened," she said, pointing up to one of the rooms. "I was hospitalized here when suddenly I was notified that he wanted to see me—after all those years. I was very ill, about to undergo an operation. My family was with me. I refused to see him. I was adamant about it. The members of my family also told him it was a bad time, that I shouldn't be excited. That I had been through enough."

She paused, looking for the right words. "The next day, I was about to be taken to the operating room. The king came into my room and said only one thing: 'Forgive me.'

"That's all. What could I do? It doesn't matter what he did. When a person stands in front of you and says 'forgive me,' you have to accept it. I forgave him."

"After everything he did to you?" Amalia was disbelieving.

"After everything," she answered softly. "I have nothing against him anymore. I know now that he suffered too. And besides, he is Alia's beloved father and today Alia is my best friend. So I have to take that into consideration too."

Dina started up the car again. On their way home they stopped off at Hamley's, London's large toy shop. Three children were waiting for their return: Reyout and her small brother, Or, and little Hussein, Alia's son and Dina and Hussein's grandson, who is somewhere in the line of succession to the throne of Jordan. Ta'mari and I were also waiting—as was one more person: Mrs. Greig, now a gray-haired woman in charge of Alia's little boy. Alia and her son, together with Mrs. Greig, had come to visit Dina and Salah in London by chance, just when we were there. They didn't know that there was an Israeli couple in the house, with their two children. When Dina and Amalia left for a while, the children immediately found a common language.

After the women returned, the children began playing with their new toys. Amalia and Ta'mari sat in a corner having one of their endless arguments. Alia and I were discussing purebred Arabian horses. Soon after, Hussein got up to go for his daily Arabic lesson and Mrs. Greig held out his raincoat for him. Dina, who was standing at the door, suddenly put one arm in Mrs. Greig's and the other in mine. Turning to everyone else in the room she said with an embarrassed smile: "These are the two people in the world to whom I owe my sanity. To you," she said, turning to Mrs. Greig, "for being close to Alia when I was far away, and to you, Aharon," she said, turning to me, "for being with Salah when I couldn't be there."

Fortunately for everyone, the children began to make a rumpus and attention was diverted from three pairs of wet eyes.

6

"I hate that queen!"

As'ad Suleiman Hasan, a tall, thin, good-looking boy of about twelve, was walking up and down the aisles of the Bethlehem movie house. It was intermission and he was hawking refreshments: cold drinks, candy, peanuts. He liked his new job. He worked evenings, which didn't interfere with school, and he made enough to give some of his earnings to the family and still have pocket money left over. But best of all, he could see all the movies free.

That night something went wrong. One of the customers got tired of waiting for the boy to reach his row and he began to shout impatiently: "Move your ass a little faster, stupid." The boy walked over to the gentleman, raised the wooden tray on which all his wares were carefully arranged, and dumped them on the man's head. With nothing left to sell, he left the movie house.

The next day he went to his boss to apologize. The owner of the cinema knew the boy's family and, under the circumstances, was prepared to accept his apology on condition that . . . As'ad bristled at his tone of voice. He told the owner he was quitting. His pride did not go before a fall, never did and never would.

As'ad was born in Bethlehem on October 27, 1942, to a large family from the Bedouin tribe of Ta'mara, which to this day lives near the ancient

81

fortress of Herodium. Like most of his kin, he had beautiful bright green eyes. His father was named Abu Daud (father of Daud), in accordance with custom: Daud was his first son. He had worked as a cook in Jaffa between 1942 and 1948, returning home once a week to his family. But after 1948, unable to commute between Israel and Jordan-occupied Bethlehem, he lost his job. He was unemployed until he was given the concession for a small kiosk in the courtyard of the police station on the Bethlehem-Hebron road.

As'ad's mother, a strong woman in every sense, was particularly partial to As'ad, among her many children, because of the fact that he had suffered from asthma ever since birth. As a small child he was tied to his mother's apron strings long after he should have been self-reliant.

But the most important object of his childhood adulation was an uncle, his mother's brother, who still lived with the tribe and served as their judge, a mark of dignity and seniority. It was his custom to ride into town on horseback, a sword dangling from his side, and he often took little As'ad with him, for a ride back to Herodium.

The family—father, mother, and ten children—all lived in one room in the vicinity of the Church of the Nativity. The proximity of the church was not without effect. Every Sunday, the children of the Moslem Suleiman family were dressed in blue and white and sent to sing in the church choir. Apparently the parents' attitude was that a little more religion, Christian or Moslem, could never hurt. During the week, the paved plaza in front of the church was As'ad's playground. And when he and his friends had a homemade soccer ball to kick around—a large sock tightly stuffed with rags—it was also their soccer field.

One day when As'ad was thirteen and a soccer game was in progress, a few policemen appeared and began to shoo the boys off the plaza. They were setting up police barriers at strategic points, and the boys were told, in no uncertain terms, to "beat it."

As'ad, who never liked to be told what to do, at least not without a reason, wanted to know why.

"Queen Dina is visiting the city," was the reply. "There'll be a motorcade passing through here soon."

"So why do we have to go home?" the boy still wanted to know.

But the policeman had run out of patience. He had work to do.

"Either get out of here," he said angrily, and then pointing to the police van, "or we'll take you out." Most of the boys ran off. As'ad simply strolled away, muttering: "I hate that queen!"

In addition to the plaza, As'ad and his friends had a hideout, a neighbor's backyard used primarily as a junkyard. The junk didn't bother the boys and they would sit there whenever they wanted to meet in seclusion, for intimate talks or, as was the case when they got older, to read classical Arab poetry to one another. One day, when As'ad was about eleven, the owner of the house decided to put his property in order. He cleared the yard, told the kids to get out and stay out, and planted shrubbery around its periphery.

"I used to examine the shrubbery every day, watching it come up. I was really upset: we had been dispossessed. One of the kids said that there was another place where we could hang out, in an olive grove down near the wadi. I was against. I didn't like the idea of giving in. It was my feeling that the yard was more important to us than it was to the owner. So one morning, before dawn, I sprinkled the shrubs with kerosene and then lit a match. Nobody ever knew how the fire started and the owner never got the energy to plant another round of shrubs. The place reverted to a junkyard and we got our hideout back."

As'ad was devoted to his friends and couldn't bear to be on bad terms with any of them. He later attributed his sense of justice to his highly developed sociality. He constantly worried about other boys. For example, there was an orphan who worked in the bakery on his street, "the street of a thousand steps." Because the boy had no home, he would sleep on the warm floor near the ovens, without a blanket. As'ad would bring him candy and fruit from time to time, and when winter set in he begged his mother to let the boy sleep in their house, to no avail, of course. In her humble opinion, twelve people in one room were enough.

"When I was six years old," Ta'mari remembers, "I first became aware that there was such a thing as a Palestinian problem. I saw it every day, at home, in the street, all over. Thousands of homeless people appeared at the time in the main square of Bethlehem, refugees from what had been Palestine and was now Israel. Almost everybody was involved in collecting food and clothing and blankets, including my own family. You could find these refugees everywhere, in caves, in abandoned houses, in people's yards. Eventually they set up a colony of tents and makeshift tin huts under the steps of the street and you would find whole families living in tiny, filthy quarters. My entire surroundings had suddenly changed and there was just no way of not becoming involved—whether you wanted to or not. No one could remain aloof. We were only kids then and really didn't understand what had happened. We didn't know what politics was all about. All we knew was that there had been a 'catastrophe,' and that it was connected with Jews, Zionism, Israel. The source of all evil was the State of Israel which had just come into being."

There is another vivid memory of childhood that always remained with As'ad. Very often he would go to visit his father at his kiosk at police headquarters. Scenes of brutality were a common, everyday occurrence there. The Jordanian police had little compassion for their prisoners, most of whom were Palestinian refugees. Prisoners were beaten and cursed. One day, when he was nine years old, As'ad arrived at the kiosk and found it closed. He was told that his father had been arrested "for talking back to a policeman."

He dashed down the corridor of the prison wing and from a distance saw his father locked behind bars. He stopped and waved to him. His father saw him and beckoned, but the child couldn't bear the sight of his father's humiliation. He ran out. "I never forgave myself for not going to him. He needed me at that moment and I failed him. Strange, he never once mentioned the incident later. He was a man of enormous pride."

As a result of his arrest, As'ad's father lost the concession and had to find work somewhere else. Together with four friends, he made his way by foot through the desert from Iraq to Kuwait where he found work as a cook again. Once a year he would return home to visit his family. This continued until his death in 1981, just a few months before As'ad-Salah found himself a prisoner-of-war in Israel.

In 1955, when he was thirteen, As'ad and his friends took part in a demonstration in Bethlehem against Jordanian participation in the Baghdad Pact. Whether or not they were completely aware of the political implications of the pact—to reduce Soviet influence in the Middle East—they were convinced that they had to take part in the demonstration.

Ta'mari remembers very clearly just how the Jordanian soldiers opened fire. Four of his friends were killed, the oldest of whom was fourteen. In the wake of the demonstration, Jordanian authorities closed down the school they attended and it remained closed for a year, which only increased the militancy of the youngsters.

Some weeks later, Israeli forces carried out a retaliatory action against the village of Housan, which was adjacent to Bethlehem and served as a base for *fedayeen* raids into Israel. The following morning all the boys from the high school went to see what had happened.

"The sight was terrible. There were dead Jordanian soldiers lying next to dead villagers. The houses had been blown up. People were running around crying. Some were hysterical and screaming. So in a matter of weeks I had seen Palestinians murdered, first by the Jordanians and then by the Israelis. Both scenes were deeply shocking and it made you wonder. In any case, it certainly sharpened our political awareness."

It was obvious to As'ad, even as a youngster, that the regime in Jordan was interested in decreasing the number of Palestinians on the West Bank. Palestinians were much more developed socially and politically than the original Transjordanian population, which was largely Bedouin. A large number of heads of family—like As'ad's father—were forced out of their jobs and businesses and compelled to seek work in distant countries. The most attractive places to the migrating Palestinians were the rich Persian Gulf states. Many young people followed in their fathers' footsteps. As a high-school student, As'ad became aware of the fact that the West Bank was largely a country of women, children, and old people.

"We were born with gray hair," Ta'mari recalls. "We went straight from childhood to old age. The only thing left was to dream and to see if we could make those dreams come true through political action." But open political organization in Jordan was against the law.

Palestinians who worked in Syria, Lebanon, and the Gaza Strip, and came home on visits, reported that the situation in those countries was even worse. At least on the West Bank, they said, you were able to maintain your national identity.

The Algerian war for independence was crucial in shaping the views of the younger Palestinian generation. Support for the FLN (Front Libération Nationale) was widespread and the Palestinians often held rallies and collected money for them. Yet As'ad never joined any of the existing parties, most of which were clandestine. He was biding his time: "I wanted to join a party which was exclusively devoted to the cause of the Palestinians. But there was no such party. It was abundantly clear to me that Palestine was the heart of the Middle East conflict."

In high school As'ad was a good student. In math and English he was outstanding. His favorite subject was history and he dreamt of continuing his studies in Cairo. One of his close friends, who was a little older and already a student at Cairo University, had excited his enthusiasm for university life. As'ad, although perfectly aware of the fact that his father's eighty dinars a month were not sufficient to feed and clothe the family and

finance a university education as well, nonetheless, was determined somehow to get his father's blessing for the scheme. His friend—after a little bit
of prompting—convinced Abu Daud that a student could easily manage
on ten dinars a month. He wasn't lying, just grossly exaggerating. Abu
Daud was ready to invest ten dinars in his son's education, and As'ad was
the first and only one of his children to get a university education.

As'ad went to Cairo with twenty-seven dinars in his pocket to start with.
Every month he received ten dinars from his father, which he would turn
into twelve Egyptian pounds. And, somehow, he did manage. He paid
eight pounds for his lodgings and used the rest for books and food. Sometimes he went hungry, but he was neither the first student nor the last in
this world who was nourished by the challenge.

As'ad hoped to study either economics or political science, but unfortunately those were the most popular departments at the time. Enrollment
was limited and, if that were not enough, Palestinians were put at the end
of all the waiting lists. He didn't have much choice; he might have studied
these subjects at the American University in Cairo, but it was a private
school. Instead he chose English literature at the free university of Ein
Shams and figured that when he finished he would be able to teach English
language and literature in Bethlehem.

He was an excellent student. Word of his academic success reached the
ears of an uncle of his living in Panama, and the uncle forthwith invited
him to complete his studies in Panama at his expense. As'ad refused. The
family urged him not to turn down the offer. But he was adamant. "I didn't
want to cut myself off from my roots. I tried to explain to them that I loved
the area of Herodium and that my greatest dream was to build a house
there on one of the hills. I knew exactly where. But they just laughed."

It didn't take long before As'ad became active in the Palestinian Students' Association (GUPS) in Cairo. Within a year, the handsome and
energetic young man was elected general secretary of the organization.

The GUPS numbered twelve thousand students, most of them from the
universities in Cairo but some from other Egyptian cities, and had been
founded some ten years earlier by a student from the engineering faculty of
the Cairo Polytechnical Institute. His name was Yasir Arafat.

The new general secretary, As'ad Suleiman Hasan, headed the only
legal Palestinian organization in existence at the time. The Fatah was still
an underground movement and the PLO, which was to become the
umbrella organization of all the Palestinian movements, had not yet been

born. As'ad organized local and international student conferences and worked hard to get international figures sympathetic to the Palestinian cause to attend them. Such well-known people as Krishna Menon, India's foreign secretary and one of the leaders of the third world, were among them. So were some leading British politicians. As'ad himself attended international conferences held in Europe, most but not all of them in countries of the Eastern bloc.

As'ad was following in the footsteps of his predecessors in the job: Arafat, Salah Halaf, and Khalil el-Wazir. All three had "graduated" to positions of importance in the Fatah. It was, in fact, only natural.

Ta'mari spelled this out for me much later. "Joining the Fatah in 1965 was self-understood, in terms of both political necessity and conscience. No decent person can ignore the sufferings of his people. That would be selfish. If you didn't join it meant that all you were interested in was a career and money."

In 1966, when he had completed his M.A. studies, he ignored the requests of his professors at Ein Shams to stay on for a Ph.D. He returned to Bethlehem as an underground fighter, with a new name: no longer As'ad but Salah. Salah was the name of the twelfth-century conqueror Saladin (Salah a-Din el-Ayyubi), who defeated the Crusaders in Palestine, and it was suggested to him by one of his friends in the Fatah. He took a new family name as well, Ta'mari, after the Ta'mara tribe of his ancestors. He explained to his family that an alias was necessary for underground work. Salah Ta'mari thus joined the founders of the Fatah, Abu Amar, Abu Jihad, Abu Ayyad, and Abu Loutuf.

His family worried about him. And rightly so. One night, Jordanian soldiers knocked at the door and took Salah away. He was accused of being in possession of official receipts from the Fatah (for use in raising funds). Salah was jailed—for the first time, for membership in the Fatah—and his passport was confiscated. But a few days later he was released.

By 1967, Salah Ta'mari was a full-fledged commando. He had done military training in Algeria and Syria. He was now what Israelis began to call a "terrorist."

When the Six Day War broke out on June 6, 1967, Salah Ta'mari was in Cairo: he had stopped off on his way back from Algeria to Bethlehem to finish some work for his degree. He dropped everything and tried to get home but he was too late: the Israelis had closed the bridges on the Jordan River. The West Bank was occupied territory.

7

"Suddenly he was standing opposite me . . ."

On the last day of the Six Day War, Ta'mari arrived in Damascus for the Fatah congress. There was only one item on the agenda: the renewal of armed struggle in the Israel-occupied West Bank and Gaza Strip. All of the founding members of the Fatah were there and this was Ta'mari's first personal encounter with them.

"Most of them were militant activists, like me, not military men but intellectuals who had joined to work for the Palestinian people. We were not a junta that wanted to take over a radio station in some Arab country. We were all university-educated, aware of the injustices being perpetrated against our people, looking for a way to preserve Palestinian identity. Every single individual there was capable of performing a wide variety of functions—organizational, operational, or educational—and fighting, too."

The PLO, created by the Arab League in 1964 and headed by Ahmad Shukeiri, was still a separate organization, and the Fatah had no connection with it. It was only in 1968 that all Palestinian organizations united under the umbrella of the PLO.

After a few days of discussion, the congress decided to establish Fatah bases along the East Bank of the Jordan River, with the central command in the town of Karameh. Salah Ta'mari was appointed head of the central command.

Their plan of action included infiltrating units into the occupied territories in order to organize civilian resistance to the occupation. The people chosen for this work were Fatah members originally from the West Bank, who knew the area well and could "melt" into the population whenever necessary. The inspiration for this kind of guerrilla operation came from Mao Zedong's famous dictum: "The revolutionary should be able to operate among his people like a fish in water."

Ta'mari was one of those fish—although the word "fish" in its more literal context hardly applies to him. Although he crossed the Jordan many times between 1967 and 1968, helping to "plant" units, on one of the crossings he nearly drowned: he had never learned how to swim. In order to minimize the danger of betrayal by informers or by people caught and subjected to interrogation, no one in a unit knew anyone in another unit, or in his own unit for that matter. The details of these operations were kept absolutely secret by Ta'mari, even from his closest comrades. They are secret to this day.

"The occupation hit us very hard," Ta'mari recalls. "We were absolutely determined to raise the morale of the population and to organize resistance. Our main job was to prove to them that they hadn't been abandoned." But for the most part the effort failed. Clandestine cells and a popular resistance movement never materialized. The large majority of the local population was not ready to cooperate and the Israeli intelligence network was extremely efficient.

For the first time in his life, Ta'mari realized what it meant to be a fugitive in one's own country. Nonetheless, efforts continued. He knew that Arafat was operating on the West Bank, but the Israelis were soon on Arafat's tail and he had to flee his hiding place in Ramallah and return to Transjordan. That was in September 1967.

In January 1968, headquarters in Karameh were bombed by Israeli planes, and not long after, the town was besieged by the Jordanian army: Hussein was becoming uneasy about Palestinian "autonomy" on Jordanian soil. At that point Ta'mari returned to Karameh; a change in tactics had been decided upon. Instead of trying to organize civilian resistance from within the territories, the Fatah would cross the river in order to carry out attacks on Israeli targets, and then immediately return to base.

On March 18, 1968, an Israeli bus hit a mine on a dirt road between Beer Ora and the Red Canyon, in the south of the country. It was a popular route for local tourists. There were high-school students and members of the paramilitary Gadna youth organization on board, all from the prestigious

Herzliah High School in Tel Aviv. The doctor accompanying the group and the Gadna instructor were killed, and twenty-eight pupils were injured. It was the thirty-eighth Fatah operation since the beginning of the year.

That same evening an emergency meeting of all Fatah commanders in the area was held in Karameh. Yasir Arafat and his deputy, Abu Ayyad, reported a conversation they had had that morning with the chief-of-staff of the Jordanian army, General Amar Hamash. Hamash told them that Jordan had received information from the CIA (Central Intelligence Agency) to the effect that the Fatah attack on the bus was the last straw for the Israelis. The Israelis now planned to attack and destroy all Fatah bases along the Jordan, first and foremost Karameh. The Jordanians were also told exactly on what day the attack would take place: March 21, three days hence.

The question before the Fatah commanders was what tactics should be adopted, and the subject was discussed from all angles. They could evacuate the town, taking temporary refuge in the mountains to the east, or they could remain and fight. According to the guerrilla tactics of Mao and of the Vietnamese general Vo Nguyen Giap, "If the enemy is strong, the guerrilla force should avoid confrontation. The enemy should be attacked where it is weak." It was no secret to any of them that the enemy was much stronger, in manpower, in equipment, and in experience. The obvious conclusion was, therefore, to retreat.

At that point Ta'mari asked for the floor. He was the youngest of the commanders present. "I agree that if we define ourselves as guerrillas, there is no point in our facing Israel's regular army," he began. "But we have to look at the problem from another, more crucial angle. It is up to us, right now, to provide an example for the Arab world in general and for the Palestinian people in particular. If we remain and fight, we may be able to convince the world that we are not merely 'terrorists' but fighting men, ready to sacrifice their lives for their country. If we abandon the battlefield to begin with, it will be a blow to our image. This time military tactics have to be subordinated to political strategy."

The fervor of Ta'mari's appeal was impressive and his position was adopted by almost unanimous vote. They would stay and fight. Later he learned that Arafat and Abu Ayyad had adopted the same position with Hamash that morning. For security reasons, it was decided that certain members of the leadership would leave the area immediately. But Arafat stayed as did Abu Ayyad. They would remain there with Ta'mari, who was in charge of organizing Karameh's defense.

The Jordanian commander of the area gave orders to his units to back up the Palestinians with artillery fire.

Thus, when Israeli infantry and mechanized units crossed Allenby Bridge at dawn on March 21, it was no surprise to the Fatah. The Israelis refrained from bombing the town as a softening-up action. Instead they dropped leaflets in Arabic, informing the civilians that the IDF was on its way and advising them to leave.

At the very last moment, just before Israeli paratroopers were supposed to be landed on the eastern outskirts of the town, in order to encircle it and cut off all avenues of retreat, Yasir Arafat left by motorcycle. He was in luck. A heavy fog had delayed the scheduled landing by an hour. Abu Ayyad found a hiding place in a crevice on one of the mountain ridges.

As the Israeli troops closed in on the town from all sides, Ta'mari abandoned command headquarters, leaving behind the goats and chickens and cats and dogs that he had raised in his backyard ever since arriving in Karameh. He spent the day moving among the fighters, from bunker to bunker, from trench to ditch and back again. As the Israelis advanced, street by street, house by house, gradually occupying the entire town, Ta'mari was convinced that he had seen his last sunrise. When he took refuge at the end of the day in one of the houses and survived without a scratch—no one was more surprised than he. But a hundred and twenty Fatah fighters were killed, more than a hundred were captured, many were injured, and many more simply fled.

Twenty-eight Israeli soldiers were killed in the operation, most of them by Jordanian artillery.

The Jordanian propaganda mills turned Karameh into a legend of Palestinian-Arab heroism overnight. For Ta'mari, who had witnessed the uneven match at close hand, it was hardly a glamorous affair. "There was a woman there," he later recalled, "with two small children in her arms, who tried to reach cover in one of the trenches after her house collapsed. She ran into me on the way and handed me one of the children, begging me to run with him to safety. She hadn't noticed that the child was already dead. He had been killed by a flying splinter that had pierced his neck when the house fell. The second child was bleeding. I managed to get him to the hospital later and he was saved.

"Still and all," he continued, "Karameh did something to us. It left us with a profound sense of unity, as if together we had succeeded in doing the impossible. We suffered terrible losses but we had inflicted losses on the enemy as well. It was a turning point for us. It wasn't just another un-opposed Israeli retaliation. We didn't just wait around for the next blow to fall. After Karameh, Palestinians held their heads up."

The assistance of the Jordanians was another source of pride. It gave the Palestinians the feeling that the Arab world was behind them. The next day Ta'mari went to Amman for the funeral of the Fatah dead. More than a hundred bodies were laid out under an awning on the main street of the capital. And emotions reached a new high when King Hussein declared: "We are all *fedayeen*."

Thousands of young people joined the Fatah after Karameh. Many of them left their studies in high schools and universities in order to sign up. Ta'mari was appointed "commissar" for the new recruits, in charge of political and ideological education during their military training.

He moved to southern Jordan, making the rounds of the bases together with Arafat. He was Number Two in the Asifa, the military wing of the Fatah. He initiated the establishment of a center for refugee children near the base in Ghor e-Safi, southeast of the Dead Sea. The center contained an infirmary, a library, athletic facilities, and a small farm. Israel artillery often shelled the training camps and more than once Ta'mari managed to escape only by the skin of his teeth.

During the heady days following Karameh, Ta'mari moved up in the Fatah hierarchy. He took part in the fourth assembly of the Palestinian National Council (PNC) in Cairo in July 1968, when all the Palestinian movements became federated in the PLO. It was at this meeting that the Palestinian Covenant was reworded to read: "Armed struggle is the only way to liberate Palestine." Ta'mari was one of the most enthusiastic sup-porters of the new wording.

The Fatah was the largest and most influential of the fighting organiza-tions in the PLO (and, indeed, at the PNC's fifth assembly, in February 1969, Arafat was elected chairman of the PLO executive). But in the wake of the Six Day War and the upsurge of Palestinian nationalism, there was a significant growth in all of the other Palestinian organizations as well. The most notable among them was Dr. George Habash's Popular Front for the Liberation of Palestine (PFLP). This organization specialized in attacking targets in the occupied territories and inside Israel proper—and this was in line with Fatah policy.

On July 22, 1968, however, the PFLP initiated a new form of action: its people hijacked an El-Al airplane on its way from Rome to Lod, forcing the pilot to land at the airport in Algeria. For five weeks twenty-one Israeli passengers and eleven crew members were held as hostages until Israel agreed to release dozens of terrorists in exchange. Non-Israelis on the plane had been released immediately.

This new form of terrorism aroused Ta'mari's ardent opposition—and still does. When it took place, he was on a mission for the Fatah in London and was absolutely livid: "It is madness," he said in an interview with British television. "It is completely immoral." The reporter interviewing him was, on the other hand, sympathetic to Dr. Habash's new tactics. "Imagine," Ta'mari recalls, "I, the Palestinian terrorist, didn't agree with the British reporter on the subject."

He expressed this opinion in Fatah forums as well. "Instead of hijacking the plane," he contended, "it would have been better to lie down on the runway, thus preventing the plane from taking off. In that way we would have gained the same attention." He explained to his comrades that while expanding their fields of action they had to maintain their belief in human values. He was convinced that Dr. Habash and his followers no longer had any faith in humanity. They were calculating people who wanted to produce immediate results. "I have faith in mankind," Ta'mari explained. "I believe that they will listen to me only if I fight in an honorable way. Hijacking planes is not humane."

It was Ta'mari's opinion that hijackings did not serve the interests of the Palestinians. He claimed that the struggle had to be useful and advantageous to the movement, not injurious. Such actions, he believed, put ammunition in the hands of the enemy, thus boomeranging against the Palestinians.

"If we *could* liberate Palestine by hijacking," he went on, "then we should go ahead and do it properly. We should train three hundred efficient hijackers who would bring us nearer our goal. But you all know that Palestine isn't going to be liberated that way. Hundreds of our fighters are living under miserable circumstances in mountain caves, waiting for the opportunity to really strike a blow at the enemy. Why should we destroy their morale? Why must they witness this mad exhibition which turns a single terrorist into a national hero?"

Ta'mari remarks were not concealed in the classified files of the PLO. They were published all over the world, reported in the Arab media, and even found their way into books.

In the middle of October 1968, he went from Karameh to Amman for the funeral of Abd el-Fattah Hammud, one of the first Fatah members and a friend of his from his GUPS days in Cairo, who had been killed in an automobile accident. All the other Fatah leaders were there as well, and it was the first time that they had appeared together in the Jordanian capital. Abu Ayyad used the opportunity to make an impassioned speech in praise of the PLO in general and the Fatah in particular.

The funeral exacerbated Hussein's fears. He suddenly realized how extensive the Palestinians' armed strength was and how much of a threat they might prove to his kingdom. Ta'mari and his comrades also began to feel the friction.

The presence of the various organizations in the south had increased and PLO people were moving into areas not specifically allotted to them. In part this was the result of frequent Israeli shelling of their bases in the Jordan Valley. They had no alternative but to move eastward.

It was then, for the first time, that the PLO began to implement its new system of moving its commands into the heart of the refugee camps, where they were surrounded by large concentrations of civilians.

A month after Hammud's funeral, Hussein forced the Palestinian organizations to sign an agreement whereby they recognized the sovereignty of the Jordanian government and its responsibility for all security measures. They would be allowed to continue their raids against Israel from Jordanian territory but within Jordan itself they would be restricted. They would no longer be allowed to wear uniforms, carry weapons in public places, or set up roadblocks for searching suspicious vehicles.

The agreement was one thing, the reality another. In the next two years, until the summer of 1970, Ta'mari attended scores of meetings with PLO heads who were trying to stave off what appeared to be an inevitable clash with the king. If it became necessary, he would fight, that was certain. But he had more than political reasons to hope that it wouldn't come to that: Ta'mari was involved in a passionate love affair with Princess Dina, the king's first wife.

Dina and Ta'mari had met in London, at a cocktail party given for a joint Jordanian-Palestinian delegation to the British parliament. Dina was the guest of honor at the party.

Dina became active in the Palestinian cause after the Six Day War. "I had grown up in a home where being an Arab was central to our existence," she told me years later, "and I was hoping that there would be a renaissance in Arab life. Something very basic happened in 1967. The injustice to the Palestinians shook me to my very foundations. Not long after, Golda Meir declared that 'there is no Palestinian people, there is no Arab people, there is no Arab unity.' I was desperate to find a way to disprove her pronouncements, not with words but with deeds."

Living and studying in London, Dina decided to establish a Palestinian-Arab cultural center there, which would be able to present Arab achievements in various fields: art, literature, poetry, music, handicrafts, etc. Every month, or so she planned it, the cultural achievements of a different Arab country would be featured. "In a small way, I wanted to show that Arab culture and Arab unity existed."

The center never materialized. Instead, in the center of London Dina opened a boutique called Arabesque, which specialized in handmade clothes and crafts, most of them produced by Palestinians. The proceeds from the shop went to the Fatah, which had just recently come into existence. Their ideology and program appealed to her. Although the income was small and the boutique barely covered its expenses, it nonetheless remained in existence until 1987.

Dina looked forward to the cocktail party, where she would meet for the first time some of the leaders of the people on whose behalf she was working. For her they were the symbol of an ideal, a national mission. She had heard Ta'mari's name and was eager to meet him.

Ta'mari, on the other hand, was not especially eager to attend that particular cocktail party. His childhood memories of the Jordanian royal family did not incline him toward the ex-queen. He informed his friends that he was staying home for the evening.

One of his friends took the matter in hand. He realized that as a child Ta'mari's pride had been hurt and that he still bore the scars, but in his opinion Ta'mari was carrying matters too far. He threatened that if Ta'mari refused to go so would everyone else, and the entire reception would be a flop.

Reluctantly, Ta'mari went. Reluctantly, he agreed to shake hands with the guest of honor.

"Suddenly he was standing opposite me," Dina recalls, "proud and pure. And that was that." For a few days she wasn't sure whether he was a Christian or a Moslem. It almost didn't matter. She knew that the terribly appealing young man was a devoted soldier of the cause who had miraculously survived the destruction of Karameh and had not given up.

From that time on, and Dina was over forty, she became attached to Ta'mari and tried to assist him in whatever way she could. She had at her disposal a great store of understanding for him and for their common political aims. Now, whenever she went to Jordan to visit her daughter, she had another person to see. On one of her visits to the palace, she told Hussein that there was another man in her life and even told him who it was.

Hussein's response was generous: "You deserve the best and I hope that he is a good choice."

Dina had never thought of a second marriage after her divorce from Hussein. First of all, her life revolved to a great extent around her daughter and, secondly, "In accordance with family tradition—and I was an ardent believer in the sacred traditions of my family—I could only marry a Hashemite. A second marriage was simply out of the question for me."

But all that changed after the traumatic events of Black September, 1970.

Despite his hope that the friction between Hussein and the Palestinians would not come to a head, Ta'mari's logic told him the opposite. "Even if the Fatah had behaved like angels," he later reflected, "Hussein would have tried to destroy us." And the Fatah were not angels. Far from it. They had actually created in Jordan a state within a state. Territories under PLO control considered themselves beyond the jurisdiction of Jordanian law. This was true of the refugee camps, of the PLO training bases springing up like mushrooms all over the desert kingdom. It was even true for Palestinian quarters within the large cities. In blatant defiance of the agreement with Hussein, the PLO militias set up roadblocks on every road and intersection. PLO soldiers walked around in public in uniform, carrying arms. They had their own independent infrastructure: police, courts, prisons, even a public welfare system dispensing medical care and social services.

In Ta'mari's opinion, many of his own people—not to mention the PFLP or Nayif Hawatmeh's Democratic Front or the Sa'iqa—had fallen prey to primitive instincts and wrongly believed that Hussein was their main enemy. Those who were intent on bringing things to an open clash were, he thought, making a big mistake. They lumped all their enemies together—Zionists, imperialists, and reactionary Arab regimes—thus blurring the identity of the real enemy.

"Suddenly he was standing opposite me . . ."

On September 1, 1970, at 5:40 in the afternoon, the first shot was fired in the bloodshed that was to lead, ultimately, to the destruction of the PLO in Jordan. The king, accompanied by a convoy of vehicles, was on his way to the airport in Amman to welcome his oldest daughter, Princess Alia, returning from a visit to Europe. On one of the hairpin turns in the road, automatic fire was opened on the convoy and bazookas were launched at close range. Some of Hussein's bodyguards were hit by the first blast, others began to return the fire. The king issued telephone orders to his troops who soon appeared on the scene, and he himself used his own pistol until the Palestinian units were silenced.

Within an hour, Jordanian artillery units were shelling all Palestinian bases and commands in the vicinity of Amman.

Both sides were ready for the confrontation. Hussein had—a few hours earlier—established a war cabinet headed by a Palestinian general. The PLO had established a unified military command for all its component organizations. Ta'mari was recalled from southern Jordan to Amman and put in charge of the central command. The city had been divided into sectors.

Ta'mari arrived in Amman in a rage. His anger was aimed primarily at the PFLP, which was responsible for the fact that the situation had so suddenly and radically deteriorated. Three commercial flights had been hijacked the week before by the organization and brought to the old British airfield near Zarca where they were blown up. His rage was further inflamed when he heard one of Habash's people broadcasting Marxist propaganda through a loudspeaker on the roof of one of Amman's largest mosques.

It was Ta'mari's opinion that Habash and Hawatmeh were providing Hussein with an opportunity to root out the Fatah, which was the organization that really threatened him. The king would be able publicly to justify his actions on the grounds that he was being attacked. The Fatah would lose its grass-roots support among the Palestinians because of the insane actions of the two extremist organizations. According to Ta'mari, they had managed to expand only because the Fatah was so strong.

Ta'mari's contentions sounded a bit hollow in light of the devastating shelling of those parts of the city under PLO control. The Jordanians were indiscriminately and mercilessly pounding all Palestinian sections of the city, even those with a dense civilian population.

Very shortly after the opening volley, the Jordanians occupied the main

Fatah command at Jebel Hussein. The entire city was placed under curfew. Arafat, who had been at the central command, had to flee. The other leaders of the organizations dug in at headquarters in the Ashrafia quarter of the city.

Ta'mari reached the northern part of the city and tried to organize resistance in the refugee camps, where fierce fighting had broken out. The camps were being shelled without letup. There had been some hope, at first, that they might stave off the attack, but as the hours wore on it became clear that their hopes were misplaced. Jordanian tanks and artillery encircled the Palestinians, who had only RPGs, Kalashnikovs, and mortars. Ta'mari tried to maintain radio contact with Arafat, but was unsuccessful.

It was during this period that Abu Musa joined the Fatah, defecting from the Jordanian army where he commanded a brigade. His real name was Sa'id Meghari. When the fighting began he was stationed with three hundred troops in one of the southern sections of the city, and it was there, on the PLO radio station, that he heard the personal appeal of his cousin, Abu Daud, a veteran Fatah leader: "Abu Musa! Join our ranks! Immediately!"

Abu Musa ordered his troops to cease fire. Five hours later he was placed under arrest but he managed to escape with his troops. They crossed the lines and joined Ta'mari's forces. Abu Musa's defection may have delayed the end for a while but it didn't change the final outcome.

For ten days Ta'mari tried to hold the line with his men, moving from one point to another, encouraging them, giving them hope. On the third day of the fight he made his way to one of the positions, where he found an unmanned machine gun on a sandbag elevation. The post had been hit very hard. Ta'mari manned the position for as long as he could until he was relieved. He had been on his feet for three days and without sleep for two nights. He slid into a deep trench and closed his eyes. Suddenly a tremendous explosion rocked the position. When he raised his head a few minutes later, nothing was left either of the fighter or the machine gun. The entire position was in ruins.

Ta'mari was considered by most of his comrades to be a relentless fighter, a man who refused to concede defeat. He was also known as a lone wolf and someone with an exaggerated notion of what he was able to achieve by himself.

After ten days, Palestinian resistance was completely broken. There were thousands upon thousands of dead and wounded. Members of the various organizations who had succeeded in surviving fled to northern Jordan. Under pressure of the other Arab states, Hussein was persuaded to stop the bloodbath—even though he had not yet finished the job. The total annihilation of the PLO in Jordan continued, on and off, until July of the following year with the massacres at Jarash and Ajloun. Only then was Jordan really PLO-*rein*.

The PLO leadership had to begin rebuilding their force from scratch, in another place. The next chapter of their history would be written in Lebanon.

A few hours before the outbreak of hostilities between Hussein and the Palestinians, Dina had left Amman with Alia, stopping in Beirut for the night on their way to London, where Alia had to report for school. It was in Beirut that they heard the news. Dina continued to London, settled Alia in at her boarding school, and took the first flight back to Amman. She was not worried about being caught in the fighting: she was worried only about Ta'mari.

During the ten days of Black September and for a few days after, Dina had no idea whatsoever of Ta'mari's whereabouts or if, indeed, he was still alive. Of one thing, however, she was absolutely sure: if and when she found him, she would stay with him and they would marry at the first opportunity.

"My situation at the time," she later told us, "was absurd. I came to Jordan because of Salah, but of course I was expected to see the king—who had, in a manner of speaking, ordered the death of the man I loved."

The wedding took place in the dark of night, under the stars, near a makeshift PLO position, not far from a blacked-out Amman under curfew. A number of Ta'mari's friends had gone out to find a sheik to perform the ceremony. That wasn't so simple. Perhaps they recognized Dina and took fright or simply didn't want to get involved. In any case, three sheiks had to be brought in before the wedding actually took place. There were no crystal chandeliers to light up the wedding ceremony and the guests were not offered wild strawberry juice as refreshment. The only illumination came from candles.

For Dina the wedding was a compromise between what she wanted and what was possible at the moment. "I didn't want to get married in secret. I

99

was proud of marrying Salah. Only there was really no other way. Everyone was frightened at that time—of the king, of his agents, of everybody. The sheiks were even frightened of me."

Before the ceremony Ta'mari had informed Arafat of his intentions, and the PLO leader was justifiably amazed. But he knew that there was no way he could convince his headstrong lieutenant. Ta'mari made a joke of it. "I promised you that I would win control of half the Hashemite kingdom. Well, I did."

In November 1970, more than a month after the event, the UPI (United Press International) office in Cairo issued the following news item to the world: "Dina Abd el-Hamid, the first wife of King Hussein, divorced from him in 1957, secretly married a month ago. Her husband is one of the leaders of the Fatah. Dina received the king's permission to marry. The Fatah command in Amman informed the foreign press that Dina's new husband was one of the foremost people in the Fatah's information services."

The press made no mention of the unusual timing of the wedding and it was only later that the affair was given political overtones.

Ta'mari's friends in the Fatah, with the exception of one or two, did not look kindly on his marriage. "I was severely criticized. I was accused of marrying her for her money. They wanted to know what a simple guy like me was doing with a queen." Later, he himself coined the self-deprecating phrase "she's a queen and I'm the son of a cook."

The age difference between the two—over ten years—was another subject of speculation and gossip. Ta'mari dismissed it as totally irrelevant. "For me Dina is sixteen years old and always will be. I married a woman who is my wife, my friend, my mother, my daughter, and my love. We may be diametrical opposites. We may look at things differently, and it's true that over the years we have had arguments that sometimes go on for days. But that's only one side of our relationship."

At times, Ta'mari expressed this differently. "Dina is the head and I'm the heart. I'm afraid of being the head. But people should understand. When I see a rose, I see a rose. I can smell it and enjoy its beauty. If others see something other than a rose—that's their problem."

Dina knew that the public's imagination was something uncontrollable. She remembered all the myths, good and bad, that had been woven around her at the time of her marriage to Hussein. Her only advice to her young husband about the stories going around was: "Ignore them."

Some of the stories that appeared in the press were unusually inventive.

It was said that Hussein was behind the marriage: because he was fighting the PLO, he wanted to prove to the rest of the Palestinians that he really had nothing against them and therefore approved of his ex-wife marrying a PLO commander. Another version, somewhat similar, was that he approved of Dina's second marriage in order to win sympathy from the Jordanians, who still adored their first queen.

According to Ta'mari, Hussein was never asked his opinion about the marriage nor, certainly, was his permission ever sought. "Dina is a very independent person, with a will of her own. She always was, even as queen." According to Dina, "It is true that I always had a tremendous amount of respect for my family, including the king. I would never take a step that might harm his reputation. But just as I wouldn't do anything to harm him, he wouldn't do anything to harm me. There was only one person that I had to consider when I decided to marry—and that was my daughter." Alia, it turned out, was a source of encouragement in this respect. She herself was fond of Ta'mari and always hoped that their relationship would be lasting.

After Black September, it became more and more difficult for either Dina or Ta'mari to remain in Jordan, and they went underground. Ta'mari was forced to change hiding places frequently.

Despite the dangers, he wanted very much to remain in Jordan. He wanted to be close to the Palestinians in the refugee camps, and in fact toured them all secretly with his fellow activist Abu Daud. He no doubt wanted the masses of Palestinians to realize that their leaders had not deserted them. But at one point he insisted that Dina leave. She agreed, and a friend of hers, a woman pilot, flew her out in a two-engined light aircraft.

Meanwhile it was becoming more and more difficult for Ta'mari and Abu Daud to evade the Jordanian authorities, and they finally left the south of the country for Jarash. It was there that Ta'mari received an order to come to Lebanon. He stole over the Syrian border and from there reached Beirut. He thought he was going for a few days, but he stayed ten years.

Dina was waiting for him there, and without either of them being aware of it, they began what turned out to be the longest period of their lives spent together.

Dina went into her second marriage with her eyes wide open. She knew what the Fatah meant to Ta'mari and what the objective situation was. She knew that he would not always be at her side and that it was she who would have to nurture the marriage with understanding, devotion, and love. But as Ta'mari often pointed out, it was not only his responsibilities that produced long separations. "Dina has so many burdens to carry," he told us more than once. "The truth is that she carries half the Arab world on her back."

8

"RPG kids"

By the time Ta'mari reached Beirut, Arafat had set up PLO headquarters in the Fakhani quarter of the city and Fatah commands in the nearby refugee camps of Sabra and Shatilla. Other Fatah units had been relocated in camps in the south of the country, around Tyre and Sidon.

Ta'mari's first assignment was in Arqoub, an area which soon became known as "Fatahland." Most of the raids against Israel originated from that area until 1978, when the IDF carried out Operation Litani, a limited invasion into southern Lebanon. But in 1970 Ta'mari "set up house" in a field tent there, on the slopes of Mt. Hermon. With all the good will and idealism in the world, it was hardly possible for Dina to remain there with him. They had to find a more civilized place to call home. Their first plan was to acquire an apartment in Beirut, near headquarters in Fakhani. But in the end Ta'mari preferred somewhere closer to his men. By then he had been appointed commander of the Fatah militias in southern Lebanon and political chief of the movement in all of the refugee camps south of Sidon. They decided to look for a place in Sidon, capital of the south.

They found a large house in the center of the city, opposite the main mosque, and moved into one of the apartments. From the yard, there was a view of the two Crusader fortresses on the sea and the nearby Phoenician Temple of Eshmun, son of the goddess Astarte. For the next ten years Dina and Ta'mari's home was to become a combined Grand Central Station and community center, for itinerant and local Palestinians as well as for the residents of Sidon—Christians, Shiites, and Sunnis. It was "open house" at all hours, a place to discuss one's problems, get advice, have a coffee, smoke a narghile, or just take a rest. It was also a base for both of them in their frequent travels.

"During all those years," Dina recalls, with obvious nostalgia, "I don't think that Salah ever finished a meal. Every time he picked up a fork, either the phone or the doorbell would ring."

Ta'mari's scant spare time was spent between his two favorite pastimes, animals and gardening. He kept ducks and chickens outside and stray dogs and cats inside. In front of the house he planted flowers, in back fruit trees.

Fakhriyya, Dina's mother, who came to live with them, also had a green thumb and did most of the regular upkeep. She was particularly fond of flowers and shrubs and spent a good deal of time cultivating a kitchen garden. Even after she developed cancer she refused to give up her plants, and Ta'mari often had to carry her into the house like a small child when it became obvious that she was overdoing it.

The living-room floor was covered with Persian rugs. The furniture was all Damascene—carved wood inlaid with seashells. Of all the rooms in the house, Ta'mari's favorite was the library, which he had built and furnished by himself. There were bookcases covering all the walls and an antique writing table set squarely in the middle of the room. The desk was Ta'mari's pride and joy. The rest of the furniture reflected Dina's impeccable taste.

Dina also owned her father's house in Cairo, in the Mo'adi section of town, where her mother had lived until she joined her daughter and son-in-law in Sidon. The house was kept up by servants and a chauffeur, all of whom were retained permanently. Dina did a lot of traveling. First of all she regularly visited Alia, who was at school in London and who later settled in Amman. She continued to supervise the work of her boutique, Arabesque, although the shop was managed during her absences by her friend Mrs. McKay, the wife of a former British ambassador to Cairo.

Ta'mari, too, was frequently abroad, most often on short missions to attend conferences or to speak at political seminars for Palestinians living in Europe or America.

In the summer of 1970, Yasir Arafat and his deputy, Abu Ayyad, visited the commander of the North Vietnamese forces, General Giap, and following this visit Fatah commanders were sent there regularly for training.

Among the first to go was the commander of the southern militias and the Asifa, Salah Ta'mari.

Ta'mari spent six months in Vietnam, where he underwent training in guerrilla warfare in the jungles, which in his opinion was not too applicable to the situation of the Fatah in Lebanon. He observed the work of the political commissars, since it was similar to work that he had done over a long period. Their job was to instill in the fighters the proper national-political motivation. In the main, however, they coordinated work between the party and the army—another feature which was not strictly parallel with the Palestinian setup.

Ta'mari returned to Sidon with two mementos from Hanoi: a small monkey and a brightly feathered parrot. On the plane back, he devoted himself to teaching the parrot a little Arabic. When he reached the door of the house, the monkey on one shoulder, the parrot on the other, and Dina cried out the traditional welcome, *"Markhaba,"* the parrot responded in kind. From that day on, Markhaba ruled the roost.

During his frequent visits to Europe, Ta'mari used to visit two of his friends, Issam Sartawi and Sa'id Hamami. Sartawi, Arafat's adviser, and Hamami, head of the PLO's London bureau, were the most notable figures in the PLO who inclined toward recognizing Israel. Both paid for it with their lives: murdered by the Abu Nidal group.

Ta'mari knew Abu Nidal, or Sabri el-Banna, from the days following the Six Day War in Jordan, when Abu Nidal was still in the Fatah and before he was appointed representative of the Fatah in Iraq.

Like most of the Fatah leadership, Ta'mari disapproved of the man's views. Abu Nidal and his core of followers left the Fatah and went to work for Iraqi intelligence. Of all the Palestinian organizations that emerged and eventually formed the "rejectionist front," Abu Nidal's was the most extreme. Their specialty was eliminating moderate PLO leaders. They murdered Sa'id Hamami in London, in January 1978, and Ez a-Din Khalaq in Paris, in August of the same year.

Ta'mari was appalled by the murders. Friends of his who knew of his ideological proximity to Hamami advised him to take care, to be on guard for his own personal security. One of those who so advised him was Sartawi himself. Ta'mari remembers that he laughed at him. "I told him that I couldn't possibly walk around under a security shield. It would be too much of a blow to my ego."

Issam Sartawi was murdered by Abu Nidal in April 1983, in Portugal. Ta'mari heard about it when he was in prison in Israel.

Quite a number of Israelis and Jews have been victims of Abu Nidal's terror, among them a toddler outside a synagogue in Rome, a group of elderly people at a synagogue in Vienna, two Israeli women on a plane hijacked to Malta, and the Israeli ambassador to London, Shlomo Argov, whose injury in 1982, by the way, gave Israel the ostensible justification for invading Lebanon. The most recent victims of Abu Nidal and his gang, some of whom were bystanders, were people mowed down at the El-Al counter at Rome airport in December 1985, and twenty-seven Jews at prayer in Istanbul in 1986.

When Ta'mari settled in Sidon, the PLO was already in full control of the refugee camps in southern Lebanon. At that time, sixty-five percent of the Palestinian population of the camps were under the age of twenty-one, the large majority of them children. When this became evident, Ta'mari decided that children and youth would be the major focus of his efforts.

"From all the reading I did on the history of Zionism and Jewish settlement in Palestine, I reached one important conclusion: the worst enemy of the Arabs in general and the Palestinians in particular is their backwardness, mentally, culturally, and intellectually. The Jewish pioneers who came to Palestine at the beginning of the century were for the most part from the European elite. They came to the East with brains from the West and conquered us. They didn't have 'Jewish brains.' A Jew from Yemen is just as backward intellectually and culturally as an Arab from Yemen. The Jews who came to Palestine were the products of the European milieu in which they lived. That's where their strength and abilities came from.

"That's why I felt it was so important to begin to educate the younger generation," Ta'mari explains. "Their welfare and progress had to be our first priority. The real revolution begins with education." These ideas were to reach fruition when he founded the Fatah youth movement.

Ta'mari took his model from—the Israelis. He had read a book, translated from Hebrew into English, about the Gadna (an acronym in Hebrew for "Youth Battalions") who were given paramilitary training at high-school age. The book both fascinated and inspired him.

Ta'mari set up the youth movement, provided it with its nomenclature, its guiding principles, its rules and regulations, and its activity program. He decided what kind of uniforms the kids would wear, what songs they would sing, and what their anthem would be. The boy's movement was called Ashbal (the young lions) and the girls' Zaharat (flowers). During the war in Lebanon, the members of the movement became known to the world, after their weapons, as the "RPG kids."

Ta'mari claims that he always considered the central goal of the Ashbal educational. Military training was secondary. He wanted to familiarize the children with the history and culture of the Palestinian people through the creation of a complementary after-school framework. The activities included sports, music, handicrafts, and art. During the summer months, the children went to youth movement camp, in the mountains east of Beirut. There, naturally, activities were on a broader and more intensive scale.

Ta'mari also set up summer camps for children from the Palestinian diaspora in Europe, America, and Australia. Every year scores of children from abroad joined their Palestinian brothers and sisters in the Ashbal and Zaharat camps at Suq el-Gharb and Behamdoun. They were instructed by youth leaders in their Palestinian heritage. They were taught the poetry of the pre-Islamic poets Anatara Ibn Shaddad and Abu Zaid el-Hilali, and the contemporary Palestinian poets and writers Mahmoud Darwish, Ghassan Kanafani, and Fadua Touqan. They also were given "home hospitality" in the refugee camps so that they could learn the customs and traditions of their people, as well as experience their plight. At the basis of Ta'mari's educational philosophy was the motif of love—love for their people and homeland—rather than hatred of the enemy.

To what extent Ta'mari succeeded with his educational plans is a subject of some controversy. Incontestable, however, is the fact that in the early seventies, Palestinian children of eight or nine years were able to use a rifle and operate an RPG. By the age of twelve they were, for all intents and purposes, full-fledged commandos.

Ta'mari once explained his rationale to me. "Those kids were born into refugee camps. That's the first thing you have to understand. They were exposed daily to air raids, strafing, and shelling. The fundamental responsibility of every parent was to teach his child how to reach the nearest shelter in the shortest possible time or how to take cover in an air raid. In other words, their most sacred responsibility was to teach their children how to survive. This kind of teaching comes under the name of training and it includes teaching them to follow explicit orders, drilling them, and helping them to develop physical stamina.

"The parents couldn't take their kids out for picnics or into the woods to teach them the names of flowers and trees. The fields and the woods were full of mines, delayed-action bombs and other lethal traps. Those were the 'fruits of the earth' they had to recognize. Instead of bird-watching, they had to react to the chirping of a Phantom or a Skyhawk. If you live at the edge of a river, you have to teach your kids to swim."

Still, the Ashbal and Zaharat children benefited from Ta'mari's other educational aims. They had their own orchestra, again on the model of the Gadna, and it was considered the best in Lebanon. One of its members was known as "the little drummer girl" and was the inspiration for John le Carré's book of that name, just as Ta'mari himself was the inspiration for the character of the Palestinian protagonist.

"But if you were a parent in a refugee camp," Ta'mari continued, "and had the choice of sending your kid to play in an orchestra or teaching him to defend himself against tanks with an RPG, what would you do? The fact of the matter is that in the massacre at Sabra and Shatilla, most of the members of the orchestra were slaughtered whereas the kids from the snipers' unit managed to survive, defending themselves with the best weapons they had—the RPGs."

It was the parents themselves, according to Ta'mari, who insisted that self-defense be given precedence over educational activities. "Not that they were against music. They just wanted their kids to survive."

The real impetus for military training came after the Christian Phalangists slaughtered Palestinians in the refugee camp of Tel e-Za'tar in Beirut in 1976. That was the first time thousands of children were killed simply because they didn't know how to defend themselves. "Older people may find ways of saving themselves in extreme circumstances," Ta'mari said, "but kids ordinarily just lose their heads."

After Tel e-Za'tar, Ta'mari allowed even four-year-olds to watch the older kids train. Instructors would observe the reactions of the small children, and if any of them showed aptitude, their parents would be approached to allow them to join in. Children wore uniforms from kindergarten on. "Khaki was the cheapest and strongest material there was anyway, so economically it was a sound idea."

Once a year, on March 8, prizes were given to the children with the best school records. Each year at a different camp, twelve hundred Ashbal pupils were awarded certificates of merit.

Some of the outstanding pupils were sent at the PLO's expense to international summer camps abroad, usually in countries of the Eastern bloc that trained PLO fighters and supplied them with weapons and ammunition. Prior to the Lebanon war, some of the children were sent to science camps as well.

All PLO leaders attended the March 8 ceremonies. Yasir Arafat would deliver a short speech (usually composed by Ta'mari), in one of which he said: "Remember that for you school is the first most important thing, the second most important thing, and also the third. The revolution only comes after."

In his book *The Palestinians*, Jonathan Dimbleby wrote that more than anything else the gun set the pace and the tone among the youth of the camps. "It is by means of the gun that the PLO hopes to liberate Palestine and it is the gun which serves as inspiration for their children. It may be that the PLO people are right. But adults have an advantage over children: they have a sense of discrimination. Adults can distinguish between the weapon and the goal; children cannot. They tend to mix up means and end. The gun and the return to Palestine have become one and the same thing."

In the war in Lebanon, more than two hundred RPG operators between the ages of twelve and fifteen were taken prisoner. How many more there were who escaped, or who themselves were killed while launching rockets, no one can estimate.

As a result of his work among the youth, Ta'mari became one of the most popular people in the camps. Whenever he entered a PLO base, he was immediately surrounded by admiring young fighters. Memories of this kind are those he cherishes most.

The civil war in Lebanon was central to the experience of the Palestinians during the mid- and late seventies. "All war is despicable," Ta'mari told us more than once, "but civil war is indescribably so. It is by its very nature the dirtiest of all wars. You have easy access to your enemy or to whomever you think is your enemy. It's not hard to plant a bomb or shoot under cover of darkness. The war takes place practically in your backyard. It's the most drawn-out kind of war because the fighters are generally inexperienced and lack confidence. Terror reigns, blood is spilled, and the war gathers momentum like an avalanche. One act invites retaliation and then you retaliate against the retaliators. In the end you don't know where it all began. Everyone is swept up in the storm."

In retrospect, Ta'mari believes that a lot of the suffering in the civil war could have been averted.

He became involved in the civil war after a friend of his, Ma'rouf Sa'ad, a Sunni Moslem and a member of the Lebanese Parliament from Sidon, was killed. He was shot dead in March 1975 by soldiers in an incident at the fisherman's wharf in the city, after a dispute between a group of left-wing Moslem fisherman and a unit of the Lebanese army, led by a Maronite general, all of them trigger-happy. As a result, Ta'mari began to take part in demonstrations against the cruelty of the Lebanese army. He was forced to take up arms as well when he realized that the Lebanese regime wanted only one thing: the eviction of all Palestinians from the country.

At the beginning of 1976, the Christians carried out a pogrom in the Palestinian refugee camps of Maslah and Karantina in Beirut. Ta'mari was alerted to a meeting of the PLO High Military Council at headquarters in Fakhani. The subject on the agenda was retaliation and Ta'mari was fervently in favor. It was decided that PLO fighters would march on Damour, a Christian town located on the coastal road between Beirut and Sidon, and occupy it.

"It wasn't hard to mobilize fighters from all the organizations after the pogrom in Beirut. Almost every single Palestinian was eager to take revenge. The reasons we chose Damour were rather complicated. But basically the reason was that it had strategic importance, linking the Palestinian and pro-Palestinian south with Beirut."

It was also an opportunity to close an old account. "The population of Damour and the neighboring Christian towns of Al-Jiyya and Ne'ma were supporters of Camille Chamoun's party and the Christian Phalangists and every other anti-Palestinian outfit whose main business was to terrorize Palestinians on their way to work. They would set up roadblocks for a few minutes, stop cars, and kidnap Palestinians or Lebanese Moslems. Snipers would take potshots at any Moslem who went through the city. Dozens of people were killed that way. It was their favorite pastime."

Ta'mari had no idea how catastrophic the Damour action would turn out to be. He himself did not take part in the occupation of the city as he was stationed in nearby Al-Jiyya, which was occupied only later.

In any event, an enraged and vengeful mob of Palestinians "joined" the military units and fell on Damour. Matters were soon completely out of hand. Apart from the organized shelling of the city, a massive and indiscriminate bloodbath was under way. When Ta'mari was informed "Mission accomplished," the mission was apparently not entirely over. Some hundred Christian women, children, and elderly people had taken refuge in a church in the center of town. Abu Musa, in charge of the Fatah's military operation, found himself helpless in the face of the bloodthirsty Palestinian mob. He sent a message to his friend asking him to come immediately from Al-Jiyya. Ta'mari reacted instinctively: "We've got to save those people and fast."

Ta'mari and Abu Musa took a jeep in the direction of the church but were held up on the way by the continued shelling. They had no alternative but to wait until nightfall. Ta'mari began to plan a rescue operation that involved Dina as well. She had just returned from Cairo and was totally unaware of what was going on in Damour. But in the first stage of the operation, Abu Musa and his men would try to reach the environs of the church and prevent the mob from entering.

Meanwhile Ta'mari returned to Sidon. When he reached home, as Dina recalled, it was after midnight and she was awakened by a loud knocking. Salah was wearing traditional Bedouin dress, the *abbayeh*, and was as pale as a ghost. "I asked him what was happening, where he had been. Suddenly I noticed something bulging from underneath his gown and asked him what he was carrying. He took out a wounded little white lamb. 'This is the only thing left alive in Damour. Do something with it. I have to return.' He then gave me an idea of what was happening."

Ta'mari asked Dina to round up as many cars and drivers as she could and drive immediately to the church in Damour without attracting any attention. She succeeded in getting a dozen or so friends and neighbors to help in the rescue operation, and by dawn they had evacuated most of the Christians from the church. They took them to the nearby monastery of Deir e-Mkhalles Brahamia, northeast of Sidon.

"The last one out of the church," Dina recalled, "was an elderly professor. He was distraught because he had left all his research at home when he fled, and it was his life's work. So the next day Salah went to look for his house. The work was gone, the house was gone. Everything had gone up in flames."

When the slaughter and the destruction were over, the mob turned to looting. According to Ta'mari, those days showed him the ugliest side of his people.

"There was nothing that those incensed people would stop at. They were dragging charred furniture out of the houses, tearing doors and windows off their hinges, and piling them up in trucks and cars. Their appetite for loot was simply insatiable."

On the road back from Damour, Dina and Salah passed a Lebanese gentleman, a Moslem, standing by the open trunk of his car and loading it up. He had torn windows out of the ground floor of a nearby house. "I never saw Salah so enraged," Dina told us. "He got out of the car, took a stick, and began to smash everything the man had put in his car. A crowd gathered around, all of them with loot of one kind or another. He screamed at them, telling them they should be ashamed. But he was like Don Quixote tilting at windmills."

The next day Ta'mari returned on the same road. This time he was with his driver, Abdallah, in a Mercedes he had purchased from a traveling Indian circus that had once performed in Sidon. In the middle of Damour the car stalled, and Ta'mari and Abdallah got out and began pushing it. No one came to help. Everyone was still busy pillaging. But one or two people began throwing them admiring glances accompanied by caustic remarks. "They were sure that we were stealing the car, doing what everybody else was doing," Ta'mari explained. "I said to Abdallah: 'Let's get out of here. To hell with the car. I can't have these people thinking that a Fatah commander would preach one thing and do the very opposite himself.' "

During the occupation of Damour, Ta'mari again found himself involved in a rescue operation—only this time he came to the aid not of women and children but of two Phalangist militiamen, his sworn enemies in fact.

A unit of the PFLP had captured the two Phalangists, who had been operating a machine gun. "The commander had no qualms about tying up his two prisoners and putting them up against the wall," Ta'mari recalled. "I happened to know all of the people involved, the two prisoners, who were from Sidon, and the PFLP commander. I got into an argument with the Palestinian commander while he was readying his prisoners for execution. I tried to convince him that once you take prisoners, you become responsible for them. Disarmed, they're no longer a danger to you. When they surrender, they give themselves up to your protection.

"But the PFLP commander was intent upon finishing them off. I realized that he would think no more of killing me in cold blood than he would of killing them. He called me 'chicken.' I told him that if he thought that what he was doing was heroic, he should call in lots more people so that they could witness his bravery. He could even bring over the prisoners' wives and children. 'Kill them in front of their kids,' I said. 'That would be real heroism.'

"That apparently convinced him because he put away his Kalashnikov. I untied the two Phalangists and sent them over to the French Mission where I knew their wives and children were."

There is an epilogue to this story.

Six years later, during the Lebanon war, when Sidon was already in Israeli hands and Ta'mari in prison, members of the Phalange appeared at his house, took the keys, locked it up, and declared it confiscated Phalange property. A few days later the regional Phalange commander knocked at the door of the house. Mahmoud Faris, Ta'mari's upstairs neighbor, opened the door, frightened that he might have to pay with his life for being Ta'mari's friend. He was surprised when, instead, the officer returned Ta'mari's keys to him. "Take care of the house. I owe my life to Ta'mari. I've given orders to my men to keep out of here. From now on, I'm personally responsible for the safety of the house."

Ta'mari's talent for human relations was a rare phenomenon in the civil war, and he was known far and wide in Lebanon for his "erratic" behavior.

Tel e-Za'tar proved to be the decisive blow struck against the Palestinians in the civil war. In June 1976, the Syrian army entered Lebanon at the invitation of the Christian-dominated government. With the Syrians backing them up, the Phalange militias surrounded the camp and embarked upon wholesale massacre. The Palestinian refugee camp was literally wiped off the face of the earth. The Syrians, at that particular moment in time, were wary of the growing strength of the Palestinians in Lebanon.

The PLO did not have much of a chance against them and no one knew this as well as the PLO leadership. Tel e-Za'tar didn't augur well for the future. The Phalange and the other Christian militias were one thing, the combined might of the Syrians something else.

Ta'mari was of the opinion that little could be done under these circumstances, but his friend Abu Musa, now in command of PLO forces in the south, thought differently. If the Syrians couldn't be prevented from entering Beirut, at least they could be prevented, in his view, from moving into the southern sector of the country. He was determined to hold the line against the Syrians in Sidon.

Abu Musa organized an ambush of the Syrian tank convoy moving south. At the entrance to Sidon his men destroyed four tanks, killing six Syrian soldiers. Syrian revenge on Abu Musa took two years in coming.

One day, two armed men suddenly appeared in front of his house in Sidon as he was about to leave, and opened fire. He collapsed on the steps. His house was not far from Ta'mari's. Ta'mari heard the shots and rushed out to see what had happened.

He found his friend lying unconscious, splattered with blood, his body perforated with bullets. The assassins had fled. Ta'mari drove Abu Musa to the hospital, where he was immediately operated on. His life was saved but he remained a cripple, forced to move around on crutches for the rest of his life.

The lesson of the attempted assassination was not lost on Ta'mari. The Syrians had taken revenge on Abu Musa even though they had by this time transferred their support from the Christians to the Palestinians. The Palestinians, he concluded, could depend on no one but themselves. The Arab countries only used them as pawns. The hard truth was that their fate was of interest to no one but themselves.

Years later, when Ta'mari was a prisoner in Ansar, Abu Musa rebelled against Arafat's leadership. Ta'mari received the news with a heavy heart. "The PLO," he said, with some bitterness, "can't even depend on itself."

On July 10, 1981, after a few weeks of relative quiet on Israel's northern border, the Israelis renewed their aerial attacks on PLO bases and Palestinian refugee camps in southern Lebanon. On the fifth day of the attack, the PLO heavily shelled the city of Nahariya from bases in Tyre. The Israelis retaliated: PLO commands in Fakhani, Sabra, and Shatilla were bombed.

In response, the PLO began a kind of war of attrition which lasted twelve successive days. The "Two-Week War" was how it was referred to in PLO history. Sixty-eight Israeli settlements along the northern border, from Nahariya in the west up to Kiryat Shmonah in the east, were hit by 1230 shells and Katyushas. For the first time in Israel's history, residents of the north began to flee their homes.

For the PLO it was an achievement. Their system was simple. An artillery or Katyusha launcher would fire a number of shells and then move rapidly to some other location, thus escaping Israeli detection and bombing. But in the end the IDF beat the system and destroyed the PLO's launchers. After two weeks, the PLO in southern Lebanon was left with only two launchers still functioning. All the others had been hit or moved north.

The Palestinian leadership had no alternative but to accept the cease-fire proposal of the American mediator, Philip Habib. It was the first of its kind ever signed between Israel and the PLO. Arafat viewed the agreement as an intermediate stage in the struggle, and presented it as such: "With the cease-fire in force, we will have the unique opportunity of rebuilding our military infrastructure in the south and seriously preparing for the next round."

Ta'mari was one of the enthusiastic supporters of the cease-fire when it was raised at the High Military Council. He had more reasons than Arafat for supporting it. He was worried about the people in the south—his own fighters among them—who had been paying heavily for the war of attrition. The PLO people in Beirut who were opposed to the cease-fire were, in his opinion, unaware of what was going on. He invited them all to pay a visit to the south and see what it was like during Israel's massive bombings. "Only people who live in the south can understand what the cease-fire means. Here in Beirut, in relative comfort, it's easy to adopt hard-line positions."

The opposition to the cease-fire, which included people from the Fatah, claimed that by agreeing to it the PLO would be heralding its own end as a revolutionary movement. It would mean the end of armed struggle.

When Habib notified them that Israel agreed to the cease-fire without demanding a freeze on the existing military situation in southern Lebanon, Arafat was able to muster the necessary votes. The cease-fire went into effect on July 24, 1981.

Arafat and Ta'mari were of the opinion that the smaller organizations in the PLO would try to breach the cease-fire and carry on the armed struggle from the Lebanese border. It may well be that Arafat's public pronouncements to the effect that the cease-fire on the Lebanese border in no way obligated the PLO on other fronts was purposely designed to give his extreme flanks enough room for action.

Ta'mari, however, passed on explicit instructions to his lieutenants in the south that any Palestinian attempting to breach the cease-fire was to be opposed by force. And, indeed, during those first weeks, Fatah officers confiscated ammunition from units loyal to Ahmad Jibril and George Habash. Sometimes they had to insist at gunpoint. Sometimes they even had to open fire.

In one case, news reached Ta'mari that Azmi Zghayyer, a Fatah commander in the Tyre region, was planning to dispatch a unit to the border to launch Katyushas at Israeli targets. He got the news from his brother-in-law, Nur Ali Abd-el-Khalek, an officer in Azmi Zghayyer's regiment, who was married to Ta'mari's sister Rihab. He told Ta'mari exactly what route the unit was planning to take.

On the night of the planned attack, Ta'mari led a unit of his own people to the south to wait for Zghayyer's men at an intersection. When their Land Rover reached the intersection, Ta'mari stopped it and ordered the surprised passengers to get out and follow him. They did exactly as told when they saw that the orders were being given by a superior officer and that Nur Ali, from their own regiment, was with him.

Zghayyer was not popular in southern Lebanon from the time he ordered the execution of a soccer player who had refused to join the Palestinian team. He was considered an insensitive and imperious man, with a streak of cruelty in his makeup. In any case, Ta'mari herded the men into his car, took them back to Sidon, and locked them in his bathroom. Later, the Palestinian military police took them to Beirut on charges of disobeying orders. Ta'mari insisted that their commanding officer also be charged and Zghayyer was called to Beirut. He based his defense on an order he had received from Arafat six days prior to the cease-fire, claiming that he had never received a countermand. In the end, he was reprimanded and he and his men were released.

In the files of Israeli intelligence, Azmi Zghayyer's name was written in blood. He was responsible for blowing up the Savoy Hotel in Tel Aviv in 1975, and for the massacre on the coastal road in 1978 in which thirty-five men, women, and children were killed. Both times the attackers came from the sea: Zghayyer was in charge of the coastal unit in Tyre.

The IDF closed accounts with Zghayyer during the war in Lebanon. He was in command of twenty-five hundred PLO fighters on the outskirts of Tyre. When he realized that his forces were no match for the IDF, he fled to an orange grove, where he was later discovered by an Israeli unit.

Zghayyer was killed. Ta'mari was to hear of his death in an Israeli prison.

The royal wedding, Amman, April 19, 1955. Sharif Abd el-Hamid Aal-Awn kisses his daughter Queen Dina, as King Hussein stands beside her. At left is King Faisal of Iraq, Hussein's cousin. The children are Basma, King Hussein's younger sister, and Prince Hassan, the king's younger brother. (Cover of the Egyptian weekly *Al-Mussawar*)

Dina before leaving Cairo for her wedding.
(*Al-Mussawar*)

The Jordanians welcome their queen-to-be. (*Al-Mussawar*)

The royal couple after their wedding. (*Al-Mussawar*)

A happy Dina holds her newborn Princess Alia, February 1956. (*Al-Mussawar*)

Salah Ta'mari on his way from the interrogation camp in Sidon to an Israeli prison, June 1982. (Israeli Press Photography Agency)

Salah Ta'mari and Aharon Barnea, summer 1982.

Salah Ta'mari and Aharon Barnea at Kibbutz Hulda after visiting Amos Oz, summer 1982. (Michal Heiman)

Field tents at the Ansar POW camp in southern Lebanon. (Havakuk Levinson)

Prisoners pass requests to a Red Cross representative during demonstration in Pen 10 at Ansar. The photo was taken from the car window of Lt. Col. Yehuda Shatz.

Prisoners' graffiti on Ansar tent.
(Fouad/SYGMA)

Ta'mari rallies his fellow prisoners at Ansar in this painting made by a prisoner on a piece of wood from a vegetable crate.

Carved wooden box decorated with colors made from spices mixed with toothpaste. Inside, a radio set used by the prisoners without the knowledge of Israeli authorities.

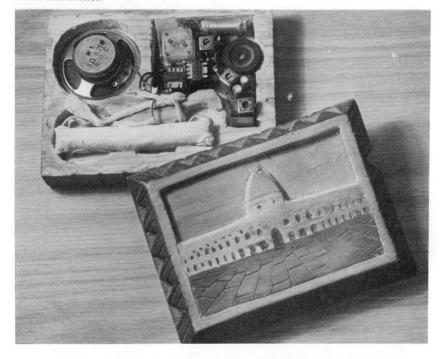

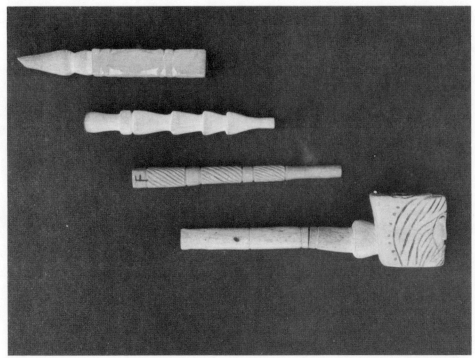

Smoking paraphernalia carved by prisoners at Ansar.

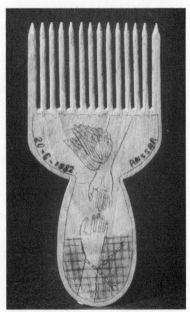

The "comb of coexistence" carved by Ta'mari.

Ansar in flames, June 6, 1983.

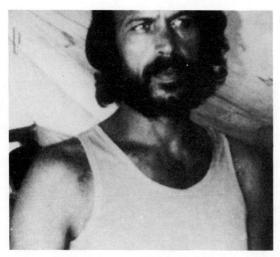

Ansar's leader, summer
1983.

Ta'mari and other members of the group of freed Palestinians at a press
conference at PLO headquarters in Algiers. (AP)

Dina Abd el-Hamid and Amalia Barnea at Dina's house in Cairo, April 1984.
On the table are photographs of Princess Alia and Ta'mari.

Princess Alia with her son, Hussein (Dina and King Hussein's grandson), and Reyout Barnea, the authors' daughter, London, 1985.

Or Barnea, the authors' son, with Hussein, London, 1985.

Salah Ta'mari, July 1982. (Michal Heiman)

9

"Mom, Dad, I'm all right."

"September 3, 1982," begins one entry in Ta'mari's diary. "It's Friday evening and everything is quiet. The cell is terribly hot despite the fact that summer is practically over. I wish I had some peanuts.

"I am still dragging my tired feet along the paths of unending time. Often I look back trying to trace my unformed steps in the byways of the past. My satisfied smiles at the changes which took place in me here—if there really were such changes—are evaporating in the face of the emptiness which the future holds. How long can this last?"

The next entry reads: "Saturday, September 4. No news from Aharon. I hope this doesn't mean that his attitude toward me has changed. Next week I'm going to begin a hunger strike. Why are they keeping me in solitary confinement? Are they planning to accuse me of taking part in terrorist actions?

"Tuesday, September 7. Time is absolute. My calendar is faceless. There is no way of distinguishing one day from the next. I'll have to invent something and it's not easy. I find that all too often I am becoming either forgetful or tense.

"Thursday, September 9. I didn't sleep at all last night. I listened to Julio Iglesias's guitar music coming from the warden's radio."

At the beginning of September, Amalia and I were busy planning a vacation. We hoped to spend a week or so in Crete. The tension and excitement of the Ta'mari-Dina affair, in all of its ramifications, had taken its toll, if only in pure nervous energy. Since her visit to Israel, and, as a matter of fact, even before, Dina had been in touch almost daily. We were her "lifeline" to Salah, her only channel of communication, and she called even when she knew that I had not seen him and had no news to give her.

We realized that our absence would affect them both adversely but we needed a breather and needed it badly. The war in Lebanon was already three months old and there was no sign that it was going to end. In fact, it was already apparent that it was going to get a lot worse before it got better. So in addition to my "extracurricular" activities with queens and PLO leaders, I still had my regular beat: Israel radio's correspondent for Arab affairs. And, sad to say, there was never a dull moment.

On September 13, Dina wrote to us from Cairo: ". . . I found someone I can trust who's going to London so I can send you a few words. I realize you'll receive this letter only after you return from your vacation—which I hope you enjoy. I want to thank you and Reyout, priceless Reyout—if we can be allowed to call her that—from the bottom of my heart. Only of course I am worried and frustrated and frightened. When you two are not there I'm deprived not only of news or contact or information. I am deprived of hope.

"I try to minimize my feelings. But who am I to even think in terms of 'patience' or 'stop worrying' or 'only a little longer,' when it comes to someone else's suffering, especially when that someone else is so dear to me. . . .

"Believe me, Aharon, you don't have to tell me things you are not supposed to. All I want is a sincere estimation of the situation, the way you have been doing up to now. And in whatever way you want to formulate it. I'll understand. I myself won't do anything until you return, until you tell me what to do.

"I only want to help Salah, to do whatever has to be done for his release and for the release of his comrades. Without any excess publicity and without causing you—or anyone else—any embarrassment or discomfort. All I want is to see my husband. So don't worry. Just tell me how he is. I'll be all right."

On September 4, 1982, eight Israeli soldiers were discovered to be missing from their lookout post in the Behamdoun area of Lebanon, northeast of Beirut. It was assumed that they had been captured either by the Syrians or the Palestinians. There had been as yet no official announcement although rumors were rife. According to one version, the soldiers had been duped into crossing the border and were then captured without showing any resistance.

The families of the eight men were, naturally, staggered by the news and worried about their sons' fate. Teams of army psychologists were called in to help. But more to the point the entire country was in shock. The soldiers had been from one of the elite branches of the army, the Nahal, where training goes hand in hand with work in the kibbutzim. Members of the Nahal are known for their strong social and ideological dependability. Their apparently unopposed surrender was practically a national disgrace.

Three days later, at a press conference in Damascus, Abu Jihad, Arafat's deputy, announced that the eight had been captured by the PLO. They would be ready to exchange them for PLO prisoners held in Israel from before the war. Abu Jihad further announced that the prisoners were being treated in accordance with the Geneva Convention.

The announcement was double-edged: there was comfort in the knowledge that the soldiers were still alive and consternation over the fact that they were in the hands of the PLO. Never before had an entire unit of Israeli soldiers been captured by Palestinian fighters.

On September 9, five days after the capture, the commander of the unit, Reuven Cohen, appeared on Israeli television in a clip from Syrian TV. He was revealed to the world sitting comfortably and eating grapes, in a PLO media bonanza. For Cohen's parents it was comforting: at least they had proof that he was alive. The other parents were not so lucky.

In Dina's letter of September 13, full of longing for Salah and gratitude to us for keeping her informed, there were two enigmatic sentences scribbled in the margin: "Meanwhile and without trying to sound dramatic, if something untoward happens to me, please take care of Salah."

We spent Rosh Hashanah, the Jewish New Year, in Crete, enjoying the peace and quiet. We were hoping against hope that our week's interlude would pass without any great international crisis that would drag me back to my desk. Our last vacation, in Italy, had been cut short by Sadat's murder.

Our luck didn't hold but our nerves did. On our third day in Crete the new president of Lebanon, Bashir Jamail, installed with the active assistance of Ariel Sharon, was murdered. The Lebanese mud was getting thicker. But we decided to stay the week anyway. Not even Israel radio's indefatigable correspondent for Arab affairs was inexpendable for four days. We remained on the island till the end of the week, swimming, sunbathing, playing tennis, and eating yogurt and honey. We "comforted" ourselves with the thought that by Yom Kippur we would be back.

Yom Kippur that year fell on September 26. In Israel, it is a day of almost deathly silence. No cars, no radios, no TV. Everything is closed. Nobody moves for twenty-four hours. Believers and nonbelievers alike respect the sanctity of this holiest of Judaism's holy days.

We were surprised, therefore, when the telephone rang.

It was Dina and she began by apologizing—for calling us on Yom Kippur, for calling us so soon after our return home, for disturbing us in the middle of the day.

I began to apologize too. "Dina," I said, "I just got back. I haven't even finished unpacking. I haven't had time yet to visit Salah."

"That's not what I'm calling about," she said, cutting me short. "I want you to listen to something. Hold the wire a minute."

I held on and listened. At first all I heard were the crackling sounds of a tape, static, and background noises. Then I heard a voice say clearly: "I, Danny Gilboa, twenty-one years old, from Tel Aviv, would like to send regards to my parents and to my sister. Don't worry. Everything is fine. I feel good and hope to be home soon." Silence followed.

"Are you listening, Aharon?" Dina asked.

"I'm listening," I said, hardly believing my ears. I had broken out in a cold sweat.

Another voice followed. "I am Reuven Cohen, twenty years old, from Holon. Mom, Dad, I'm all right. Please don't worry. We are being treated well. I hope the whole thing is over soon."

There was a short interlude, more background scratching, and then: "My name is Eli Aboutbol. I feel okay. Tell my folks not to worry." And following this another three: Avi Montebilski, Raffi Hazan, and Avi Kronenfeld, six of the eight captured boys.

"Did you make the tape, Dina, or did somebody give it to you?"

"I taped them," she answered, "myself."

"Where, when?" I didn't know quite what to ask first.

"A few days ago, where they're being held."

I tried to keep calm but by now I was a nervous wreck. "Dina," I managed to say, "I'll call you back. Where are you? I've got to see you."

Dina remained calm and collected. She apologized again for disturbing us on the holiday, then added: "I wanted you to be able to tell those boys' parents that they're all right. It will help make things easier for them."

For me as a journalist, it was, of course, a sensational scoop; for me as a human being, it was an opportunity to alleviate the agony of six families. It was, in combination, the Ta'mari-Dina story in reverse.

For Dina, it was a way of saying thank you, payment in kind.

The minute Yom Kippur ended—with twilight—I called the IDF Missing Persons' Bureau. I informed the officer in charge that I planned to meet Dina abroad in order to get more details and to bring back the cassettes.

"Good luck," she replied. "It's really a good deed."

Unfortunately, I had to be in Beirut early the next morning. The world was in an uproar over the Sabra and Shatilla massacre. I left my Beirut number with Amalia in case Dina should call.

Two days later, she called. She didn't realize that I was in Lebanon since the Kol Yisrael office number in Beirut was hooked into the Israeli telephone network.

"When can we meet?" I asked her. "I would like to broadcast the boys' voices over the radio."

Dina couldn't grasp the reason for my urgent tone of voice. As far as she was concerned she had made a humane gesture toward the parents of the boys, and that was that. The idea that it was a scoop for me, a feather in my journalistic hat, was peripheral.

"I'm in Athens now, on my way from London to Cairo," she answered, somewhat confused.

"Could we meet tomorrow in London?" I was persistent.

There were a few seconds of silence before Dina spoke again: "Okay," she said finally, "I'll turn around and go back to London."

I got permission to get a replacement in Beirut. When I got back to Tel Aviv, I cut out pictures of the eight boys to take with me. The next day, a few hours before the flight, I dropped by to say hello to Ta'mari. I wanted to be able to give Dina "fresh" regards.

I arrived in London in the afternoon and called Dina from my hotel. We arranged to meet in the cafeteria of the Clive Hotel.

At 7:30 I was already in the cafeteria on my first cup of coffee. The picture window of the place looked out on the entrance. Between one cup of coffee and the next I maintained a steady vigil, despite the fact that a gloomy drizzle impeded visibility. It was a little after eight when Dina drove up behind the wheel of a brown Jaguar.

121

She ran the short distance from the curb to the hotel entrance, out of the rain. I got up and went to meet her. She was wearing a black woolen cape.

In all our conversations up to then, in person and on the phone, Dina had always been the one who was anxious for information, although she never dispensed with the outward forms. She had always exhibited admirable patience. Now our situations were reversed. I could hardly contain myself. I wanted to know everything about our prisoners of war—where, what, how. But I too was able to contain my impatience.

We sat down and ordered some more coffee and exchanged pleasantries.

All of a sudden someone else was standing at the table, smiling. I looked at her and it wasn't difficult to identify the young woman. She was the spitting image of her mother. Alia was wearing the standard duffel coat of the London student. She carried an oversized cotton bag on her shoulder and her hair was coiled into a single braid.

"Meet Sweetie," Dina said, smiling and full of warmth, and I shook hands with King Hussein's oldest daughter. "I asked her to join us if she didn't hear from me after a while, just to be on the safe side." I wondered what Dina had been afraid of. . . .

Alia sat down and we ordered still more coffee. Our conversation continued on the lines it had started and I soon found myself revealing to Dina and to an acquaintance of five minutes' duration, and not without some emotion, that Amalia and I were "expecting."

Alia smiled and said she hoped the second would be like the first. "She's a wonderful example to follow," she said, fishing in her bag and pulling out a photograph of Reyout, on her first birthday, a wreath of flowers on her head.

"How did you get that picture?" I wanted to know—and then remembered. When Dina had visited us, we had shown her Reyout's photograph album and she requested a copy of one of the pictures. Alia apparently had "appropriated" it. Her own son, Hussein's first grandson, also called Hussein, was Reyout's age.

The ease with which Alia joined our little coterie was amazing. She didn't stay long that evening, but a few days later, Amalia received a plant through Interflora. The accompanying message read: "Best wishes for the coming event. Take care of yourself. In friendship, Alia."

Dina and I got down to "business." I told her that I had seen Salah for a few minutes before I left and informed him of her visit to the Israeli POWs.

Her face was suddenly transformed into a mask of restrained expectancy. I told her that he approved of what she was doing and had absolute faith in her judgment. What I didn't tell her was that he asked me to caution her against doing anything that might be interpreted as an attempt to obtain his release before or independently of that of the others.

Now it was Dina's turn. She took a cassette out of her handbag and immediately apologized for its poor quality. "Everything was done under pressure and conditions were not optimal." Still, she went on to assure me, the boys were being well treated. She also told me that in addition to the six she had recorded, there were another two being held somewhere else whom she was unable to meet and record.

I asked for a description of the boys' condition and she told me that they received the same food as their guards and that they were given Marlboros to smoke. One of them, she said, needed new glasses; another was wounded but not seriously. "I think that's the one called Eli," she said. "He is being cared for by a nurse who speaks Hebrew. Her name is Fatma Barnawi. She learned her Hebrew when she was in jail, in Israel."

The name rang a bell. Fatma Barnawi had been in prison, together with her sister, for twelve years. She had been sentenced to life imprisonment for planting a bomb in a Jerusalem cinema.

"Where did you get to see them?" I asked, hoping against hope that she might tell me.

"I can't say exactly—and I'm sure you understand why."

I took out the newspaper photos of the eight prisoners and Dina identified six of them by name. She put the salt shaker over the picture of Yosef Groff and the pepper mill over the picture of Nissim Salem. "I never saw these two."

That night I was unable to sleep. I listened to the tape over and over again. The quality was really bad but it made no difference. The message was clear: the voices belonged to our boys. What Dina referred to as "a small gesture of my gratitude to you personally," was, I began to realize, a great and noble act.

When I landed at Ben-Gurion, I went straight to the Tel Aviv studios and closeted myself with a sound engineer until we were able to produce a master-quality rendition of the voices. That night we delivered a copy of the cassette to the IDF Bureau of Missing Persons. Gen. Moshe Nativ later told me that from then on Dina's name was on the lips of everyone involved in the affair.

I prepared a bulletin for release on the early morning news magazine. It ran: "Six IDF soldiers held by the PLO have sent live regards to their families for the first time since their capture. The tape with their voices reached the hands of our correspondent."

The news item was never released, nor was the cassette ever played on the radio. The military censor blue-penciled them both, as he blue-penciled all subsequent information relating to the prisoners and the negotiations for their release. The media in Israel accepted the verdict.

A few days after I returned from London, six couples, the parents of the boys, were called to the office of the Bureau of Missing Persons to hear their sons' voices. The parents were naturally greatly affected, and asked to hear the tape over and over again. They were also curious: how did the tape arrive? To this question they received no answer.

One day in July 1983, the father of one of the boys, Zvi Gilboa, called me at the office. He didn't know me personally: he knew me only through my reports and commentaries on the radio. At that time there was heavy fighting in the Bekaa Valley between Arafat's men and Abu Musa's rebels. Gilboa wanted to know if I would mind talking to him for a few minutes: his son, he told me hesitatingly, was one of the PLO prisoners and he was anxious to acquire a greater understanding of just what was happening.

I sat with Gilboa for some time in his office in Tel Aviv. He was a broken man. All he wanted to know was if and how the fighting would affect the chances of his son's release. I couldn't provide him with any inside information. I could just offer him the kind of analysis that appeared logical, namely, that the rebels were forcing Arafat to retreat, under fire, from their bases and positions in the Bekaa in the direction of Tripoli, in the north. We could only hope that developments would prove propitious for the return of the boys.

Gilboa showed me three large files in his office. They contained every scrap of information from the press, both local and international, that had ever appeared concerning the prisoners. He spoke of the efforts being made for their release by Bruno Kreisky, the chancellor of Austria, of the Red Cross visits to the boys, of the interviews with them on Arab and American TV. He also spoke of the difficulties the parents had in carrying on. During the conversation, he also told me confidentially about the first tape of their voices that had reached Israel. "That tape brought me back to life," he added.

After fourteen months in captivity and complicated negotiations between Israel and the PLO through a variety of mediators, the six were released. They remembered Dina's surprising visit very vividly. She was their first outside visitor and saw them even before the Red Cross did.

"We were in the same room we were kept in all the time," Danny Gilboa recalled. "It was in Shtura, or at least that's what they told us. A couple of minutes before she came in, the guards told us that an important person was going to visit. We understood the word 'queen' but we couldn't make much sense out of it. Everybody around us was in a dither."

"The guards infected us with their excitement," Raffi Hazan added. "At first we were indifferent. Her name didn't mean anything to us, but when she came in everybody stood to attention. The respect she was shown was beyond anything you could imagine. One of the guards who had been with us since the beginning was practically kissing her hand."

"She spoke English and Raffi and I were the interpreters," continued Danny. "She asked us how we were feeling and all of a sudden she pulled out a tape recorder and put it on the table. I can see that tape recorder now.

"We didn't know at the time that her husband was a prisoner in Israel. She never said a word about that. She just went over to each of us separately and had us say something into the tape. She asked Eli Aboutbol about his wound and if he was being treated for it. After she finished everything returned to normal."

Raffi had one more piece of information to offer. "We asked her about Nissim and Yosef. She said that as far as she knew they were all right." And then as if conjuring up the visit in his mind's eye, he added: "Her English was perfect and her manners, the way she was dressed—she was really something. She certainly didn't fit into the surroundings. Before she left, she shook hands with each of us as if she really meant it."

Dina never tired of inquiring after the six boys, long after they were released. She remembered them well. She wanted to know if Eli had fully recovered from his wound, if Danny had put on weight, if they were working or at school, if they had readjusted psychologically. She also followed developments relating to the other prisoners, Yosef, Nissim and a third, Hezi Shai, who had been held by Ahmad Jibril and was released long after her own private prisoner, Salah Ta'mari, had become a free man.

10

"I'm going to kill myself."

The library in Salah Ta'mari's cell was not large but it was diversified. From Sidon he had brought with him an Old and New Testament in English, the Koran, a volume of the complete works of Shakespeare, a number of spy thrillers by his friend John le Carré, a book of Greek mythology, and two books on Plato, A. E. Taylor's *Plato, the Man and His Work*, and G. C. Field's *Plato and His Contemporaries*. He had a few books on the history of Zionism which I had brought him—on request—such as Ben-Gurion's *Letters to Pola* and Golda Meir's *My Life*. He had also asked for and received a number of books by contemporary Arab writers and some classical Arab poetry. Two books that he read over and over again were Aldous Huxley's *Eyeless in Gaza*, and Jabra Ibrahim Jabra's *The Ship*. Jabra is a Palestinian poet and novelist from Bethlehem who has lived in Baghdad since 1948.

The prison authorities had given him permission to keep the television and radio-recorder Dina had brought, as well as a small collection of light and classical music cassettes. There was a lot of Julio Iglesias, his favorite singer. Once when I was visiting I pulled out my own favorite—Mozart's Fortieth. Ta'mari, watching me, remarked: "I'd trade them all in just for that one."

At first he spent his evenings listening to the news, from Monte Carlo, Damascus, Amman, and Israel's English and Arabic broadcasts. But with time his interest flagged: the news of the world and the war in Lebanon merely intensified his feelings of frustration. On September 3, 1982, two days after President Reagan announced his peace plan for the Middle East, Ta'mari's diary reads:

"The wealth of distorted and inaccurate news broadcast by the Israeli media is making Israel look like an Arab country. Israeli public opinion is shaped entirely by the goals of the present government—and that can only result, ultimately, in a catastrophe for the Jews and for the Arabs.

". . .Again, the Jordanian regime is still complicating the whole business. Reagan's peace proposal is a great step forward in that it attempts to save the Arab state from being swallowed up by the Jewish state. The Arabs would be foolish to say 'no' to Reagan."

A month later, on the 113th day of his imprisonment, at seven in the evening, he wrote: "Glued to the radio and never missing a single news broadcast seems to make a profoundly serious person out of me. Yet what I really need is a little entertainment. It's not a bad thing at all to be involved in politics but the fact of the matter is that I'm involved without being really involved. In my present circumstances, following the news like a bloodhound is just a provocation. And it's becoming intolerable. There's not a single person here that I can talk to."

He likened himself to a spectator at a football match who gets a heart attack just from watching the game, or to a man in a car sitting next to the driver: "I keep pressing on the gas and on the brakes, but they're not there. The truth is that I can't do anything and the radio is killing me. I have to find some way to protect myself." He "came to the conclusion" that the Israelis allowed him a radio in the first place just for the purpose of destroying his sanity. The only thing to do, therefore, was to stop listening.

His relations with the guards at the time of his so-called war from within were a major concern. He considered them representatives of the younger generation of Israelis, for better or for worse. When his relations with them were at a low point, which they frequently were, he became miserable and bitter. Ta'mari needed people. Without them he was like a fish out of water.

He was always trying to drag them into an argument or a discussion. "When I was first imprisoned," he told us later, "I had a very pointed view of the young Israeli. I was sure they were all supermen. I was convinced that in addition to being courageous they were all steeped in history in general, and Jewish and Zionist history and culture in particular. I was sure that every Israeli played at least one instrument and knew at least a thousand lines of poetry by heart."

It didn't take long for the myth to be shattered, and Ta'mari found satisfaction in shattering it over and over again, every time he talked with one of his guards. He was also very anxious for them to listen to him. One of his guards was from Rumania. Once he got into an argument with him on whether or not the Bible gave the Jews their "alleged" right to Palestine.

"I don't give a damn for the Bible," was the answer he got. "I don't believe a word that's in there."

"So why the hell are you here?" Ta'mari wanted to know.

"Because I can afford it," came the answer.

Later, turning over the answer in his mind, Ta'mari saw it as the familiar logic of the white man. That was power—not to give a damn about anything. That's the way it was in Johannesburg, in Capetown too.

He discovered that another one of his guards didn't have the faintest idea of the connection between Abraham and the Arabs. Ta'mari tried to explain that Abraham, the father of the Jews, was also the father of the Ishmaelites, and that the sanctity of the Ka'aba in Mecca sprang from Moslem belief that Abraham had built it. "In Arabic," he explained, "Abraham is called Ibrahim el-Khalil. *Khalil* means primordiality and connotes love as well. God is also called 'the merciful el-Khalil.' "

He tried to explain to a guard called Uzzi that Jerusalem once belonged to the Jebusites, a Canaanite people, and was a thriving metropolis long before it was conquered by King David. Uzzi, like most of the others, couldn't have cared less.

There was only one guard whom Ta'mari found to his liking, a Moroccan by the name of Albert. Not only did Albert bring him home-cooked food, he was the only one of the young Israelis who showed an intellectual interest in anything. He was ready to listen to Ta'mari, to argue with him, to look through his books. But with the exception of Albert, Ta'mari was forced to the conclusion that the young Israeli not only had no idea of his own history but that he was not particularly interested either. His major interest was the disco music that blared from the transistor permanently glued to his ears. They were a Coca-Cola generation, imitation Americans. Jewish history was totally irrelevant to them. They liked to listen to Julio Iglesias, he told me, "but they didn't understand a single word." They also liked to play with the electronic toys that Dina had brought.

Although I tried to explain to him that the guards were not necessarily a true cross section of Israeli youth, Ta'mari remained unconvinced. He believed that the average Palestinian youth was of a better caliber than the average Israeli, and this belief gave him a certain amount of inner strength.

"What the average Israeli knows about his own history," he wrote in his diary, "is similar to what Arabs once knew about theirs. The schools used to teach that Shakespeare was really an Arab whose name had been distorted from Sheik Zubier. . . ."

Ta'mari's ideal "Zionist enemy" was personified by Zuri Ben-Nun, the section warden. He and his ideology were what the PLO had to fight against, and during that period in prison Ta'mari fought him—at least on a personal level.

Relations between them were complex, ambivalent. They stood at opposite poles. Each represented total dedication to his beliefs and each believed that his own ideology justified whatever means were adopted to achieve its sacred ends. Each believed that if he could just pinpoint the weakness of the other's ideological structure, he could stave off its potential danger.

Ta'mari, however, had good reason to be afraid of Ben-Nun. One word from him and his daily life could become hell. Still, this didn't prevent the prisoner from trying to provoke his captor all the time. However much they deplored one another's views, it is quite possible that, at some level, each admired the other's zeal.

Zuri Ben-Nun had been a prison warden for long years. Born in Jerusalem to a religious family, he served in the army in one of the special religious combat units. He was married and the father of four and lived in the Jewish settlement of Kiryat Arba, built after the Six Day War as a thorn in the side of Arab Hebron. The philosophy of his movement—the Gush Emunim (Bloc of the Faithful)—was "possessing the land," a phrase which, in Hebrew, has unmistakably aggressive sexual overtones. Ben-Nun had a reputation among his colleagues as both a man of vision and a man of action. He carried a weapon with him wherever he went. Since settling on the West Bank, he had picked up a good deal of spoken Arabic from his neighbors in Hebron.

Once, while visiting Ta'mari in his cell, Ben-Nun told him the story of an old Arab peddler in Hebron who prevented a Jewish child from Kiryat Arba from eating a guava that had been sprayed with a particularly lethal insecticide. It was one of his favorite stories and he told it ostensibly to prove that Jews and Arabs could live together peacefully.

Ta'mari's response was less than enthusiastic. "The kid probably tried to steal the guava. What's a guava after you've already stolen his land and his house?"

"Hold it a minute," Ben-Nun retorted. "Nobody stole anything. My comrades and I came to fulfill the biblical injunction to 'settle the land,' where the Kingdom of Israel existed two thousand years ago. We came to rebuild an area where your grandfathers murdered our grandfathers in 1929. The Lord, blessed be He, gave the Land to our father, Abraham, Abuna Ibrahim. The Jewish people have always been tied to this land, from time immemorial. And there's one more thing. I see your people in Hebron going out to work every morning and coming back. They never had it so good. They've been able to build villas with fancy bathrooms and buy television sets. The Israeli occupation is the best thing that ever happened to them."

Ta'mari was ready for him. "All Abraham bought in Hebron was a burial plot from Ephron the Hittite, and he was a Bedouin like me. If you guys continue with all of your insane schemes, the whole country will be a graveyard—for you and for us."

Later that day, Ta'mari wrote in his diary that people like Ben-Nun "should wear much larger skullcaps to cover their lousy helmets. I really believe that the destruction of the Mosque of al-Aqsa is only a question of time. They can always find excuses, claiming that the guys who did it were crazy. But Ben-Nun and his friends really believe deep inside that the mosques on the Temple Mount have to be destroyed in order to prepare the ground for the building of the Third Temple. Whether this is Jewish imperialism or Jewish redemption—they really don't care.

"I'm sick and tired of listening to the stories they tell you about Jewish history," he continued. "Millions of Moslems and Christians also believe that they're true, actual facts. For me they're literature, art—two fields which have little connection with fact. I think it's tragic that Ben-Nun keeps looking for a factual cover for his fairytales. The bloodiest invasions and occupations have always been carried out in the name of some great and holy ideal. There were always geniuses around to invent great coverups—crosses or Jewish stars or Arab crescents at the end of the bayonet or on the crest of the helmet."

Further on, he wrote, in greater heat: "I want to shout and scream and break down the ugly walls of this cell. . . . There is no limit to the Israelis' greed, no limit to their contempt for 'goyim.' There's no limit to their arrogance. They think that they are so perfect that they could bottle their urine and export it as eau de cologne. If Ben-Nun's dream comes true, the amount of suffering imposed on the world will be the direct result not of the Third Temple but of the Third Jewish Reich."

It was Ta'mari's opinion, in retrospect, that Ben-Nun never got the better of him in their arguments. Nor did he ever succumb to Ben-Nun's mockery of his belief that coexistence between Jews and Arabs was possible. He was further convinced that Ben-Nun and his comrades were totally against any rapprochement between Jews and Arabs for the simple reason that it threatened to destroy the walls of the mental ghetto in which they had so firmly, and defensively, entrenched themselves.

While still in prison Ta'mari had once summed up the situation to his own satisfaction: "Ben-Nun is always trying to prove to himself that what he thinks is infallible, not to mention just and good. He is trying to prove that the Palestinian is an inferior being. I am living proof that he is wrong and he can't escape my presence. I'll have scored a victory on the day that I succeed in destroying his cool—and that day is bound to come."

One day Ben-Nun went so far as to agree with Ta'mari that the Palestinians had certain rights in Palestine. But, in his opinion, "the realization of your rights will be the destruction of mine." At that point, Ta'mari could only pity his adversary.

It was Ben-Nun, however, who granted Ta'mari extra privileges, who made routine life in prison easier. It was Ben-Nun who saw to it that Ta'mari got fresh air every day and even took him for his first walk outside in the prison yard. The minute that they were outside Ta'mari began to inhale deeply and to sniff the air.

"What do you think you're sniffing?" Ben-Nun wanted to know.

"Horses," answered Ta'mari.

"Don't be silly," Ben-Nun put him down. "There's not a horse for miles around."

Ta'mari was certain that Ben-Nun was lying and was just trying to belittle him.

A few days before Ta'mari was taken out of Ben-Nun's jurisdiction, the two men were playing chess in the same yard. Ta'mari, playing with the white pieces, had opened with the queen's gambit. After eight moves, he

131

had trapped one of Ben-Nun's knights, a decisive move in the game. Ben-Nun suddenly looked up.

"You know," he said, "you were right. There used to be a stable in these parts a couple of years ago."

Ta'mari looked Ben-Nun straight in the eye. "You know what," he began, "you look a lot like one of my younger brothers. That made things pretty hard for me. Even when you really put me off with your views and ideology and your ideas about me—and I knew exactly what you were thinking—there was still something about you I liked."

Ben-Nun's response was unexpected: "Tell me, Salah, have you ever thought about which one of us is the prisoner here—you or me?"

That night Ta'mari had a dream. The day the Israelis reached Sidon he had been leafing through a book of poetry by Jacques Prévert. When he left the house, the book was open to a page on which there was a drawing of a colt. It was the last thing to catch his eye. The colt appeared in his dream. "I saw the colt leaping out of the book and beginning to gallop away. I jumped on his back and we rode away. It was a wonderful feeling. I felt myself getting stronger and stronger as if a million atoms were exploding their energy into my system. The colt seemed to be carrying me to the sun. As we got closer and closer, the intense light blinded me. When I woke, I was looking at the fluorescent light in the cell. But I still felt that immense energy, and it kept me going for a while."

Ta'mari's occasional sojourns outside the prison, during his interview at the TV studios, his visit to Amos Oz, and his visit with Dina, invariably and understandably had bad repercussions. His return to the confinement of his prison cell depressed him. The same reaction would set in after every single one of my visits.

"I just can't bear these extreme transitions," he told me. "I can't spend time with you and your family, or walk in the street and see ordinary people, or sit here and talk to you—and then just stay here by myself in this lousy cell not knowing if I'll ever get out. I can't take it anymore. I think I'd prefer knowing that I'm doomed to remain in the cell forever. Then I would find some way to cope with it. But being privileged to go out or have you here—it's debilitating."

Before Amalia and I left on vacation at the beginning of September 1982, I had come to say goodbye. Ta'mari did his damndest to cover up his feelings in front of me but he wrote in his diary: "Aharon's going away—even for a short time—is unbearable for me. What else have I got to do?"

Another time when I was unable to visit him for two weeks, he wrote: "Aharon hasn't come, either yesterday or today, although he promised. Maybe he's not allowed to anymore. Actually, I really don't want to see him anymore. It would be better to break off with him. Not that I don't trust him. It's just that I've become so dependent on him and I hate that. I've become an infant again in prison. I can't buy anything by myself. I've got to ask for everything—even food and water. I'm gradually becoming less and less independent and I hate it. I hate that feeling.

"When Aharon doesn't show up, I become frightened. I'm so disappointed. I really shouldn't hope for anything from anybody. I shouldn't let myself be so vulnerable. I shouldn't let anything affect me negatively. It's better for me to be alone, to learn to depend on myself and only on myself."

The chinks in his protective shield became gaping holes. There were signs of a complete breakdown. He refused to leave his cell. His relations with the guards deteriorated. He no longer tried to get them to argue with him. They were all sick and tired of him by now. His eyes weakened from too much reading and writing. He began to get headaches.

"Since the day before yesterday," he wrote on October 16, 1982, "things are deteriorating rapidly. No 'good-mornings' or 'good-nights' from anyone . . . my headache is so bad it seems as if my head is going to explode. I can't read anymore or make even the slightest physical effort. Whatever I do sets off a hammer in my head. Everything hurts—even my pulse beat. I seem to forget things. I can't concentrate.

"One idea gives me no rest: the idea of a free zone somewhere in the Arab world. Not a tax-free zone but an idea-free zone. I dream of someplace like that where the authorities won't interfere with people's thinking. Everybody living in exile will come there—from London, Paris, wherever. There they'll be able to live out their ideas, to express them. We could establish a special radio station to transmit the truth to the Arab people. It's their right to know the truth. They'll begin to think differently, examine and discuss everything. A station like that will light a small candle, illuminate some dark corner of our ugly Arab world. But where? How? Who?

"What has to be decided is not the fate of Palestine but the very existence of the entire Arab world. If they only knew what the future holds in store for them, they would send their women and children out to the battlefield.

"Everything is still. It seems that they don't want to leave me any alternative but *Shahada*."

Shahada means a martyr's death.

"The silence is oppressive," he continued. "I'm almost finished reading the last of my books. I left a few pages to enjoy later. It reminds me of when I was a kid and was given a piece of chocolate. I would eat so slowly so that the taste would linger as long as possible. We didn't have chocolate often.

"The hardest thing for me is to decide on some idea that will be oriented toward a goal. A goal is encouraging and the process of attaining it helpful. This doesn't work when I only think about myself: about my family, about love. Those subjects only produce pain and sorrow and, ultimately, self-pity.

"It's seven in the morning. I didn't sleep and my eyes are stinging. Have I become part of this cell or is the cell part of me? The little bird and the prisoner. That's a wonderful tale for children, to be told in the middle of winter, in front of the fire. Is there still such a thing as a burning fireplace in winter? Do people still know what the art of conversation is? We used to stop and think about other people and only later complain about ourselves. Now we only complain and use our last shreds of strength for what we still think is important. We invent all kinds of meetings just to give us the impression that we are busy.

"How will the little bird be able to transmit her song through the rusty chains? How will she be able to feather the bed of the poor wounded knight instead of feathering the nest for the fledglings she is expecting? Even the little bird is lamenting. She doesn't encourage anybody anymore. Her song is just a vocal phenomenon, like the Arabs—God's unfinished symphony.

"If something happens to me, I hope they understand that they didn't leave me any hope. I would prefer that Dina live with one single memory than with an empty sack. I refuse to allow them to insult me. I have to win.

"If something happens to me, will they give my diary to my wife? I doubt it. Maybe Aharon would. The little mouse has returned. Let's see if I can train him."

My last visit to Ta'mari in his cell was on October 22, 1982, in the evening. Meanwhile political developments had taken a dramatic turn. Yasir Arafat was in Amman for the first time since 1970. He and Hussein had embraced in front of television cameras. The news of the rapprochement, when added to Ta'mari's frustrations, loneliness, and isolation, was too much for him. First of all, a new chapter in Palestinian history was being written without him. Furthermore, less than two months after evacuating Beirut, Arafat had made an about-face, approaching the person who was the PLO's worst enemy.

I knew that Ta'mari would be furious but it was the first time that I saw him raging like a bull. The political situation provided the background but his rage was directed against us.

The minute I walked in, even before I had a chance to sit down, he shouted at me imperiously: "Take a pencil and write down what I tell you."

"What happened?" I wanted to know.

"Just write!"

"I'm not your secretary." I was annoyed. "You know how to write yourself."

"I asked for a priest to come and take down my last will and testament but they didn't bring me one! So you can do it!" He was practically screaming.

"I'm not a priest and you're not a Christian!" I also raised my voice. "And nobody is trying to kill you."

"I'm going to kill myself. I have to do it. I've decided."

He wasn't shouting anymore. I could see that he meant every word he said. Desperation was in every syllable. I looked at him. His face was haggard and gray. His green eyes, which usually blazed, were dull.

I decided on a different tack. I tried to calm him down. "Come on. Sit down. I'll make us some coffee."

"For God's sake, no. I'm serious. Can't you understand that?"

"I can try," I said feebly.

Ta'mari started to explain. "In a few days I'll be forty. My most important tie to life was Dina and the rest of my family. My responsibility for Dina was my first priority and I've failed her. Dina's visit to Israel, which was dangerous for her, only strengthened my sense of obligation. I wasn't there when her mother died. I wasn't able to help my own mother and sisters in Kuwait after my father died. None of my obligations are worth a damn anymore.

"The second most important thing in my life are the kids from the Ashbal. In my will I want Dina to sell the house in Sidon and to distribute the money to the kids in the orchestra. I want each one of them to get a new instrument. I want them to have the motivation to continue after I'm gone.

"Nobody, Aharon, but nobody," he was almost shouting again, "has put me on trial. Therefore I have to judge myself. I have no other way out.

Everything has crumbled. I turned myself in so that the civilians who were looking out for me wouldn't suffer. Meanwhile thousands of civilians in southern Lebanon have been killed. So what was the point of my surrender? Where is the Israelis' word of honor? Where is the end to the bloodshed?"

I listened in absolute silence. Ta'mari continued to settle accounts with himself and with the rest of the world.

"Aside from all that, the man who stands before you today is an empty shell. Empty and guilty. Some of our people made terrible mistakes. No matter what I do for the rest of my life I won't be able to change what has already been done. Some people did terrible things. They murdered innocent women and children. Someone in the PLO should have stopped them. I was a member of the PLO and a senior commander and I did nothing to stop them. Now I have judged myself for that."

I was astounded. Anger, despair, fright, and agony were alternating in his voice. His eyes turned a deep, threatening red.

"In short, my friend, I have nothing to live for. I no longer have any goals . . . or hopes. Even if they don't bring me a priest I'll finish myself off. I have a plan. I'll tape my will. I'll tape a message to Arafat. Then I'll kill myself. I have some cyanide. Don't ask me where I got it from. My decision is final. On October 27, my birthday, I'll come full circle and I'll go to my death with my eyes open."

He went on for some time without letting up. It was apparent that he had been mulling over these things for quite some time, during long, lonely days and even longer and lonelier nights.

"My message to Arafat—in case you're interested—is simple: he should release the eight Israeli soldiers that were captured near Behamdoun. That's all. What I want from you, Aharon, is to get my diary to Dina. I could also have asked you to make sure I was buried on the land of my father's tribe near Herodium. But it's obligatory to fulfill a last wish and I doubt that you could do that."

Ta'mari went over to the bed and pulled out a thick notebook from under his mattress. "This is the dearest thing I have here, the diary I've kept since I arrived. I don't know what will happen to it if I leave it here, so take it with you. I'm sure I can trust you to get it to Dina. If you want, you can read it."

The whole situation was disturbing, almost intolerable. I was already familiar enough with Ta'mari's love for the dramatic but I was hard put at that moment to decide where the acting ended and the truth began.

Furthermore, I wasn't particularly anxious to delve into it too deeply. I had a feeling that he wasn't lying about the cyanide. I had a feeling that he had really reached rock bottom—and I cared. His well-being had become crucial to my own existence. I had to take his threat seriously.

There was something else: this scene took place after Dina had already visited, on her own initiative, the Israeli prisoners held by the PLO. In his "will," Salah recommended that Arafat release them; this recommendation was not unconnected with Dina's involvement.

I walked out of the cell with a heavy heart. Salah had thrust a responsibility on me that put me in an impossible situation. I was both frightened and worried. He had given me five days. Only then would I know positively if he was really serious. I had to do something and do it fast.

I couldn't possibly do it by myself.

It was after midnight Friday night. Zuri Ben-Nun was surely at home in bed in Kiryat Arba. Even if I called he wouldn't pick up the phone on the Sabbath.

I asked the guard for a tranquilizer and gave it to Ta'mari. He took it like a kid who is too tired to argue. I promised to come to see him the next day. "Don't do anything rash. Just take it easy."

I only hoped that Dina wouldn't call. What could I tell her—that he had given himself only five days to live?

On the way home, thinking about what had happened, it occurred to me that Ta'mari was probably scared to death to die. But with his pride and sense of honor, he couldn't be trusted not to do it. Months of despair and frustration had eaten away at his strength. Now, in order to overcome the fear of death, all he needed was one moment of utter determination.

When I got home, I woke Amalia up and told her the whole story. She was more upset than I. We sat down and I repeated to her, word for word, everything Ta'mari had said. She took notes and by the time I finished she had filled five pages in tiny script. We put the pages into an envelope. I picked up the phone to the same IDF officer who had helped arrange Dina's visit. That same night, he sent a messenger to pick up the envelope.

The next morning at five o'clock, the door to Ta'mari's cell was opened and he was ordered to pack his things. After that he was handcuffed. He "celebrated" his fortieth birthday at the Ansar POW camp in southern Lebanon.

He was no longer alone.

11

"Our Respected Brother Salah"

The helicopter circled over the small landing strip for the third time before coming down. The strip had been built by the PLO at points equidistant from Tyre and Ansar in southern Lebanon.

"That's the place," said Colonel Rosenfeld to Brigadier General Katz, pointing to a wheat field to the east of the strip. The wheat field extended up to the village of Duweir and was just about ready for harvesting.

Col. Meir Rosenfeld was already past the age for active duty. Nonetheless, he had been called up to head the department for POWs in the Military Police, and had left with General Katz to find a suitable area for constructing a POW compound.

The decision to set it up on Lebanese soil had been taken a few days earlier, in the first week of the war, by Maj. Gen. Moshe Nativ. Within days of the invasion, the temporary compound in the A-Safa warehouse in Sidon had become congested. Because of its location, the IDF faced enormous difficulties in supplying food and water to the thousands of prisoners. As a result it was hard to keep the POWs under control—not to mention the hundreds, perhaps thousands of women and children who stormed the gates at all hours demanding to see their loved ones. The compound in Israel, at Meggido, near Afula, was also full and a steady stream of new prisoners was arriving daily. However, legal advisers to the IDF made it clear that the transfer of prisoners to Israel contravened international law. The central compound had to be in Lebanon.

As the IDF advanced further into Lebanon, every day hundreds of Palestinian fighters surrendered or were rounded up by the army. The situation was so bad that the prisoners and their families began to impede the progress of the IDF. Furthermore, the interrogation of prisoners under these conditions was, of necessity, cursory and ineffective.

According to Sharon's blueprint for the war, Israel expected to help establish a new Lebanese government with which it would sign a peace treaty. As soon as that occurred, and it wasn't expected to take long, the occupied parts of Lebanon, together with all the prisoners, would be handed over to the sovereign Lebanese authorities. The camp was conceived, therefore, as a large but temporary compound.

The landing strip near Duweir offered a reasonable solution, since equipment and supplies could be readily flown in. For security it also seemed a good choice. In case of trouble, reinforcements could be flown in too. Nor was it far from Israel's northern border. But few security problems were envisaged. What could possibly happen in the three or four weeks until the camp was dismantled?

On June 12, one day after Rosenfeld and Katz viewed the area, an advance force of MPs arrived together with a gigantic combine. The wheat fields belonged to two Arab families living not far from one another. The IDF cut the wheat and stored it in a large tent set up for the purpose. The Arabs were informed that the IDF had harvested their wheat for them and that they could have it all. But—one of the families had to evacuate its house for the duration and move in with its neighbor. The military police would supply the two families with food, water, and fuel. The first house was turned into camp headquarters and Colonel Rosenfeld set up an office on the roof of the house to supervise the construction.

A few days later, the stubble was covered with a thin layer of limestone gravel brought in in big army trucks. It took another month to get the Ansar camp in working order: barbed wire, pens, outhouses, lookout towers, tents.

On July 14, 1982, the first contingent of those "rounded up" were brought to Ansar and Colonel Ben-Shahar took over command of the camp. When more than three months later on Saturday, October 23,

Salah Ta'mari reached Ansar, there were already ten thousand prisoners there, and Colonel Rosenfeld was back, as commander.

The prisoners were divided into two subcamps, Ansar I and Ansar II, referred to as "tubs" by the MPs. Each tub contained fifteen pens, and each pen—enclosed by barbed wire—250 to 300 prisoners and a sentry tower. The pens were 44 × 44 yards and had 10 or 12 large field tents in each; that is, there were about 25 prisoners to a tent. A 20-foot-wide road separated the pens and was used for patrols. The two tubs were also encircled by barbed wire and by a high earth embankment where sentries kept watch night and day.

Ta'mari could not see the tent city from where he sat as the car drove into the camp: he had made the trip in the back of a Black Maria.

He was taken into the concrete prefab used to house the guards. The guard on duty that Saturday "registered" him but decided not to assign him to a pen until the camp commander returned from his day off.

Ta'mari soon found himself locked in a room with four bare walls, a table, a bench, and a shuttered window. The difference between being in prison in Israel or in Lebanon was very small. An MP let himself in a few minutes later, bringing a few blankets—which he tossed onto the army cot—and a plate of food. He left without closing the door and Ta'mari noticed a short, bespectacled, gray-haired man standing outside. He was in uniform and had captain's rank.

"My name is Captain Sela," the man introduced himself, "and I represent the IDF spokesman in the camp. I'm responsible for coordinating visits by the press and media. May I sit down?"

Ta'mari shrugged his shoulders indifferently. Captain Sela, a lawyer in civilian life, had not received any information about the new prisoner. The man on duty had merely told him that he had arrived unexpectedly and looked "important." Sela thought that a talk with the newcomer might liven up the monotony of his long, uneventful Saturday afternoon. Ta'mari did not disappoint him. They talked long into the evening.

"The man fascinated me," Sela told me months later, in his office in Tel Aviv. "I understood him immediately. First of all, he was charismatic. Secondly, he deeply believed in the justice of his cause. He talked to me in a language I understood, in concepts taken from Judaism. He began by comparing himself to Joseph, thrown into a pit by his brothers who wanted to sell him to the Ishmaelites. I felt a deep sense of identity with him, although he looked like the dregs of humanity. He was in rags and hadn't washed or shaved for days. But his eyes would light up from time to time as he spoke of the need for coexistence between the two peoples."

Late in the evening, before Captain Sela left, Ta'mari apparently hinted to him that he was no longer able to stand total isolation and might do something desperate. Sela took him seriously and begged the guard on duty "to keep an eye on the new prisoner" until the camp commander returned the next morning. Sela waited impatiently for Rosenfeld's return and collared him the minute he appeared.

Colonel Rosenfeld was not at all sympathetic to Sela's intervention: "They sent him here without clearing it with me first and they can have him right back. The only thing he can do here is make trouble."

Sela was not deterred. "Rosenfeld," he persisted, "this guy is a real leader. He's intelligent. You should be interested in someone like him. If all the bitterness and pressure building up here explodes one day, you won't be able to calm down ten thousand men over the loudspeaker. You'll need a mediator, someone who can represent them. It's my opinion that Ta'mari is just the man. Only right now he is in a deep depression."

Rosenfeld wasn't convinced. Sela continued to entreat him. Rosenfeld remained adamant. Sela went in to speak to Ta'mari again and then returned to Rosenfeld. In the evening, Rosenfeld relented. "Okay," he told Sela, "I'll go talk to him. You're driving me nuts."

Ta'mari was lying on the cot, dozing. Rosenfeld touched him and he sprang to attention. "Commander," he said, and saluted. He had immediately identified the elderly man's rank. Rosenfeld was short and stout and red-headed, like Ben-Nun, but his red hair was turning gray.

"You can go," Rosenfeld said to the two guards who had come in with him. To Ta'mari he said: "What's with you?" He didn't sit down or motion Ta'mari to sit down.

"Nothing, Commander," Ta'mari answered faintly, in English. "I'm not a problem."

"Sit down," Rosenfeld commanded, "and listen to me carefully. I've heard all sorts of things about you. They say you're a troublemaker. Is that true? They also say you're a very intelligent guy and understand things. I don't know you and you don't know me. But it's worth your while to understand a few things. You people are staying here and it's my job to make sure you stay put. If anybody ignores this very basic fact and tries to incite the prisoners to riot, I'll have to open fire. And there's plenty of firepower in this camp. If you can grasp that simple fact, you can use your influence to keep things here under control."

"No, no," Ta'mari protested in a weak voice, almost whispering. "I'm finished. I don't have any influence anymore. Just forget about me."

Rosenfeld began to sense Ta'mari's acute distress. He realized soon enough that Sela was right. Ta'mari seemed altogether indifferent to his own fate, and this stirred something in the old soldier.

"Listen," he said after a few minutes' thought. "I'm transferring you to the officers' pen."

Ta'mari was incredulous.

"If you do that," he said to the Israeli officer, "I'll be more than grateful."

Rosenfeld noticed that Ta'mari's eyes had lit up for a second. "Let's go," he said, "right now."

The two men walked over to Pen 5, where officers of all the Palestinian fighting organizations were held—from the units of Ahmad Jibril, George Habash, Nayif Hawatmeh, and the Sa'iqa, up to and including the Fatah. Ta'mari, joining them now, was the highest-ranking officer.

"Open the gate," Rosenfeld ordered the MP stationed there.

The soldier stuck the key into the lock—and then stopped dead in his tracks. Inside the detention area, the officers seemed to be springing up from all sides, moving like a tidal wave in the direction of the gate.

Rosenfeld kept his eyes on Ta'mari. The tall man in rags looked for a long moment at the hundreds of men on the other side of the gate and gave them some slight signal—no more than a raised eyebrow. But it was enough. The men turned and walked slowly back to their places.

Rosenfeld was completely astounded. He had never seen anything like it in his entire life. "A man shows up, signals with his eyebrow, and they all obey him."

The gate was opened and Ta'mari walked in.

The prisoners waited until Rosenfeld left before crowding around the newcomer. A group of Fatah officers led their commander to one of the tents. One of them had already prepared coffee. Ta'mari sat on the ground at the edge of one of the mattresses. Somebody brought him two rolled blankets. Ta'mari looked around. He realized that officers from the other organizations had not joined in the welcome.

The men expected to hear something from Ta'mari. Instead he began shooting questions at them: "How many prisoners are there here?"

"Ten thousand," answered one.

"Five thousand," answered another.

Other figures were also given, ranging from four thousand to twelve. Ta'mari was astonished. "You mean you've been here all this time and have no idea how many people there are?"

Ta'mari wanted the situation in the camp explained to him—what the setup was, what they did all day, how the Israelis treated them. The men responded willingly. They told him that the Israelis appointed a *mukhtar* [headman] in each pen who was held responsible for what went on. They told him of the underground communications system established throughout the camp: a note was written on a piece of paper with the addressee's name on the outside, tied around a stone, and then tossed into the next pen.

Ta'mari requested paper and the total number of pens. In a few minutes he had formulated a letter to the mukhtars in which he requested an answer by "return mail": he wanted to know how many there were in every pen, what their demands were, and if they had any special problems. He ordered two of the officers to start copying the letter and to make sure the "mail" went out. "In half an hour we'll know how many people there are here."

It was as if he had breathed new life into the men. Senior officers began giving orders down the line to the lesser officers. Ta'mari signed all the letters with "Revolution until Victory"—the motto of the Fatah—and his name. He himself didn't leave the tent.

Within a short time, stones began falling into the officers' pen. They were all addressed to "Our Respected Brother Salah" and all contained the number of the pen, the name of the mukhtar, the exact number of prisoners, and what they needed (such as blankets, books, medication); special mention was made of sick prisoners in need of medical care and prisoners who were being interrogated all the time.

List after list was brought in to Ta'mari, still sitting on the edge of the mattress. He called over Maj. Ahmed Abu Leila, from Nayif Hawatmeh's Democratic Front, and asked him to add the figures up. Abu Leila was thus informally appointed Ta'mari's first deputy.

Colonel Rosenfeld went back to headquarters. It had been almost dark when he left the new prisoner in Pen 5 and by now the camp was lit up by hundreds of bulbs and floodlights. He wasn't sure he had done the right thing. Ta'mari was a born leader—he had seen that much with his own eyes—and those qualities might just boomerang. If anything happened, the trouble and the responsibility would be his. It was hard enough just keeping 10,500 men crowded into such a limited space on enemy soil without inviting extra headaches.

Rosenfeld was fifty-five years old, the oldest reserve officer in the military police. Although as head of its department for POWs he had chosen the site and supervised its construction, it was only recently—three weeks before to be precise—that he had actually taken over its command. The camp was in a perpetual ferment. After the initial period in July, when they were still shocked and frightened, the prisoners had become nervous and impatient.

They had begun to hoist PLO flags and display pictures of Arafat all over the place. There was constant shouting between one pen and the next, twenty-four hours a day. At times all the voices would blend together into one thunderous shout, which would then turn into a flow of abuse against the State of Israel. The Israelis on duty at the camp were largely from the reserves and Rosenfeld knew that most of them were uneasy. He was not sure that the manpower at his disposal was actually equal to a security emergency.

He also knew that a section of Israel's political and military leadership was exceptionally sensitive to the very existence of Ansar. The massacre at Sabra and Shatilla—which was followed by a mass demonstration in Tel Aviv's main plaza, demanding an inquiry—was still fresh in everyone's mind. "Everyone was traumatized by Sabra and Shatilla, including us," was the way General Nativ put it later. "If we were forced into a situation in which we had to open fire, we wouldn't be able to explain it to the world." Nativ told Rosenfeld that he personally would have to answer for whatever happened in Ansar.

"I was in a bind," Rosenfeld told me afterward. "The responsibility for Ansar was mine. The government would not be anxious to back me up if something happened. Furthermore, I knew that the PLO was holding our prisoners. If we did anything rash, they would too. I was frightened that the mothers of our prisoners would hold me responsible if anything bad happened to their kids."

Rosenfeld couldn't fall asleep that night. It was after midnight when he got up, got dressed, and walked over to Pen 5. He ordered the guard to open the gate. The guard hesitated. It wasn't customary for an Israeli officer to enter one of the pens alone, without a security escort. For morning inspection, no less than five men and an officer went in and they were heavily covered from behind—by armed soldiers, a half-track with a primed machine gun, and sentries with their fingers on the trigger.

"Open immediately," he repeated, and walked in.

One of the sentries shouted the news to his buddies: "The commander has gone into the officers' block," and sounded the alarm. Within seconds, the area was alive with half-tracks, tanks, and armed soldiers. Pen 5 was flooded with light. Emergency precautions had been set in motion.

Rosenfeld paid little attention to the tumult. He stood in an open area and told one of the prisoners to get Ta'mari.

"You're a brave man coming here alone at this hour," Ta'mari greeted him, in English.

Rosenfeld noticed hundreds of heads sticking out of the tents.

Rosenfeld answered in Arabic. He wanted everybody to understand what he was about to say. "I'm not brave. I'm in charge of this camp. I can go wherever I please, whenever I please."

He stood there talking to Ta'mari for about an hour. At one point Ta'mari informed him that there was a prisoner in Pen 28 with only one kidney, in need of urgent treatment. Ta'mari wanted Rosenfeld to see that he was in command of all the particulars and prepared to take responsibility for what was going on.

"Come and see me tomorrow and we'll discuss everything," said Rosenfeld, and left.

"I had to feel my way in that situation," he later said. "After I saw that I could stand and talk with him for an hour and nobody interrupted or made a rumpus, I calmed down a little. I realized that there was someone to talk to."

The emergency precautions were canceled. The tanks and half-tracks departed. The floodlights were dimmed. Colonel Rosenfeld went back to his room to sleep and Ta'mari returned to his tent. Ta'mari was impressed: "He's got guts, that commander."

When dawn broke over Ansar, every prisoner in the camp knew that Salah Ta'mari had been taken prisoner and was in Pen 5.

As was the custom every morning, five MPs and an officer, carrying billy clubs, entered Pen 5 for inspection. At the sound of the key in the gate, all the prisoners jumped off their mattresses, rolled their blankets up, and placed them at the foot of the mattress. Then they sat down in two rows, oriental fashion, their backs to the tent opening, and, with their hands on the back of their necks, dropped their heads between their knees.

Ta'mari rose from his mattress and watched his fellow officers. He was appalled. He couldn't believe his eyes. The Israelis came in and began to count the two rows of men. "You too," one of them shouted at Ta'mari in Arabic.

"I'm not sitting anywhere, goddamn it! You can count me standing up! If you don't like it, shoot. Then you can count me lying down."

The soldier moved threateningly in Ta'mari's direction. The prisoners were holding their breaths, wondering what they would do if Ta'mari were hit.

The Israeli officer defused the situation immediately. "Leave him alone," he ordered. "He's a special character. Don't answer him. Just count and let's get out of here."

Nobody in the tent moved until the count was finished. But once the soldiers left the tent, one of them turned to Ta'mari and pleaded with him: "*Minshan allah* [for god's sake], we don't need trouble. Don't do anything rash."

"Don't worry," Ta'mari answered them. "I won't give you more trouble. You've got quite enough already."

His jugular vein was pulsing. "You are human beings and not numbers. From now on I forbid you to sit with your heads between your knees during inspection." He was giving them orders. It was clear to him that they were being ruled by fear, senior officers and junior alike.

He walked out of the tent and into daylight for the first time since arriving. The sight that met his eyes only exacerbated his anger. In the center of the pen, inlaid into the path between the tents and the barbed wire, was a large Star of David, made of small whitewashed stones. Next to it was a candelabrum, the symbol of the State of Israel. Nearby was a miniature of the Dome of the Rock, with a Star of David at the top and over it the word "Shalom" in Hebrew, English, and Arabic.

"Who made this?" he asked one of the prisoners standing nearby.

"We all did," was the indifferent answer.

"It can't stay here!"

The prisoner walked away, as if he hadn't heard a word. Ta'mari stood there for a moment, thinking. Then, changing his tack, he began to move from tent to tent, reminding everyone that it was already late October and there might be rain soon. "If we don't do something about the paths here, we'll all sink in the mud." He enjoined everyone to get out and start paving the paths with whatever gravel was available.

146

He himself bent down and began collecting small stones. Others soon joined in. As if inadvertently, he took some of the pebbles from the Star of David to use for paving stones. The transition from words to deeds seemed to melt the fear. More people joined in. Within an hour the Star of David had disappeared, as did the candelabrum and the word "Shalom." Instead, the path in the center of the pen had been covered with gravel.

The sentry on duty became aware of the unusual industry of the prisoners and reported to his superiors. Word reached Rosenfeld.

When Ta'mari was escorted out of the pen by five MPs—as ordered by Rosenfeld—the prisoners were sure that some form of punishment was in the offing. A number of prisoners who had refused to collaborate in the "road-building" began exhorting their fellow prisoners with various versions of "I told you so."

Rosenfeld addressed Ta'mari sharply: "I see you're beginning to make trouble. That doesn't square with our talk last night. This morning you refused to follow orders during inspection and now I understand you ordered your people to destroy something which they worked very hard to make. I saw in that design a symbol of brotherhood. You thought it was something to incite the prisoners against?"

"What kind of brotherhood are you talking about?" Ta'mari erupted. "There's no brotherhood between people standing outside the barbed wire and turning their guns on those inside! If you want to maintain peace and quiet here, Commander, the first thing you have to do is stop humiliating the prisoners. It's humiliating to make them sit with their heads between their knees while you count them. It's your right to count your prisoners but not to humiliate them. I'll never agree to that—even if it means that you're going to shoot."

Rosenfeld studied Ta'mari carefully. "I'll tell you what," he said. "I'm ready to change inspection procedure for a trial period, on one condition: that order is maintained during inspection and that my good intentions are respected."

"Tomorrow morning, Commander, everyone will be lined up in threes for inspection. Like soldiers. As for art, decorating our living quarters with a Jewish star is another form of humiliation. If you force frightened prisoners to make Jewish designs, don't be surprised if one fine day they use their imaginations and whitewashed pebbles to make the word 'Auschwitz.' "

Rosenfeld's blood went to his head but he held his tongue. Ta'mari, apparently, had not yet finished. "One last thing," he added. "Captain

147

Sela showed me the Geneva Convention and explained to me just how it was being violated here. I have no illusions that we'll be treated like prisoners-of-war, but we do have the right to representation."

"Okay," said Rosenfeld, "you're the committee."

"Oh no, Commander." Ta'mari shook his head. "If I continue to meet with you privately, I won't be of any use to anybody. I have no intention of representing all the prisoners by myself. There are people here from different organizations, from different countries, and with different problems. In the Fatah we are used to democratic procedures. . . ."

"So who do you propose?" asked Rosenfeld, ignoring Ta'mari's barb.

"I'll have to consult with the others. Tomorrow I'll give you an answer."

The new system for inspection instituted the next morning indicated to the prisoners that the newcomer had, indeed, taken over and was going to get things changed. It also helped Ta'mari convince the other officers that a committee was necessary. The prospect of improved conditions prevailed over differences of opinion that might have cropped up over candidates for the committee. Ta'mari had his own list prepared. It included Major Leila of the Democratic Front as representative of all the organizations outside of the Fatah: Nabil Masri, a medic from Gaza who spoke Hebrew and would serve as a kind of minister of health; Ne'me Jum'a, a Lebanese Shiite lawyer from the Amal organization, to represent all the non-Palestinians, and, of course, Ta'mari himself as chairman. Ta'mari suggested that the committee be called "The Committee for the Defense of Prisoners' Rights."

The committee was recognized by the commander of Ansar and soon began to meet regularly with representatives of the International Red Cross. Every evening at eight o'clock, following a meeting of the Israeli officers, Colonel Rosenfeld convened the prisoners' committee in Captain Sela's room.

Ta'mari brought a long list of demands to the first meeting but, in view of the attention accorded to the committee, decided that it was unnecessary to make them all at once. It would be better, he thought, just to get things moving in the right direction.

To begin with he demanded, and received, permission to enter all of the pens freely, in order to keep in touch with the prisoners as a body and hear what they had on their minds. Rosenfeld was later to say that freedom of movement was the only right he granted Ta'mari: "The rest were his own achievements." All of the guards were instructed to let Ta'mari in and accompany him on his rounds.

After making himself familiar with the camp as a whole, Ta'mari mod-ified his original demands, made impulsively on the first day. Instead, he worked out a plan based on two guiding principles: to make the authorities aware of the fact that the prisoners had a unified leadership, and to make the prisoners aware that the committee was looking after their interests. Demands were made in two areas: those concerning the morale of the prisoners and their status as POWs; and those concerning their physical conditions and daily routine. For Ta'mari, problems of morale had priority.

The problem of the sick belonged, in fact, to the first area. There were prisoners who were invalids, afflicted with heart disease, cancer, diabetes, or kidney trouble, and prisoners who were crippled. They all required daily treatment and Ta'mari insisted from the very first that they be released immediately. There were also dozens of mentally ill. During the war a hospital for the mentally ill in Nabetiya had been bombed. Most of the patients fled and had been rounded up by the IDF. Among them were drug addicts who, according to Ta'mari, not only endangered their own lives but made life difficult for the others.

Another problem that contributed to the low morale of the prisoners was the separation of brothers, and fathers and sons who had been assigned to different pens. This problem and its solution afforded Ta'mari the oppor-tunity of enlarging and reenforcing his power base in the camp, a situation which the Israeli authorities favored: they preferred dealing with Ta'mari rather than with the dissidents of Habash and Hawatmeh.

Rosenfeld empowered Ta'mari to move fifteen prisoners daily from one pen to another within the framework of family unification. The families thus reunited were beholden to Ta'mari and became his staunch sup-porters. At the same time, he was able to "plant" certain of his Fatah followers in pens where the dissident organizations were in the majority, and thus keep abreast of developments. Ta'mari proved not only a leader of men but an astute politician as well.

As his grasp of the situation in the camp crystallized, he began to define long-range goals for himself and for the committee. He usually formulated them in ideological terms: "Ansar is providing us with a unique oppor-tunity," he told them. "There is an enormous concentration of PLO organizations here. There are also members of Lebanese resistance move-ments and ordinary Lebanese citizens sympathetic to our cause. We have all the conditions for teaching our revolutionary ideas and educating the people here. We can use the time for political activity, for lectures, even for physical training. We can give the prisoners the tools for self-expression. Instead of drawing Jewish stars, they can be encouraged to express their own identities. Even if the result is primitive, at least it will be their own. It will give them a way of expressing their national aspirations."

Ta'mari never let up on questions of morale, and as far as he was concerned the unity of the ranks was a prerequisite for high morale. Furthermore, he believed that the higher the morale of the prisoners, the lower the morale of their Israeli captors. "This has to be the motivating force of our psychological warfare, of our counteroffensive. That way we can be victorious, even behind the barbed wire of Ansar."

The first days of November heralded the coming of winter. Up to then, the prisoners slept on mattresses on the ground, each with one blanket. Now this was no longer enough. "It's cold at night," Ta'mari explained to Rosenfeld. "We need more blankets. We need camp beds to put the mattresses on, otherwise we'll soon be sleeping in mud. You can't keep healthy people in such conditions, not to speak of the sick. If you don't take care of it soon, the situation might really deteriorate."

A word to the wise was sufficient. A few days later, a convoy of trucks unloaded an enormous quantity of cots, blankets, warm jackets, sweaters, socks, and heavy underwear for the inmates of Ansar. "I had the whole army jumping," Rosenfeld recalled, "from the chief-of-staff down to the quartermaster corps. It was quite an expensive operation. Imagine, five blankets per prisoner. That turned out to be seventy-five thousand blankets at one go. Not to mention ten thousand loaves of bread a day and water and everything else. Ansar cost the government of Israel about a million dollars a day."

In general, both Ta'mari's position and that of his committee became stronger. Everyone realized that because of them they would suffer less that winter. Still, there were prisoners who were not yet ready to accept either Ta'mari's or the committee's authority. Those unwilling to concede anything of their organizational identity were allowed to carry out activities independently. But everyone else was now drawn in through the establishment of a "joint command" of representatives from all the PLO factions, with local commands in every pen. Subcommittees were set up in every pen to deal respectively with politics, religion, sports, food distribution, and so on.

Later, yet another committee was set up—to plan ways of escaping.

Once winter set in there was a further demand—for kerosene heaters. Rosenfeld was amenable to the idea but there was strong opposition from some quarters of the IDF. They were afraid the prisoners would use the fuel to burn up the camp. Rosenfeld said he was in control and would take full responsibility. But this time his concern for the prisoners backfired.

The heaters arrived and with them a contingent of civilians, employed by the army, to install them in the pens. The civilians refused to enter the pens while three or four hundred terrorists were inside. Rosenfeld had to think fast.

There were at the time another ten pens being built in Ansar II to alleviate the crowding. Rosenfeld ordered the civilians to install the heaters first in the new, empty pens. When they finished, he ordered the temporary transfer of prisoners from Ansar I to Ansar II. This way, the stoves could now be installed in the old pens. When the installation was completed the prisoners were told that they were being transferred back to their old pens and a rumor was circulated that the old pens had no heating. This was enough to foment a riot. The prisoners pulled out kitchen knives and began to rip up the tent sidings.

Rosenfeld was raging like a bull and gave orders to get the prisoners out but they refused to move. An emergency was declared and tanks and MPs surrounded the rebellious pen. Rosenfeld walked right in and began to shout at the prisoners—above the noise of the tanks and half-tracks. "Either you evacuate this place immediately or there's going to be bloodshed!"

Slowly but surely, the men began to move out, their aggression somewhat vented. They walked out to the patrol path which, after the first few rains, had turned into a quagmire. Rosenfeld ordered the prisoners to sit down, in the mud, and not to move. "You're going to sit here until you drop dead or until I find out who cut up the new tents." The tanks moved in as if to emphasize the gravity of the situation.

The prisoners crouched in the mud like animals. But their mouths were sealed. And they stayed that way for more than an hour until the mukhtar stood up and said to Rosenfeld: "Do us a favor and call Ta'mari."

Ta'mari was brought over from the other end of the camp. Rosenfeld told him what had happened. The tanks and half-tracks and the men in the mud told him what was happening now. Rosenfeld's expression left no room for doubt. The situation was grave.

Ta'mari's first, spontaneous impulse was to sit down in the mud with the other prisoners, which is exactly what he did. He sat there and was soon shaking with cold. But after a while he got up and turned to face his own people. "I suppose you think you're great heroes?

"You want to know what heroism is? I'll tell you. To get up and walk in the direction of those barbed wire fences, knowing full well that you'll be shot dead before you make it to the other side. If that's what you're after, let's go! I'll lead the way. What good is ripping up tents?" By now he was shouting and his bitterness was evident. What had actually infuriated him was the fact that the people who had ripped up the tents—men from George Habash's organization, the PFLP—had consistently refused not only to cooperate with the committee but even to coordinate their own activities with them. By their partisan action, they had destroyed the principle of unity that Ta'mari had worked so hard to instill.

Rosenfeld admitted much later that at the moment he was overcome with pity for Ta'mari. "First he sat there freezing. But even worse, he was absolutely helpless. I couldn't stand it. I didn't want *him* to suffer. I decided to end the business. I got them all on their feet and sent them back to the torn tents. Let them live there and freeze from the wind and the rain. I figured that maybe that way they would get Ta'mari's message."

Ta'mari's authority was firmly entrenched but Ansar was still seething all the time. The discontent operated like a brush fire—you put it out in one place and it immediately erupted in another. Soldiers stationed in the camp, regardless of rank or corps, were affected by the oppressive ambience of the place. It was depressing, loathsome, vile—whether you sympathized with the prisoners or wished them all dead. And among the men from the regular army and the reserves, there were all kinds.

The very existence of such a gigantic prison camp was problematic. "We understood very well the human problem that we were up against," said General Nativ. "All kinds of Israelis ended up there for various periods of time. There were people who got rid of their aggressions easily by cursing the prisoners or throwing stones at them. But there were others who simply could not countenance the idea of a camp, run by Israelis and surrounded by barbed wire, tanks, and sentries. It reminded them of a concentration camp. This comparison was made by Israelis, foreigners, the media. It was almost natural especially when added to the fresh trauma of Sabra and Shatilla."

In addition to the obvious associations, the frustrations, and the revulsion, there was something else—fear. It hung in the air. People were afraid of what would happen next, where the next brush fire would erupt, what toll it would take. "And fear," added Nativ, "is not a sign of good health."

The first fatal incident occurred the week before Christmas.

It happened on a routine patrol. One of the soldiers, sitting on a half-track with his finger on the trigger of his machine gun, went berserk. He squeezed the trigger as the half-track passed Pen 20, emptying the whole magazine. Three prisoners sitting and eating their lunch were killed on the spot. Another twelve were wounded. The soldier went into shock as did all the people in the pen.

Within minutes, the news had spread over the whole camp. Reaction was spontaneous. Thousands of agitated prisoners threw themselves on the barbed wire and began to shout, cursing the State of Israel, the IDF, and the guards.

Colonel Rosenfeld wasn't in the camp that day. It was Saturday and he had taken the day off. He was alerted from his home in Nazareth while the regional commander ordered reinforcements sent into the camp.

As his helicopter dropped down on the airstrip, Rosenfeld was able to see what was happening. The pens were surrounded and the patrol paths were choked with tanks and half-tracks. The hysterical cries of the prisoners hanging on the barbed wire added an animal-like grotesquery to the scene.

Rosenfeld was of the opinion that a different approach was needed. The presence of such massive force might just set off the powder keg. He immediately requested that all reinforcements evacuate the camp. He didn't want another soldier losing control.

Once this was done, he himself made the rounds of the pens accompanied by his deputy. His appearance was effective and the hysteria was slowly defused. Still, Rosenfeld was afraid that the prisoners might want to take revenge, and he was especially worried about morning inspection in the blood-spattered pen.

The next morning, a half hour before the scheduled inspection, Rosenfeld arrived at the gate of Pen 20 and ordered the guard to open up. Ta'mari's friend Saruji, the school principal from Sidon, ran toward him and tried to warn him not to go in. "They'll kill you." Rosenfeld paid little attention to the warning. The prisoners came out and moved dangerously close to the camp commander. He began to shout: "Get back into your tents!! All of you!! Immediately!!" The prisoners had been expecting the usual detail of five soldiers plus officer, but Rosenfeld's toughness was enough. They realized that he would use his gun if he had to. With Saruji imploring them as well, they reentered their tents.

In the center of the pen was an improvised coffin. Rosenfeld knew what this meant: it was the Bedouin call for a blood feud. He made it his business to go from tent to tent with his message: "It was a tragic accident and the guilty will be brought to trial."

Morning inspection passed without further incident. Later that day, Ta'mari made it clear to the occupants of Pen 20 that Rosenfeld had not been in the camp at the time of the murder: he had seen his helicopter land. That evening, at their regular meeting, he also warned Rosenfeld that it would be dangerous for him to enter a pen alone now under any circumstances.

Ta'mari realized that next time he wouldn't be able to guarantee anyone's safety.

It was the custom in Ansar to take a number of prisoners out every day for interrogation. Interrogations were conducted either in what the prisoners called "the cesspool," an area near the camp, or on firing ranges inside the borders of Israel.

Israeli intelligence had been handed a tough assignment: they had to identify every prisoner, find out what organization he belonged to, and then drag out as much information from him as possible: the type of actions undertaken by the organization, quantity of weapons, where their bases were in Lebanon, who the commanders were, etc.

The number of prisoners alone was staggering. Added to this was their natural reluctance to talk: most gave false names and misleading information. This was to cause a good deal of unnecessary confusion later, when the time came for the prisoner exchange. "I'm not sure we really knew who we were releasing," General Nativ remarked. "We may have had a couple of important people in our hands whom we were never able to identify."

In any event, the interrogations, and the methods employed, were a form of pressure on the prisoners. They were all frightened of being called. According to Ta'mari, the interrogations were one of the great demoralizers. He decided to launch a campaign against the whole system.

This was not an easy fight to wage. It required a very high degree of unity among the prisoners and such unity was still lacking in Ansar. The first step was taken, therefore, within the framework of the committee. It was decided that every time a prisoner was taken out for interrogation, his name would be passed on to the committee. When he returned he would report to the committee exactly what had happened. If the committee decided that the prisoner's rights had been infringed or that he had been brutally treated, an official complaint would be lodged with the International Red Cross.

Once this procedure became routine, the next step was taken. The prisoners themselves began to take an active role. They covered the outsides of the tents with inscriptions in English and Arabic, written with toothpaste: "Stop the interrogations!"

Ta'mari had still another idea. Every time a man was taken out for interrogation, the prisoners began to sing loudly. This form of "communal singing" became a very useful weapon.

The interrogations were not stopped, but Ta'mari came to the conclusion that the men could be trusted to take more radical action. One day, after a couple of prisoners were returned from questioning, the Israeli commander was presented with an ultimatum. Ta'mari announced that "if the interrogations are not stopped, we will begin to burn the tents. This should be proof enough that we mean what we say. If this doesn't help, we'll climb the barbed wire fences. You'll have to open fire."

Ta'mari understood that there could be no backtracking from such an ultimatum. "Either they give up trying to break us through interrogations—or they kill us. In the final analysis the question is whether we'll be destroyed from within or from without."

One morning, while Ta'mari was in Pen 6, he heard his name called by one of the prisoners. He had been seriously ill with influenza and still had a high fever. Although he was rather weak from all the medication, he left the tent to see what the man wanted. "They're taking twelve people out for questioning," he was told.

Ta'mari gave the order and the men began to sing. They were used to this. Then he gave the order to set one of the tents on fire. Nobody was ready to do it so Ta'mari himself did it. Within a few minutes other tents in Pen 6 were burning. The fire spread rapidly. The flames electrified all the prisoners, who began to sing louder, hoist Palestinian flags, and wave pictures of Arafat.

"That was a moment of truth," said Rosenfeld later. "We were scared to death. We had never seen anything like it at Ansar. What could we do if

155

they carried out their threats and started climbing the barbed wire fences? What was I supposed to do with ten thousand frenzied prisoners? Kill them all?"

Rosenfeld called Ta'mari to come out of the pen. Ta'mari refused. "I'm not ready to talk to you," he called back, to the cheers of the prisoners.

Rosenfeld ordered the guard to open the gate and he walked in, alone.

The crowd of prisoners retreated a little but stayed in one mass. Ta'mari, standing near the burning tents, saw that Rosenfeld had entered the pen alone. He was overcome—either by fumes from the burning tents, or because of his weakened physical state, or at the horror that, if Rosenfeld were hurt and the guards opened fire, there would be dead prisoners all over the camp. He fell to the ground unconscious.

Four prisoners picked him up and ran with him to the pen infirmary. He was laid out on a bed. His face and body were covered with a cold sweat. Rosenfeld entered the infirmary and went over to the bed. Hundreds of prisoners crowded into the large tent behind him.

It took a few minutes before Ta'mari regained consciousness and raised his head. He took in the situation and just managed to whisper: "Don't hurt the commander," before losing consciousness again.

The prison physician, Dr. Emad, asked everyone to leave. Only Rosenfeld remained.

"I asked you to stop the interrogations," Ta'mari said, when he had recovered consciousness. "It can't go on like this. The men can't take it. Among the prisoners you took out today is a man suffering from kidney trouble. He might die."

Rosenfeld listened.

Nobody mentioned the fire. Outside the flames were still licking the tents.

Finally Rosenfeld turned to Ta'mari. "Give an order to your people to put out the fire. I promise to meet you halfway."

Ta'mari signaled to two of his lieutenants standing at the entrance to the tent. They left to follow orders. Rosenfeld went over to a table in the infirmary and made some coffee. "Drink this," he ordered Ta'mari. "You'll feel better."

Rosenfeld was an honorable man. The interrogations were stopped.

12

"You are the kind of enemy I like."

Just as Ta'mari's move to Ansar opened a new chapter in his life, it also changed the relationship between us. Our meetings before had been frequent, almost regular, and rather intense. Now they were few and far between. One of the immediate effects of the new situation was that Ta'mari's dependence upon me, both practically and psychologically speaking, decreased. Another was that I had good reason to feel relieved: his threat of suicide had been successfully aborted; I heard through the grapevine that the new "resident" of Ansar had not only rapidly acclimated himself but had been given an impressive reception by the prisoners. History had placed him in a position where his natural leadership qualities could be properly exercised.

It was my feeling that the distance between us would be beneficial to us both. I had become a little too involved, he a little too dependent. I had been something between a family retainer, a nursemaid, and a telephone to the outside world. It was clear to me that in his new surroundings he had to "shed" me too in order to take up the position for which he was so eminently suited. Because, when all was said and done, I still belonged to the people on the other side of the fence. And the fence here was both literal and figurative: to Israel, to the enemy, to the officers and men holding a trigger to the prisoners in Ansar.

During the months of our close association, our friendship in fact, I had often thought about the anomaly of our relationship. However great the personal affection Amalia and I came to feel for Dina and Salah and they for us, our relations could never be "total." Politics, nationalism, and the ways of the world prevented this. I knew that for Ta'mari at this time that anomaly was even greater.

True I was always interested, even curious, to see him, to talk to him, but I held off. For quite a while I refrained from requesting permission to visit. But despite the physical distance and the absence of our meetings, contacts were nonetheless maintained. Practically every journalist who visited the camp brought me back regards.

One night I got a phone call from Captain Sela. "Listen," he told me, "I finished my second tour of duty in Ansar. I had some long talks with Ta'mari, despite the fact that he was busy most of the time. There's one thing he told me that I want to pass on to you: 'If you want to know, the person I consider my closest friend—among the Jews and even among the Arabs—is Aharon.' "

Our contacts with Dina remained regular, even though she knew that I didn't see Ta'mari often. She called almost daily and wrote us frequently. We talked about the possibility of a prisoner exchange and I tried to give her as much information as I could about what was going on in Israel on the subject. She likewise kept me posted on developments abroad. I often sent her news clippings from the Hebrew press about Ansar, together with a translation.

After Ta'mari had been in Ansar for three months, a friend of mine who had just returned from reserve duty there brought us a package from him: there were four gifts inside, all of them finely crafted by Ta'mari himself. He had carved, chiseled, and hand-painted four objects, using the most primitive materials and tools. There was a comb for Amalia, a cigarette holder for me, and a toy fish for Reyout. The fourth was a stone pendant on which two hearts and the name "Dina" were engraved, and we sent it off to London as soon as we could.

"Ta'mari was as powerful in Ansar as any Arab potentate." This was the opinion of Captain Sela. "Despite the fact that he and his people are always talking about democracy, I don't think that the way they're running things is exactly what I would call democratic. You could say that whatever Ta'mari decides—goes!"

He had some of the personal trappings of a ruler as well: a retinue of assistants and two personal aides to attend to his daily needs. One of them, an Egyptian named Roza, used to cook for the entire committee. There were always refreshments on the table at committee meetings and when Ta'mari received petitioners.

The Israeli army authorities outside of Ansar had a fairly good picture of the Palestinian leader and the pros and cons of his powerful position. "It was our opinion at the time," said General Nativ, "that Ta'mari wouldn't use his position in order to foment a rebellion. He might irritate us but he wouldn't engage in outright insurgency. Since we were well aware of the difference, we didn't interfere with him. He wanted to organize the Palestinians in the camp—to indoctrinate them, instruct them, keep them busy, build up their morale and their physical capabilities. And he was successful. That was clear. The arrangement also gave the prisoners a good way to let off steam: they would protest, and shout, and curse us; they held protest prayer meetings and organized demonstrations."

There were routine daily encounters between the Palestinian leader and the Israeli camp commander, Colonel Rosenfeld, which naturally produced a complex relationship. It was, on the one hand, between captor and captive but also, on the other, between two human beings—for better and for worse. Ta'mari referred to their relationship as "open poker." Despite the ups and downs that could only be expected in such a situation, their relations remained mutually respectful for the entire period of Rosenfeld's tour of duty. Each was to admit later that the other proved to be—insofar as it was possible—trustworthy and fair.

Only a short time after his arrival, Ta'mari enlisted Rosenfeld's help in strengthening his leadership base in the pens by diminishing the power of the opposition. According to Ta'mari, the opposition was preventing unification of the ranks. Rosenfeld saw no reason not to help. At one meeting of the committee with the commander, Ta'mari requested that Rosenfeld change the mukhtar of one of the pens, who refused to accept orders from the committee. It could create difficulties for both sides, he explained. That night, at midnight, Rosenfeld sent one of his deputies to do Ta'mari's bidding. It meant moving the deposed mukhtar to another pen. An hour later the deputy returned: the man refused to leave and the prisoners were carrying him around on their shoulders, creating a rumpus.

Rosenfeld took action immediately. That was the way he operated. He went over to the pen to confront the situation in person. But this time his appearance didn't have its customary effect. He was unable to calm the men down. Just the opposite: they became even more agitated. He shouted at them, "Is anybody here ready to die?"

One of the men shouted back: "*Ana* [me]!"

Rosenfeld didn't hesitate for a minute. He motioned to the soldiers guarding the pen to toss him a Kalashnikov and he fired between the man's legs. "The guy ran faster than the bullets," he added. But it was enough to convince the mukhtar that he had to move.

In order to maintain the delicate balance, Ta'mari would often make gestures of his own in Rosenfeld's direction. "He sometimes gave me advance notice that a demonstration was going to take place," Rosenfeld relates. "I knew where and when. 'They want you to know that they have grievances and want to be heard,' Ta'mari would say. When the trouble started, I would stand at the window and get reports from my men. 'Take it easy,' I would tell them. 'It'll be all right.'" And it usually was. The demonstration would run its course and there were no repercussions.

Still, everything was not a rose garden. At one of the meetings between the commander and the committee, Ta'mari walked in in a fighting mood. He shoved aside the pile of sandwiches on the table and spread out two copies of the Fourth Geneva Convention. One of them was in English and he had received it from Captain Sela. The other was a translation he himself had made into Arabic for the benefit of his committee members who didn't understand English.

"According to the Geneva Convention," Ta'mari began, quoting chapter and verse, "all prisoners are entitled to visits from their families."

Rosenfeld cut him short: "Stop wasting your breath," he said. "It's impossible. I can't have fifty thousand people coming here from southern Lebanon. We just couldn't handle it."

He reminded the committee of the near riots that took place just a few weeks before he had taken over command of the camp, when thousands of visitors had thronged the outskirts of the camp and climbed the earth embankments just to get a glimpse of their husbands and sons. "It was a miracle no one got killed," he said. "I know that I'm violating the Geneva Convention but that's the price I'm ready to pay and you're going to pay. That's all. Finished. Period."

In the pens the prisoners were awaiting good news but the news that Ta'mari brought back was not good. In Pen 4 a riot broke out and soon a large black, green, and red Palestinian flag was hoisted. It was homemade from pieces of tent canvas, colored with toothpaste mixed with various spices. The flag had been ready and waiting. All the men needed was the right opportunity to hoist it and the time had now come.

Rosenfeld was outside watching and he soon called to Ta'mari: "Give them an order to take down the flag."

Ta'mari didn't answer. He simply ignored him.

The atmosphere became more explosive. Rosenfeld gave orders—routine under the circumstances—to move in reinforcements around the pens. "If that flag isn't taken down within five minutes, there's going to be bloodshed," he warned. As if the situation itself weren't bad enough, a team of Red Cross representatives suddenly drove into the camp.

The tanks moved up to the pens. The soldiers primed their guns. The only thing missing was the order to open fire.

Suddenly the flag was lowered. The general tension was eased, but not Rosenfeld's: his anger continued to seethe.

Later, when he met alone with Ta'mari, he was pointedly unfriendly. "Why didn't you take down that goddamn flag when I ordered you to?"

"I didn't raise it," he answered, "and I won't lower a flag that someone else raises. I also argued with them, but for another reason. It was my opinion that anyone who hoists the flag has to have the strength to face the consequences. I knew that they didn't have that much strength. That's why I objected to the whole business in the first place."

"I have to point out once more," Rosenfeld told me as he recalled the incident, "that his reaction was, as usual, rational, flexible, and wise. I often realized that it was better to lose an argument with a wise man than win one with a fool."

Both men worked exceptionally hard and for long hours, and both carried a heavy load of responsibility for the lives of others. Neither was in the first flush of youth, although Rosenfeld was by far the older of two, by at least fifteen years. His days off were few and far between and more often than not were interrupted by a frantic call to return at once to stave off some potential catastrophe.

He was the first to break down at Ansar and he remembers the occasion because of something Ta'mari did.

"One day, as usual, I had called a meeting with the prisoners' committee for 9:00 P.M. I was walking in the direction of the hut where we met when all of a sudden I blacked out. When I came to everything was spinning. I

161

didn't want to call for help—after all, I'm supposed to be in charge. I finally managed to get back to my own quarters and someone called the doctor. The doctor came over and I mentioned that the committee was probably still sitting there waiting for me. I asked someone to call Ta'mari over. 'Listen,' I told him, 'I don't feel so well. I have the shivers.' 'Commander,' he said, 'you're very very tired. You're probably suffering from total exhaustion.' That's more or less what the doctor had said. There were quite a few people in the room but it was Ta'mari who went and got another blanket and covered me with it. Before he walked out, he turned to me and said in English: 'You are the kind of enemy I like.' "

When Ta'mari was in the grip of a crisis—and he had quite a few—he found the Israeli officers just as sympathetic. Colonel Shatz, to whom he first surrendered in Sidon and who served at Ansar for a long time, was one of them.

Shatz realized very early on that there were "two" Ta'maris: the enemy commander and the man with all his human weaknesses. "I was his psychiatrist," he recalls. "Not his psychologist, his psychiatrist. He used to call me: 'I've got a problem. I've got to go over to Ansar II. Come with me and open the gates.' Sometimes I used to drive him over. He would confide in me: 'Listen, Shatz, I can't go on much longer. Twenty-four hours a day I'm at everyone's beck and call. Twenty-four hours a day I listen to their troubles, their complaints, their requests. I haven't got the strength anymore.' At that point I used to turn the car around and drive back to my quarters. I knew that Ta'mari was a vegetarian and I usually had a supply of dried fruit there. I also had some classical records with me. Under those circumstances, he was able to recharge his batteries. Sometimes I would leave him alone in the room even though I kept a gun there. I just trusted him."

Yehuda Shatz was an old army veteran and a man of extreme right-wing beliefs who nonetheless made friends with his Palestinian counterpart. Perhaps it was in part subconscious. Shatz was married to a professional psychologist. One of his sons was a soldier and he had two small daughters. When he got home on his infrequent days off, he would find himself talking to his wife for hours about Ta'mari, or looking for some small thing to bring him. He would always buy him a box of Turkish delight because he knew how much he liked sweets.

On one of his vacations at home, his wife said to him: "Yehuda, you simply love that man."

"Who?" he wanted to know.

"Ta'mari," she answered.

Shatz dismissed his wife's assertion. "You and your psychology," he countered, a little angry.

That night, back at Ansar, he called his wife. "Give the girls a kiss for me," he said, and then added, "What you said this morning—I think you're right."

Despite his description of his "game" at Ansar as "open poker," Ta'mari later admitted that he had held a couple of closed cards as well. When he reconstructed for us the various strategies he'd used at Ansar, he said: "I didn't always tell the truth when I was a prisoner. One of the things I really exploited was the Israelis' constant fear that something catastrophic might happen. When I threatened them that everyone was on the verge of a nervous breakdown—that was an invention of mine. But the Israelis believed me. I knew they were scared stiff of an outburst of collective hysteria and I played on that fear to get them to let us blow off steam. The truth is that like the Israelis we couldn't let ourselves deteriorate into a state of uncontrolled hysteria. As a matter of fact the situation was never as dramatic as I made it out to be. Their fears were the same as mine, only I could never let them know that."

Ta'mari knew exactly how to use the prisoners' spontaneous reactions for his own purposes. One example will suffice.

For a very long time, the Israeli authorities had no idea that there was a radio hidden at the headquarters of the prisoners' command. Abu Leila had simply bought it—and not cheaply—from an Israeli. He had then dismantled the entire apparatus and rebuilt it to fit into a small innocuous-looking box that looked like any other hand-carved object produced by the prisoners. There was a likeness of al-Aqsa engraved on top, with hand-painted decorations adorning it. The box was always on the table, conspicuously on display. The radio supplied the committee with news of the world and they transmitted it to the rest of the pens through Ansar's unique postal system.

It was the little box that supplied them with the first newscast about a possible prisoner exchange. The news spread like wildfire around the camp and the prisoners were soon singing and dancing and shouting with joy. The Israelis were dumbfounded. They had never seen such an outburst of spontaneous joy in the camp. They called in Ta'mari and wanted to know what had happened. "I would imagine that it's the first symptom of approaching mass hysteria," he answered. "I really can't say what it's liable to lead to."

In the organized protests, in contrast to the spontaneous ones, Ta'mari had more than one aim. In addition to getting on the nerves of the Israeli guards, he also wanted to get as many prisoners as possible united in a common action. He wanted every single prisoner to contribute to the protest in the way that seemed most suitable to him. The motto of his overall strategy was: "A maximum of people and a minimum of violence."

One morning the motto was translated into a most unusual protest. When dawn broke the sentries on duty couldn't believe what they saw, or rather what they didn't see: there was not a single prisoner in sight. The entire camp looked—and sounded—like a ghost town. The thirty-two sentries all reported the same disbelief and tanks were soon closing in on the pens. Representatives of the Red Cross were just as unnerved by the "collective disappearance" of all the prisoners.

The day before, the committee had decided on an hour-long sit-down strike in which all the prisoners would participate. The first suggestion was that the sit-down strike take place in the center of each pen: thousands of prisoners would sit silently for a full hour without moving. The spectacle would be impressive.

Ta'mari had a different idea. "Five percent of all the prisoners are ill," he pointed out, "and won't be able to sit in the sun. Another fifteen percent are afraid of their own shadows and won't be seen protesting. They're afraid they might be photographed. So they'll stay inside or even pretend that they're ill. This means we've lost twenty percent to begin with. What we should do, therefore, is carry out the strike *inside* the tents. Everyone will be able to take part, including people who are ill and people who are scared."

The protest was a great success. "In an hour it was over," Ta'mari recalled. "The effect was fantastic, especially among the prisoners themselves. The biggest coward in Ansar was so proud of himself he couldn't stop talking about 'how *we* had scared them.'"

The protests improved with time and were given greater ideological meaning in accordance with Ta'mari's lights: they were the antithesis of violence for its own sake. He also incorporated songs and even a camp anthem into his strategy. "Protest," he explained, "is a kind of performance, and like all performances it has to have a beginning, a climax, and a denouement. I figured that singing at the end of an action would be the perfect denouement and would give people a really good feeling inside. The combined singing of thousands of people has a terrific effect on the people doing the singing. But I also realized that singing did not have a particularly 'masculine' appeal to the prisoners. So I began to sing first, by myself." Slowly but surely prisoners around him would join in, and soon they would be joined by people from a nearby tent, and so forth and so on, until there were thousands singing.

Ta'mari wrote two poems which became the "official" anthems of Ansar. All the prisoners knew them by heart and it can be assumed that they will remember them all their lives. The words were smuggled out of the camp and the songs were soon performed by the Ashbal orchestra in Beirut after the conductor put them to music. It didn't take long before the songs became "hits" in all of the Palestinian refugee camps in southern Lebanon.

Following is one of the anthems, "Ansar Sings to the Dawn," written in April 1983:

> Break my ribs under the butt of your gun,
> Set up the gallows, if you will,
> Let the chains and the handcuffs bite my flesh,
> Hide the rays of the dawn from my view,
> Cover my eyes with a cloth of black, the color of your hearts,
> Heighten the fences and thicken the walls,
> Round up my family and the rest of my friends,
> House them in my tent,
> Crucify a child in the burning sun,
> Or dispatch a young man to his death,
> But Ansar will always sing to the dawn!
> You can't stop the dawn from rising, can you?
> The dawn is mine,
> The dawn is mine,
> The dawn is mine.

The second anthem also refers to the need for song:

> My wounds are so deep,
> My heart bleeds profusely,
> And you sing to the future to come.
> My wound is a fountain of joy
> In the large desert of sadness.

165

Like a rainbow in the gray sky,
The colors of budding flowers
So are the wounds in my aching heart.
My wounds are deep, I know,
My heart is bleeding, I know,
But to survive even with my wounds, I know how—
To sing and to carry on.
To sing and to sing and to sing.

A few days before the prisoner exchange in November 1983, when Ansar was finally dismantled, Ta'mari submitted an unusual request to Colonel Shatz: "Allow us to tape the songs. For the sake of posterity, for the historical record. This is a unique phenomenon. Never again will all these men be together at one moment, able to sing these songs. Let us have the use of a tape recorder." Permission was granted, and for an entire day a chorus of Ansar prisoners practiced and recorded the camp songs. Neither Shatz nor the other officers were worried. They were prepared to agree to anything that kept the prisoners busy and out of trouble. It was part of prison policy.

The Red Cross was helpful in this respect: from the very beginning they had supplied the prisoners with tools for arts and crafts, and with Ta'mari's encouragement this form of occupational therapy spread rapidly and became a kind of mass activity. The prisoners carved, chiseled, and wove all kinds of useful and decorative objects: bowls, prayer beads, figurines, shawls, bags, combs, and cigarette holders. They also painted.

Ta'mari considered the art "production" of the prisoners a fairly accurate measure of their mood and morale. The motifs most prevalent at first were handcuffed wrists, barbed wire, tears, and blood. But after some time they gave way to flowers, sun's rays, white doves, wings, etc. The prisoners would also engrave or paint mottos such as "Prison is not eternal, neither is the guard," or "The enemy of the captive is his captor." Ta'mari inspired a good many of the slogans.

Among the prisoners in Ansar were those who preferred the written word, and they wrote plays, poetry, and, naturally, nationalist songs. Whenever possible, public performances were held.

Despite all this creative endeavor, Ta'mari found that the element of time or, rather, the absence of a sense of time, was the most destructive factor in camp life. "People simply lost their sense of continuity, their

166

ability to distinguish between past, present, and future." He gave two reasons for this: abysmal boredom because of undifferentiated time sequences, and being cut off from the outside world, a condition which intensified inner loneliness. For long periods at a time the men were not allowed to leave their tents, and when they went to the outhouses, they went in pairs and according to a strict schedule. "During periods like these, the men would lose their desire to live or to do anything for themselves or for the future. They couldn't see any future." Ta'mari's profound understanding of these difficulties was not hard to trace: his own recent prison solitude and its devastating effects.

Not all the men were able to survive the psychological pressures of camp life and some of them went literally mad.

Qassem, for example, was a great hulk of a man, weighing some 260 pounds. One morning the men in his pen awoke to the sound of terrible screaming. When they looked outside they saw Qassem chasing another prisoner and threatening him with an iron bar, a long tent peg that had been uprooted. The potential victim was screaming hysterically. The minute another man tried to intervene, Qassem began to chase him as well, trying to stab him with his improvised weapon. Qassem had run amok. Soon a growing band of prisoners was alternately chasing and being chased by Qassem. The sight was too much for the sentries and they alerted Colonel Shatz.

Shatz's first order was: "Get Ta'mari over here, and fast!"

Ta'mari was brought over by car, and without being given any orders by Shatz he walked into the pen, took one look at what was happening, and started walking, without a moment's hesitation, in the direction of Qassem. The minute Qassem's eye was caught by Ta'mari approaching him, he stopped dead in his tracks. The iron bar, however, was still raised threateningly.

Ta'mari walked straight over to the man, talking to him softly all the while, and reaching Qassem's side touched him with both hands. Then he requested that someone throw him a damp towel and he began to wipe Qassem's face and mouth.

Qassem suddenly collapsed. Ta'mari asked for more towels and water and began to apply compresses to Qassem's forehead. Then he requested the assistance of two men to carry Qassem to the infirmary tent.

From the minute they picked him up, the giant held on to Ta'mari's hand and wouldn't let go, even after he had been put into bed. In bed for a few minutes, he suddenly jumped up and ran over to the corner of the tent. For a moment, everyone was scared that he was about to uproot another iron peg. But all he wanted, it appeared, was the rope tied to the peg. He took the piece of rope back to the bed, tied one end to his leg and the other to Ta'mari's leg. He wanted to make sure that Ta'mari wouldn't leave him alone. Ta'mari didn't protest. He stayed with Qassem for five days and five nights. They slept together, ate together, went to the bathroom together. Ta'mari even took Qassem with him to committee meetings.

After five days, Qassem agreed to untie the rope, but only on condition that Ta'mari visit him every day. Ta'mari promised. He also had Qassem moved to another pen where he had a relative who agreed to look after him. Until the day that Ansar was dismantled Ta'mari kept his promise.

The Israeli officers were duly impressed with this side of Ta'mari's complex personality: the headstrong Palestinian commando was as gentle as a lamb. He had also shown them a quality of leadership they had never seen before.

After the Qassem affair, Ta'mari increased his efforts to secure more employment for the prisoners, anything to fill their dreary hours, even if he had to invent the work himself.

One project he initiated was a general face-lift for the camp. He organized the men into squads to clean up the pens. The first stage was garbage disposal: getting rid of all the junk lying around outside. The second was clearing the paths of weeds. The third was getting the Red Cross to provide saplings and seeds.

This last idea aroused a good deal of opposition among the prisoners themselves: "Why should we plant anything here?" they wanted to know. "You expect us to stay here until it bears fruit or is it for someone else to enjoy?"

Ta'mari considered the work an end in itself and he tried to convince his comrades that any work was better than idle boredom. "The very planting of seeds is a satisfactory act. Furthermore, watching things sprout and grow gives you a better sense of time. You begin to judge again in terms of days, weeks, seasons. I also think that if we can grow flowers here, it will give us all greater hope and it's precisely all hope that the enemy wants to quench."

Soon plots of flowers and vegetables were pushing though the earth around the tents. There was another idea blooming in Ta'mari's mind in relation to the gardening project but, at least at this stage, he kept it to himself.

Every morning he issued a daily bulletin from headquarters. He would compose the "master copy" and his deputies would copy it and distribute it to all the pens. The bulletin contained instructions for the day's schedule, including work programs, sports events, meetings, lectures, and other activities. One way he tried to shake the prisoners out of their torpor was by enlisting people with specialized knowledge to lecture on their subjects. After all, the camp was full of teachers, lawyers, musicians, and doctors. In time, the daily bulletin included news, prepared by one of the deputies whose foremost duty was to listen to the secret radio.

Ta'mari later admitted that he tried very hard to keep the tone of the bulletin from becoming too aggressive. He would write and rewrite in order to weed out any bellicosity or contentiousness that might have crept in. He also didn't want to raise false hopes because he knew that if they weren't fulfilled, reactions would be extreme. He once deleted an item referring to prisoner exchange, and when the revolt of Abu Musa against Arafat broke out, he reported it in a minor key. "I certainly didn't want to have that particular controversy played out again in Ansar. The last thing we needed was to split our ranks."

But the bulletin did contain "secret information," such as his contacts with the heads of the PLO on the outside. Ta'mari told us that he was able to maintain contacts like this almost the whole time. Prisoners who for one reason or another were released earlier transmitted messages and even letters from Ta'mari to Arafat or Abu Jihad or Abu Musa. Answers often came back with new prisoners, "planted" by the PLO for the very purpose of maintaining contact with Ta'mari. These people would purposely provoke Israeli soldiers in southern Lebanon to get themselves imprisoned.

Ta'mari tried another tack to get information from Ansar to the outside world. He attempted very vigorously to get the ban on visits from the press abrogated or at least reduced. The ban on the press had been put into effect after unfriendly reports about Israel's behavior in Ansar appeared in the world press. "It was only natural," General Nativ later explained, "that reporters entering a camp enclosed by barbed wire, and guarded by dozens of tanks and half-tracks, should have more sympathy for the prisoners than for their guards. But our conscience was clear. We did our best, insofar as it was possible, to run Ansar as decently as we could."

Ta'mari claimed at the time that it was only fair that visiting press be allowed to meet with representatives of the prisoners too. Custom was that they met only with the Israeli staff. In January 1983, when two American journalists visited Ansar, Ta'mari translated his views into a noisy demonstration. The journalists were taken up to the rooftop operations office of the camp command for a view of the setup. Ta'mari climbed up on top of one of the outhouses and led a highly vocal protest demonstration, aimed to impress the journalists.

It did. It was finally decided to allow the visitors to meet with members of the prisoners' committee. The Americans both taped and set down in writing every word that issued from Ta'mari's mouth: "We appeal to Israeli and Jewish and international public opinion to examine and investigate everything that has happened to us since we first became prisoners. Keeping us here is a war crime. Don't say at some future time: 'We didn't know!' I am making this appeal like Joseph thrown into the pit: come to our aid!"

Ta'mari, who had a great deal of experience in public relations as well as a good deal of talent, continued: "I have been here for three months and I am frightened to think what my fate and the fate of my brethren will be when we are released. We will again be forced into exile. A second or a third exile in the life of one man is too much. The irony of the situation," he concluded, "is that the Jewish people who suffered exile, discrimination, and hardship should have become so callous." The two journalists were from the *Washington Post* and the *Chicago Tribune*.

They asked Ta'mari to talk about the daily problems of the prisoners and their complaints. He did but he also mentioned those instances in which the prisoners found a listening ear on the part of the Israeli officers.

Later, after the Fatah began to allow the media almost unlimited access to the six Israeli war prisoners, Israel decided to liberalize its press policy in Ansar. Journalists were allowed to photograph the camp and talk to the prisoners. The authorities were well aware of the fact that Ta'mari was now in charge of "two" Ansars: the real one and the one he presented to the press.

Shatz, however, was no less cunning than Ta'mari. When an American television team came to visit, he suggested to one of the reporters that he put on an IDF uniform and make a preliminary tour of the camp with him—without cameras. The reporter accepted the offer and toured the pens with Shatz. Everything was in order. Quiet prevailed. The prisoners were sitting in groups eating lunch. In the supply kitchen, he saw the store of well-ordered provisions and in the tent of the prisoners committee was even offered a cup of fresh black coffee, prepared by one of Ta'mari's adjutants.

When he returned a second time, in his own clothes and with the television cameras, the prisoners were crowding around the barbed wire fences, shouting nationalist slogans and making "V" signs. In one of the pens Palestinian flags had been hoisted. In another pen, someone had started a fire. Israeli troops were put on the alert.

After the second tour was over, Shatz remarked to the reporter: "There are two sides to every coin. There are also two sides to Ansar."

The report on Ansar presented to the American public reflected both sides.

13

"It would be foolish to tempt fate . . ."

By April 1983, the Israeli authorities were beginning to have second thoughts about the advisability of the prisoners' committee, which, meanwhile, had acquired a tremendous amount of power. It was becoming potentially more and more dangerous; its disadvantages were beginning to outweigh its advantages.

At this time Colonel Rosenfeld was about to leave his job as commander of the camp, to be succeeded by Colonel Attiya. Colonel Shatz was transferred to Ansar at the beginning of Attiya's tour of duty and assigned the job of reorganizing the pens. The first thing on his agenda was a reassessment of the prisoners' committee.

The situation at Ansar had been complicated by two separate developments. First of all, Israel intended to take steps against the prisoners from Ahmad Jibril's Popular Front-General Command. Jibril was holding two of the eight Israeli soldiers captured the previous fall. They were being kept in total isolation and not even allowed visits by the Red Cross. The Israelis decided to retaliate in kind: the hundred or so members of Jibril's organization in Ansar would be placed together in Pen 31, at the eastern end of the camp, and held incommunicado—from the rest of the prisoners and from the Red Cross. It was clear that Ta'mari and the rest of the committee would do everything in their power to obstruct the transfer. For this reason, Attiya and Shatz decided to remove the members of the committee from the camp, at least temporarily, after which they would carry out the transfer. With the committee gone during this crucial change, they would then be in a better position to disperse the prisoners' Unified Command altogether. In this way, they hoped, they would be able to gain a tighter grip on the situation. All they needed was a good reason to set the plan in motion. It was provided by the second complication.

At that very same time, the committee was carrying out a stubborn struggle to get all Lebanese citizens released. They claimed that seventy percent of all the prisoners in Ansar were civilians who had no connection whatsoever with the PLO. The Israelis disagreed. They did know that there were a good number of ordinary Lebanese in the camp, and in fact in the course of time some 5,000 out of the original 10,500 were released. But of those who remained, very few were considered to be innocent bystanders.

In the middle of April, the prisoners' committee notified the Red Cross representative with whom they met daily that they were intensifying their protests: if their demands were not met they would begin by delaying morning inspection by five minutes on the first day and by fifteen minutes on the second; on the third they would refuse to report for inspection at all. If by then the "civilians" were not released, they would all march on the barbed wire fences, forcing the Israelis to open fire. They requested that the Red Cross transmit the "message" verbatim to the Israeli authorities.

The Red Cross passed on the information. Meanwhile Ta'mari had gone to the infirmary to talk to Dr. Emad about a patient who had just suffered a brain hemorrhage. The head of the Red Cross mission to Ansar, Ms. Clair, suddenly appeared on the scene and notified Ta'mari that all members of the committee were being summoned to an emergency meeting with the camp commander.

Ta'mari was wary. The committee was never convened in the middle of the day, certainly not through the offices of a member of the Red Cross.

"Remain here for an hour," Ta'mari instructed his people. "If we don't return by then, take action."

The committee did not return and the prisoners began to take action. But their protests were haphazard; there was no central organization. In some of the pens they began shouting slogans. In another, they set blankets on fire. But their message was clear: they wanted the committee members back from wherever they had been taken.

At this point, the Israelis went into action. They started with Pen 5, the officers' pen, where Unified Command was located. Their intention was to occupy the pen and forcibly remove the men to another, more distant pen, but it wasn't easy: the officers resisted. They blocked the gate with barbed wire and armed themselves with tent pegs and kitchen knives and whatever else they found. The Israelis decided to storm the pen under a cloud of tear gas. All the prisoners were removed by force and taken by truck to an empty pen.

During the next few days, other pens were forcefully occupied and the prisoners taken out. After that, the barbed wire fences were raised higher and reinforced, and the prisoners were redistributed: members of Jibril's organization were taken to Pen 31, and all non-Palestinian Lebanese prisoners to Pen 30.

The Israelis believed that they would now be able to return to the status quo ante. Instead of the prisoners' committee, they would install their own quisling mukhtars. Since there would no longer be any Unified Command, the age-old axiomatic injunction "divide and rule" would operate in its place. Deprived of their leadership, the prisoners' morale would sink, protests would stop, and Israeli control would become simpler.

"We got all the mukhtars together in one tent," recalls Colonel Shatz, "and after serving them tea we told them what was up. 'For the moment, there's no committee. Any mukhtar with a problem will call over one of the MPs who will notify me. Everything else—as before.' "

Except the mukhtars, it emerged, were not willing to cooperate. Things were certainly not as before: Jibril's men had been isolated, there were no more meetings with the Red Cross, and the disappearance of the committee was apparently not "for the moment." The mukhtars refused to follow orders and refused to meet with the Israeli command. Instead, they helped organize the spate of protests that followed.

The following morning there were signs in English on the tents and on the fences: "Bring back our committee!" And from then on there were outbursts of violence in all the pens: the Israeli MPs were constantly stoned, the State of Israel was roundly cursed at every opportunity, blankets were burned, and Palestinian flags raised. The prisoners at Ansar were not about to give up their gains: they wanted their committee and its chairman back.

It took two weeks to convince the Israelis, those in Ansar and those outside, that they would be better off with Ta'mari back in Ansar. The risks involved in running the camp through the committee were preferable to the constant necessity of using an iron fist.

The committee was brought back. They had been held for the two weeks in an isolated place. Their former powers, however, were not restored. The minute they were back they decided to repay the Israelis for the insult. They ordered the prisoners to magnify every complaint, to make as many problems as possible, and to disrupt whatever could be disrupted. The prisoners began to lodge complaints about everything—the food, the water, the cigarettes, the medical treatment, the proliferation of internal squabbles. The idea was that the flood of complaints would force the authorities to restore the committee to its former position.

The trouble was that not all the squabbling was faked. Even after the committee was granted some of its former powers, Ta'mari was not able to fully reestablish his authority. The upheaval that had taken place with the removal of the committee and the redistribution of the prisoners had taken its toll. New cliques were born and they were based not on political or organizational affinity but on family or community ties, even on national origin.

Among the prisoners rounded up in Lebanon during the war were Egyptians, Yemenites, Pakistanis, and even a group from Bangladesh who had been employed there before the war and whose sympathies lay with the terrorist organizations. Now they gravitated to each other. Furthermore, among the Palestinians themselves there were communal factions. One such faction was known as the "Syrians" because they all came from the Palestinian refugee camp of el-Yarmouk, not far from Damascus. They were all lodged together now in Pen 21.

One night one of the so-called Syrians was sitting around strumming a guitar. Guitars had been distributed by the Red Cross and it was customary to use them in rotation. One of the other prisoners insisted that it was his turn and an argument broke out between him and the Syrian. The argument turned into a brawl and another of the Syrians pulled a knife and stabbed the guitarist.

A report of the free-for-all reached Shatz. It was the worst kind of fight as far as he was concerned. "You can't just walk in and separate the main contenders. I once tried to break up a mass demonstration by dousing everybody with cold water. The men simply took off their clothes, took a shower, and continued to fight. I went over to the main gate at the entrance to the pens to see what had happened. 'Murder,' I was told. I called in Ta'mari. He also said 'murder' and disappeared. He was no good in such situations. When he saw blood he was useless."

175

By that time, most of the interior barbed wire fences separating one pen from another were in a pretty bad state. They had been breached in some places and even knocked down in others. From all the pens prisoners began running in the direction of the main gate.

"There were maybe a thousand prisoners there," Shatz recalls. "I had radioed for an ambulance. The prisoners carried the wounded man to the gate. He was bleeding profusely. Two soldiers opened the gate, took the man out, closed the gate, and put him into the ambulance. But by that time he was dead.

"I tried to find out exactly what had happened. Nabil Masri, the medic and a member of the prisoners' committee, had brought the wounded man out and he made the situation quite clear to me. He himself was in a state of shock: 'One of the Syrians killed him and now everyone is going over there.' He was almost hysterical. 'If you don't do something fast, they're going to kill all the Syrians.'

" 'How many Syrians are there?' I wanted to know.

" 'Fifteen,' he answered. 'You'd better do something fast. There's going to be a massacre.' "

The fifteen Syrians, chased by a frenzied mob, were running for their lives in the direction of the gate.

Shatz decided to let them out. It was risky but he saw no alternative. He gave orders to open the gate. But once opened it was impossible to close: the mob began pushing their way through. Shatz had to make a quick decision: he had fourteen bullets in his pistol.

"Stop or I'll shoot!" he shouted. "I've got fourteen bullets in my gun and the first fourteen out of the gate are dead men!"

The mob stopped dead in their tracks. Suddenly the entire area became deathly still. "It was the first time in Ansar that I had pulled a gun," he remembers. "Maybe that was what stunned them. Right behind me, on the patrol path, the fifteen Syrians were shaking in their boots, scared to death. And in front of me were a thousand others with murder in their eyes. In that split second I told Nabil to close the gate. He did and the soldier locked it. I put the Syrians into the camp lockup, five in a cell. The next day I handed the murderer over to the military police investigation unit, together with the knife and the body."

After that Shatz had to find out from the Red Cross the international procedure regarding a POW who kills another POW. The answer was "extradition to his country of origin." Months later, after all the other prisoners were released in the prisoner exchange, the Red Cross extradited the murderer and his fourteen friends to Syria. Meanwhile the fourteen were kept separate from the rest of the prisoners.

"From that day on, until Ansar was closed down, I had fourteen willing assistants," Shatz recalls. "They never forgot that I had saved their lives."

There was one occasion on which Ta'mari himself had to resort to force in order to maintain discipline. In a fight between two prisoners, again one of them pulled a knife and stabbed the other. The Israeli authorities didn't intervene. The injured man was treated at the infirmary.

Ta'mari insisted that the culprit be punished. He had to find some way to put an end to these internecine quarrels. The committee met and decided that the mukhtar of the pen would inflict punishment on the offender by whipping him in public. The mukhtar contended, however, that it wasn't only one man who had to be punished, that he had been aided by another five. Ta'mari didn't hesitate for a minute: "If that's the case, then all six have to be punished."

But this was more easily said than done. Internal punishment had never been imposed before and there were lots of people who didn't like the idea. Moreover, some seventy friends of the offenders banded together and informed Ta'mari that they would obstruct any attempt to carry out the "sentence."

"It was as clear as day to me," recalls Ta'mari, "that they were threatening a split—and not just a split between the people who were supporting the culprit and the others but a split down the center of Ansar between those who supported the committee and those who didn't." He decided to put his leadership to the test.

He composed a bulletin which was distributed throughout the camp. It read: "Everyone who supports my leadership is hereby requested to arm himself with some kind of weapon and join me in asserting the authority of the committee. Let's see who gets the upper hand!"

Ta'mari wasn't joking and his message was clear to everyone. It didn't take long before the opposition crumbled. The six offenders were brought before the committee. In the center of their own pen they were each given ten strokes by fellow prisoners with whips improvised from tent ropes. Their mukhtar supervised the proceedings. The prisoners from that particular pen witnessed the punishment in silence. The offenders submit-ted without a word. When it was over they were all taken to the infirmary for first aid.

That was the last time that Ansar prisoners used weapons to settle an argument.

Just at that time, reports of the rebellion in the Fatah began to reach Ansar. Ta'mari's close friend Abu Musa was leading the insurgents, who had formed an anti-Arafat coalition together with people from the "rejec-tionist front" of Habash, Hawatmeh, and the Sa'iqa. They had the support of the Syrian army, and there was news of fighting between the factions in the Bekaa Valley.

Ta'mari was worried that his greatest achievement—the unity of all the rival organizations in Ansar—was in jeopardy, and with it his own singular position. The only way he could prevent a split was to convince the pris-oners that they had only one real enemy, Israel, and that they had to close ranks against their captors.

He went from tent to tent, and spoke to larger groups from the roof of the outhouse, intent on getting his message across: "The Israelis have put us in chains and we are united by our chains. It would be foolish of us to pull in different directions." He kept hammering home one idea: "The enemy of the captive is his captor."

He knew that most of the prisoners supported him and the mainstream of the Fatah. But he was also aware of the fact that there was another man in Ansar who could undermine his position: Mohammed Abu el-Fida, commander of the Khittin Brigade of the Palestine Liberation Army. Abu el-Fida was, in fact, the highest-ranking officer of the Fatah in Ansar, with the rank of colonel. When he was captured, however, he had given a false name: he preferred being an ordinary prisoner. The prisoners in Ansar, Ta'mari among them, knew his real identity of course, but they respected his wishes and kept it secret. Now Abu el-Fida declared his unqualified support for Abu Musa.

Since Ta'mari's original internal organization of the prisoners had been based on the prisoners' affiliation to the movements outside, he had good reason to fear that the split would be overtly expressed in the camp as well. Therefore, he got the committee to issue strict orders that while it was only reasonable for the men to indulge in ideological arguments, they were absolutely forbidden to resort to violence. The use of force would be heavily penalized. It wasn't an idle threat, as everyone remembered. But he made it very clear that any attempt by the majority pro-Arafat supporters to injure people supporting the opposition would be just as severely punished.

Ta'mari's contacts with the outside at this time were fairly regular, mainly through the good offices of the Red Cross. He sent letters to both Arafat and to Abu Musa asking them to state their positions and give their reasons for the split. He wanted to keep all channels open. He notified Arafat that he fully supported him. When he received answers from both sides, he formulated the positions in the camp bulletin. Although he made his own position clear, the opposition's point of view was also given.

The fact that he was able to maintain open channels with both sides during the crisis stood him in good stead with them both later on, after he was released. But the split in the Fatah was Ta'mari's most trying experience while in Ansar, although he was able to derive some satisfaction from the fact that he prevented it from erupting violently among the prisoners.

Almost from the day he arrived in Ansar, Ta'mari dreamed of organizing a mass escape. He conceived of it in classical terms: a network of secretly built underground tunnels.

At first he kept his thoughts to himself, but as time wore on he discussed the idea with a few of his Fatah comrades who were experienced in the digging and construction of bunkers and underground munitions dumps. He needed their technical advice. The idea took some time to get out of the planning stages, because of technical obstacles as well as the need to expend energy on other pressing issues. But when the fight between Arafat and the rebels disrupted negotiations for a prisoner exchange between Israel and the PLO, and the outlook for the Ansar prisoners seemed bleak, Ta'mari decided that it was time to do something constructive. Instead of getting on each others' nerves with their endless disputations for and against Arafat, the men would be better occupied digging an escape route. And, as he believed and never tired of explaining, the more successful the operation, the more men to reach freedom, the greater the blow to the enemy.

Ta'mari estimated that if the plan succeeded, some two thousand prisoners would be able to escape within a few days.

The first condition for success was absolute secrecy. The smallest mistake or inadvertent remark would be fatal. The committee decided to appoint in each pen an "escape committee," whose first job would be to acquire the necessary tools for the work and discuss ways and means for disposing of the vast quantities of dug-up earth. They would also have to supervise all arrangements for the work, not the least of which was ensuring the absolute safety of the tunnels.

Pen 20 was chosen to begin with since it was the westernmost pen at the end of Ansar I. Work would begin in the corner tent. It was estimated that they would require nearly fifty feet of tunneling to reach the area beyond the fences. There were a few soldiers' outhouses located there but sentry duty in that particular spot was rather cursory.

The pen was divided into three contingents, for digging, for earth removal, and for security, and work was kept up twenty-four hours a day. The men used sharpened tent pegs and tin cans to dig with. A number of hatchets and hammers were also "borrowed" from the Israeli side of the camp by prisoners employed there in cleaning squads.

The earth was removed in crates after being drawn outside by a primitive system of pulleys to which broken-off sides of gerrycans were attached. The tunnels were originally lit by improvised candle-lanterns but it was discovered that they used up too much oxygen. Ta'mari designed a better system by placing mirrors at different angles to catch the daylight from outside the tent and relay it into the tunnel. Stolen flashlights, or flashlights purchased from outsiders at one time or another, were used at night, but after all the batteries were dead night work was stopped.

When the tunnel got deeper, the men figured out a way to step up the oxygen supply by pumping air through plastic gerrycans connected to a series of patched-up pipes and hoses.

Public singing became more frequent when it was found to be a simple way of drowning out the noise of the diggers at night, especially when they had to dig their way through some stubborn rock embedment. The prisoners devised all sorts of "musical" accompaniments to the singing, such as drumming on the tin walls of the outhouses or banging pots and pans together.

Within a week a large section was finished. It was almost a yard wide and about two and a half feet high. The roof of the tunnel was reinforced with slats from wooden crates and strips of tin removed from the outhouses and showers.

At the end of that week bad luck hit when an asbestos water pipe was accidently punctured in the digging and the tunnel was flooded. The prisoners started bailing the water out in gerrycans and suddenly became very industrious in watering the flower beds. But their efforts were in vain. The tunnel collapsed.

Everything had to begin again and it wasn't easy. Ta'mari tried to convince the men that at least their experience would prove useful in starting the work in other places. About one thing he had been perfectly right: all the energies that had previously gone into political infighting were now channeled into the "building" effort.

According to Colonel Shatz, "Three or four days after they started digging, we knew. One day they started digging in six pens at the same time. In our estimation, they had to remove and dispose of almost a hundred cubic feet of earth for one tunnel. At a little over three feet a day, it would take about a month to complete. We decided to keep an eye on matters and wait.

"After a week had passed, there was a proliferation of raised flower beds and vegetable gardens all over Ansar. Ta'mari asked for more seeds. 'Why not?' I answered. 'You'll have lots of fresh vegetables.'

"You could see that the floors of the tents were getting higher and that there was always dirt on the mattresses. Still, we didn't say anything. Then one day the people working on the sewage pumps began to complain that the pumps were becoming blocked. It fitted in with everything else that was going on. I called in Ta'mari.

" 'Look,' I said, 'sit down. You've said it was all open poker . . . yet you're digging tunnels. You think we don't know.'

"I took him outside, gave him a pair of headphones attached to a sensor, and said: 'Listen. The whole camp is like a busy anthill. Everybody's digging. Tomorrow morning at dawn I want everybody lined up at the gates with their belongings. I'm going to destroy the tunnels.'

"Ta'mari didn't even pretend that the situation was any different. The only thing he said was: 'Every prisoner has the right to try and escape!'

"I answered: 'It's not a question of rights. It's a question of conscience. If you let them continue now that I've told you we know, the dead will be on your conscience, not ours. If you want to try and escape—go right ahead. Our boys will be happy in either case—if you escape or if you get killed.'"

The next morning a huge cement mixer was brought into Pen 20 and the tunnel was sealed. The men stood around in silence, panic-stricken.

But in the other pens the digging continued.

Shatz continues: "That Saturday—it had to be on the Sabbath, when they figured we were resting—we decided to evacuate one of the pens by force with tear gas. We began to look for the tunnel opening but it was well hidden, under a mattress which was covered with boards and dirt. We finally cemented the tunnel. We decided to go from one pen to the next and close them all up, in an orderly manner.

"At the meeting of the camp staff that day, we decided that the next pens on the list were 13 and 8. We evacuated the prisoners from 13 and sealed off the tunnel. But for some reason we postponed the work on 8 until the next day."

That night a group of prisoners from 8 escaped. The tunnel was about twenty-five yards long and ended beyond the outer fence. The village of Ansar was about three miles away. Ta'mari still claims that about fifty people escaped. Shatz puts the number at twelve. In any case, once the escape was discovered, the Israeli forces took up positions all over the area and loosed a barrage of machine-gun fire. Four prisoners were killed and another was caught inside the tunnel. Four succeeded in reaching Damascus and another three reached other destinations.

"After that," Shatz relates, "we finished off the work in a jiffy. We evacuated all the prisoners and sealed off all the tunnels."

Ta'mari claims that the prisoner caught in the tunnel was the one who gave the whole thing away. "He was the last one in the last group. Forty people were already outside and they were waiting for the rest. It had been arranged beforehand that they would meet near the wadi behind the earth encampment. Despite strict orders to the contrary, the last guy decided that he had to take all his personal belongings with him. He had everything wrapped in a blanket. The blanket got caught on a piece of barbed wire and everything fell apart. He apparently made a lot of noise trying to work it free and gather up all his stuff because the Israeli guards saw him and opened fire. He ran back into the tunnel and was caught inside."

According to Ta'mari, four of the escapees lost their way and ended up in Mukhtara, the village of the Druze leader Walid Jumblatt. From there they tried to reach Beirut in an ambulance of the Druze militia. But the ambulance ran into an Israeli armored force out looking for the escaped prisoners. The Israelis opened fire on the ambulance, killing two and wounding two others. The two wounded men were returned to Ansar. All the others, Ta'mari says, succeeded in getting away. Some even joined the fighting in Tripoli. A number of the escapees later planned an attack against the guards around Ansar, which proved unsuccessful. They were recaptured and brought back to the prison camp.

The underground tunnels were not the only escape route used during Ansar's history. Hiding in the garbage truck was once tried. According to Ta'mari, eight prisoners hid themselves under the garbage that was regularly dumped in the wadi outside the confines of the camp. "One of the men couldn't wait until the truck had left the garbage dump," he relates. "He pushed his way out immediately and was sighted by the truck driver in the mirror. The driver ran after him, caught him, and brought him back to camp."

Shatz contends that only one man succeeded in escaping in that way. Whatever the facts, the garbage truck was regularly inspected after that.

There was another occasion when a successful escape was made. It was one night in March 1983, when the camp was without sentries for about twenty minutes. One prisoner simply took advantage of the situation, jumped the fence, and disappeared into the darkness. Shatz chalked it up to confusion. Usual procedure was for the sentry on duty to wait for his replacement and only then leave his post. That day a new reserve force had been brought into camp and they instituted a different order: the retiring sentry left his post and went to wake up his replacement. During the interim, all the posts were empty.

The question remains: Why did only one man take advantage of the situation? Ta'mari's answer is simple: "That morning Dr. Herbert Amery, the Austrian mediator in the prisoner exchange, visited Ansar. The men who saw him were convinced that the exchange would take place in a matter of days and that it would be foolish to tempt fate for a few extra days of freedom."

June 6, 1983, was the first anniversary of the outbreak of the war. Shatz was convinced that there would be some sort of mass protest that day. It was his opinion that the prisoners would start climbing the fences en masse. In anticipation, he put everyone concerned with the security of Ansar on the alert. The orders he issued were clear: "If a thousand men start climbing the fences, we have no alternative but to open fire."

The protest, however, turned out to be something altogether different. Ta'mari, who was behind it, is not particularly proud of what happened.

The main motivation of the exercise was to put Ansar back into the headlines. During the months of April and May, negotiations for the prisoner exchange had accelerated, and among the prisoners hope was running high. Toward the end of May, negotiations reached a dead end. The collective frustrations of the prisoners were vented on June 6.

At seven o'clock in the evening, the whole of Ansar was on fire.

The execution of the operation was not exactly in accordance with plans. The men of Pen 25 had suggested that the whole camp be burned down and a message to that effect had been relayed to the prisoners' committee. The committee met for consultations and Ta'mari proposed that instead of burning down all the tents at once, one tent be burned at a time in each pen and then, depending on the reaction of the Israelis, the rest of the tents would be burned down. Instructions to that end were circulated through the postal system. When the time came to start the fireworks, the men in 25 decided that their original plan was better and put it into effect. The conflagration in 25 proved infectious and soon all the pens followed suit. Torches were dipped into fuel from the heaters and used to ignite the tents. Soon the entire camp was burning—with the exception of the infirmaries and the kitchens, and the tent of the Unified Command.

The Israeli soldiers were astounded by the sight but they were ordered by their commanders not to intervene. They merely stood on the embankments and watched the camp burn down. The sight of these gigantic bonfires was almost surrealistic.

"Except for the fact that there were damages of about two million dollars," Shatz recalls, "no one really cared. They were injuring themselves more than us. It was already summer and we figured that they could sleep outside—which was true for the moment. But when the summer ended, it was going to rain again. Eventually we would have to provide new tents but we were in no hurry. They could stew in their own juices for a while."

After the fire the face of Ansar changed considerably. In place of the large field tents, the area was now covered with thousands of tiny pup tents improvised by the prisoners from blankets, and other ingenious "dwellings." Most of the internal barbed wire divisions were hardly more than a memory. The prisoners had dismantled the fences—with their bare hands—and used the wire to fashion tools and various ornaments.

A new order for the camp became imperative. As a result, the army decided to relieve the military police of its responsibility and put regular army in instead. Charge of the camp was handed over to Gen. Amir Drori, head of the Northern Command, who appointed Col. Yaacov Cafri camp commander. Cafri was the commander of an armored brigade.

"The military police was no longer able to cope," recalls General Nativ. "They themselves admitted as much. Most of their recruits were from the reserves and the tour of duty was from ninety to over a hundred days. The men simply couldn't take it. They were totally demoralized. General staff headquarters was of the opinion that fresh regular forces, especially of young soldiers, would be better able to handle the situation. The prisoners would feel the difference: instead of MPs with billy clubs, the camp would be patrolled by soldiers with guns."

The reorganization of the camp cost millions of dollars and involved renovation of the pens and the interior fencing. The new tents would be raised over asphalt floors—to prevent digging. Morning inspection, which had simply evaporated, was to be reinstituted. All loopholes, both literal and figurative, were to be closed.

In order to do this, certain arrangements had to be made. A little over a mile from the camp there was an abandoned quarry called by the prisoners Wadi Jehennom (Death Valley). It was decided to turn it into a temporary prison camp. The ground was covered with limestone gravel and the men were removed there in rotation; first all of Ansar I was emptied out, and then Ansar II. The very idea of being transported to another place aroused the resentment of the prisoners and they had to be removed forcibly and transported in closed vans.

As it turned out, conditions there were better than in the remains of the old camp. Within the boundaries of the new camp, twenty-five hundred prisoners could move freely. Shatz was to refer to it as "a summer camp."

As usually happens, summer camp eventually came to an end. It was soon time to return to the old grind. The "old grind" had been given a fundamental facelift. The fences had been reconstructed and fortified; the new tents were in place on their impenetrable foundations; and what had become a self-propelled anarchy was about to be restored to rigidity.

Shatz was of the opinion that there would be resistance when the prisoners were taken back and so he called in the committee and asked them: "Are you going back willingly or do we have to employ force?"

Ta'mari answered: "We're returning in an orderly fashion, like soldiers."

The trip back was in open trucks and everyone was compliant.

Whether or not Ta'mari knew that there would be an epilogue to this chapter is a matter of conjecture. Shatz is convinced that he did. "The bloody events that succeeded the evacuation—or the non-evacuation—of the quarry have to weigh on Ta'mari's conscience, not ours."

The evacuation ended peacefully but Shatz was sure that it had not been total. "What would I have done had I been a prisoner?" he kept asking himself, and came to the conclusion that he would have tried to escape. At least some of the prisoners, he was sure, had remained behind, hiding in the quarry and waiting for the opportunity to slip away once the last army man had left. He called in the committee again.

"Is there anyone still there? You better tell me now because we are going in there to comb the place with bulldozers. Anybody left is going to get hurt."

The entire committee was of the opinion—or at least that's what they said—that everyone had left.

Shatz repeated his warning: "I'm going to raze every corner of that quarry. The responsibility for any injuries is all yours."

The committee repeated its assurance that everyone had left.

Shatz was still not satisfied. He called in Colonel Abu el-Fida, whom he knew had his own coterie, and put the same question to him. But Abu el-Fida's response was no different from the committee's. Shatz's last appeal was to Dr. Emad, who often served as a final tribune among the prisoners. He also had no information.

Shatz now felt that he could go ahead with a clear conscience. He ordered a platoon to spray the quarry with machine-gun fire. "Two prisoners suddenly materialized from behind an embankment," he recalled. "One of them was wounded in the head, the other in the leg. Their screams were pitiful."

The two wounded men were taken back to Ansar in an ambulance. Shatz again called in the committee. "Look at these guys," he said, pointing to the wounded. "If you left any more behind you can be sure they'll come back dead, not wounded."

The committee still had nothing to say.

Shatz continues: "I had no intention of endangering any of my men. I told them: 'We're not going to look for prisoners. We're just going to shoot up the place and then call in the air force to pound it for good measure.' Ta'mari still made no move."

A platoon moved into the quarry and sprayed it with machine-gun fire from all sides and in all directions. Then a giant bulldozer was brought in to level off the area. Suddenly the bulldozer lurched to one side. The driver braked, shifted into reverse, and began moving back. He was panic-stricken: a human head had rolled in front of the shovel.

186

"We started to dig," Shatz continues, "and soon we uncovered human limbs. At that point I decided to stop. Whoever was under there was dead anyway. I sent for Ta'mari and the rest of the committee, and for Abu el-Fida and Dr. Emad and one of the mukhtars. I decided to let them do the digging. They dug for a couple of hours and uncovered four mangled bodies, all of whom they were able to identify."

Finally, the Red Cross was called in. "I told them that we had repeatedly cautioned the leaders of the prisoners and they refused to cooperate. That's what happened," Shatz concludes, with a shrug.

In 1984, a year after the prisoner exchange had been completed, a Jordanian journalist by the name of Salim el-Juneidi published a book in Amman called *The Ansar Prison Camp.* Testimony was supplied by former prisoners, among them Salah Ta'mari. The above incident is described in the following way:

"Four prisoners dug a bunker in which they decided to hide when the transfer back to the pens took place. They figured that they would be able to escape after the evacuation. They informed Ta'mari of their plan and Ta'mari advised them to forget about it. First of all it was dangerous, he told them. Secondly, it was his opinion that the exchange was in the offing. But the four men refused to listen. They remained behind in their bunker. When they saw the bulldozer approaching, they were afraid of being buried alive so they came out with their hands up, and motioned to the driver to stop. But he didn't stop and they were sliced in half by the blade of the shovel."

The author adds that that same morning the driver of the bulldozer had been evacuating the bodies of Israeli soldiers caught in the building of the military administration in Tyre. The building had collapsed as a result of the explosion of a mined car. "When he was brought to Ansar that evening, he found a way of venting his desire for revenge."

The new rules were strictly enforced in the renovated prison camp. And they were uncompromising. One of them was known as the "rule of the white line." In every pen, a white line was drawn two yards from the inner fence. It resembled the inside line on a tennis court. The prisoners were informed that the white line was the outer edge of the pen, not the fence itself. "Anyone crossing the white line gets a bullet."

Slowly but surely the prisoners got the message. The first day of the "new order" one prisoner decided to see what would happen if he put his shoes on the line. A minute later, his shoes went flying through the air. "The next day," Shatz recalls, "they tried a few more stunts. One of the prisoners let a ball they were playing with roll over the line. He went to retrieve it and got a bullet in his hand for it. Another guy, doing laps around the pen, got a bullet in his heel for trying to be smart."

There were eleven men wounded during the first three days of the new regime. But the prisoners were not yet reconciled. The twelfth paid with his life. According to Ta'mari, one of the prisoners hurled a "letter-rock" into the next pen to his brother. The rock landed in the "no-man's-land" and when the brother stretched out his hand to pick up his letter, he was shot by one of the soldiers on patrol. "He wasn't trying to escape and even if he was, the soldier was obligated to warn him once or twice, and only then to shoot. And not to kill, either, just to wound him. But this prisoner was shot dead on the spot."

Shatz has a different version. He claims that the prisoner was outside the pen, in the patrol path. "When can you consider a prisoner in the act of escaping, when he is outside the pen or when he's already at home taking a shower?"

After the death of the prisoner, no further attempts were made to cross the white line. "The 'fences,'" Shatz sums up, "were kept as shiny as nickel. Not even a speck of dust crossed them."

14

"Geneva pants"

Fall 1983. In Ansar the camp was gearing itself for another winter, to all appearances unconcerned with the intensive negotiations under way for the prisoner exchange. Salah Ta'mari and the Israelis in Ansar had one common goal: to get through each day with the least amount of trouble possible.

But appearances were deceiving: the proposed exchange was uppermost in everyone's mind. It produced tensions in the camp that were likely to erupt into violence at the drop of a hat. The waiting was unbearable, especially now that negotiations had moved into high gear.

Ta'mari was not a passive onlooker. For almost a year he had been involved in all aspects of the complicated deal, as representative of the prisoners in Ansar.

In December 1982, two representatives of the contending parties, Israel and the PLO, had met secretly in Vienna. The Israeli was the former Knesset member Aryeh (Lova) Eliav, a well-known peace activist. The Palestinian was Issam Sartawi, one of Arafat's close friends and advisers.

It was not the first meeting between the two. They had been the joint recipients of the Bruno Kreisky Peace Prize and their mutual friendship had since blossomed. Eliav had come to the meeting with the knowledge of the

189

Israeli government. His mission was twofold: to see if it was possible to find out what had happened to the five Israelis missing since the war in Lebanon, and to arrange for the International Red Cross to meet with the eight Israelis being held by the PLO.

At that meeting, Sartawi notified Eliav that "Salah Ta'mari had been appointed as the official representative of PLO prisoners in the negotiations." He asked Eliav to visit his "good friend Ta'mari" in Ansar to inform him of the appointment. He also asked Eliav to deliver a letter to him.

After this, Eliav and Sartawi walked in the pouring rain to a confectioners in the center of Vienna; Sartawi wanted to send Ta'mari "a little something that he really likes." They bought the largest box of Mozartkugeln in the shop.

That same week Eliav arrived at Ansar with the chocolates and with a video crew in tow: they had come to document the meeting between Eliav and Ta'mari on videotape for Sartawi. It was supposed to provide the PLO with incontrovertible evidence that the PLO prisoners in Israeli hands were in good shape.

The meeting took place in the Israeli staff section of the camp, in the office of the IDF spokesman, Captain Sela. Eliav gave Ta'mari Sartawi's letter. It read:

> Salah, my brother, revolutionary greetings!
> Accept my feelings of admiration for your firm stand, your heroism and your struggle. I hope my letter finds you in good health. Eliav and I are doing our best and hope that we will soon be able to bring about a prisoner exchange. I can tell you that progress has already been made. We hope that our efforts will be crowned by success in the near future.
> I saw Dina three days ago. She is taking things very well. She sends you her best wishes and encouragement. She misses you. She is proud of you. So are we all. I hope—as you do—that we all will soon meet.
> My friend, Lova Eliav, a fighter for a just peace, has done me the great favor of taking this letter to you along with a box of Austrian chocolates.
> I miss you and hope to see you soon. May God bless you.
>
> Issam.

Issam Sartawi and Salah Ta'mari were not destined to meet again. Five months later, on April 10, 1983, while Ta'mari was still in prison, Sartawi was murdered in Portugal by Abu Nidal's people.

After he finished reading the letter, Ta'mari requested that the other members of the prisoners' committee join the meeting. They did, and only after he had read the letter to them did he agree to be filmed together with Lova Eliav. Ta'mari was wearing a warm quilted jacket of IDF issue and a Russian-style hat.

"I want you to know," he said to Eliav and to the cameras, "that despite the fact that we are prisoners, our life here is meaningful. You see the hat I'm wearing? Nobody bought it for me, nobody gave it to me as a present. These hats, like so many other things, were all made here by us in the camp. We are not struggling only to survive. In order to survive one only needs one's brains. Here, we need our self-respect as well. Survival and self-respect go hand in hand. We believe that the most important challenge facing us now is to preserve love as the central motive of our existence and our struggle. We shall not let anyone take this away from us."

As was his custom when confronting an Israeli, Ta'mari made the comparison between Jewish history and the present experience of the Palestinians. "We believe that we have a good many things in common. We have a common heritage. But even more important, we have a common future. In order to fight for that future, we need brave people on both sides. Many may fall in the battle for peace but I sincerely believe that their sacrifice will not have been in vain."

One of the biggest challenges he faced in Ansar, he continued, was to prove to the Israelis that "we are as intelligent as you, as educated, and that we feel the same great love—perhaps even a greater love—for the same country."

Eliav politely interjected: "Let's not argue whose love is greater. Let's agree that our love is equal."

But Ta'mari refused to concede the point: "I agree. But let's say that your eyes are very important to you and my eyes are just as important to me. If I lose my eyesight, my eyes become even dearer, simply because I lost them. That's what I mean. As long as I am forced to live in a tent, exposed to the four winds, my ruined home is even dearer to me."

Ta'mari touched upon the problems at Ansar as well. "There is no security reason," he told Eliav, "to keep so many people here." Eliav promised that he would do his best to get the prisoners released and, until then, to see that conditions were improved.

Ta'mari made a special point of telling Eliav that under no circumstances "should anyone make any attempt to get *me* released before the others! I will be the last prisoner to leave this damn place. I'm the one who's going to take the keys of this camp and throw them into the sea. I want this to be absolutely clear."

Eliav suggested to Ta'mari that he add a few words for Dina, who would certainly see the tape with Sartawi. Ta'mari spoke as if the cameras were not even there: "I am sorry that Dina is alone now. Her mother is dead and I am in prison. When you have a wife like Dina, you expect her to do great things. You expect a nobility of spirit from her. I try to behave like that too, otherwise I wouldn't deserve her. I hope she maintains her high morale and that she doesn't lose hope. When I say that I'll be the last to leave this place, it's not because I don't miss her. The very opposite is true. She knows that I don't enjoy anything unless she enjoys it with me. Only because I love her do I want to be the last to leave."

The conversation went on for a long time. The two men discussed the long and bitter conflict between Israelis and Palestinians, each expressing his own views on the subject, while the cameras rolled.

Then Ta'mari gave Eliav a letter for Dina and some small handmade gifts: a wooden comb, a perfume bottle carved out of stone, and prayer beads made out of olive pits. He himself refused to touch the box of Mozartkugeln. They were distributed, instead, to sick people in the camp.

Eliav left with his impressions of Ansar—and of Ta'mari—and the videotape, to meet Sartawi again, this time in Paris. Sartawi brought Dina to the meeting.

The next time Eliav came to visit Ansar, he had a letter from Dina in his pocket:

> I just arrived in Paris and came straight to Sartawi's home where I met a friend who was kind enough to visit you. I received the gifts and the videotape, which I have not yet seen. So I can't say anything about it yet. We are trying to get a video tonight so that we can screen it. If I don't succeed, I'll see it in Cairo. I'm returning tonight.
>
> The negotiations seem so drawn out! I pray to God that He give me

the strength to hold out while you are gone, the strength and the patience and the faith—all of which you've always had in abundance.

You can be sure that I have left no stone unturned. I move from country to country every few days, sometimes every day. This opportunity of getting a letter to you seems like a miracle, one of those many miracles of our life together. Your purity and belief in everything that's decent and just and right make miracles your just due. I will never disappoint you.

Sweetie and I sit down and write to you every time we feel like talking to you. Our one hope is that you will be able to read everything we've written when you return to us safely and soon.

All the good wishes and love in the world are paltry compared to what I have in my heart. I am with you in every way in my prayers. May God bless you and keep you and hasten your release.

The letter was signed, as usual, "D."

After his official appointment, Ta'mari, and through him the rest of the prisoners, were kept informed of progress in the POW negotiations. Eliav reported to him regularly, as did other Israelis who were involved in one way or another.

In January 1983 the PLO appointed a special team, headed by Col. Abu Ziyad, to negotiate on its behalf. The Israelis appointed a lawyer, Aryeh Marinsky, to head the Israeli team. The "proximity talks"—as they were called—were held in Vienna and mediated by Chancellor Kreisky's assistant, Dr. Herbert Amery. The PLO people sat in one room, the Israelis in another, and Amery went back and forth between them, ironing out initial difficulties. The negotiations continued for almost a year and Amery was instrumental in bringing the negotiations to a successful conclusion, even after he had been appointed Austria's ambassador to Greece.

The conditions that the PLO proposed for the release of the six Israelis were the release of all Ansar detainees and the release of another 1,250 Palestinians who had been tried and sentenced and were now serving their sentences in Israeli prisons. Eliav was given a list of the 1,250. It was this demand that proved to be the thorniest problem in the negotiations.

The Israelis, for their part, insisted that the two prisoners being held by Ahmad Jibril also be included in the deal. Until then these two men had not even been allowed visits by the Red Cross.

Through the offices of a third party, Ahmad Jibril submitted a list of more than two hundred names, members of his organization ostensibly being held by the Israelis, some in Ansar, the others in regular prisons. He demanded that the Red Cross be allowed to meet with each and every one of his men prior to similar rights being granted to the two Israelis. According to the Israelis, not more than a third of the people mentioned were actually in their hands, and Israel's "counterlist" of names was submitted—in a highly complicated fashion—to Jibril. A special committee of ministers had had to approve the step. The names on the list had been provided by the army and the whole thing was considered top secret.

Jibril rejected the Israelis' claim. In his opinion, Israel was keeping back the names of his other people. In protest, he returned the counterlist.

At this point Ta'mari was actively drawn into the picture. His job was to compare the two lists and see if he could account for the discrepancies. He began, naturally, with the prisoners at Ansar.

The source of the discrepancy was that many of the prisoners had registered under false names. But that was not the worst of it. Some of them had given a second false name to the Red Cross. And then, just to complicate matters a little further, and to annoy the authorities at the same time, they had traded their Israeli-issued POW identity cards with each other. They had also tried to alter their appearances by either growing beards or mustaches or shaving them off.

It was now up to Ta'mari to unravel the knots. That he was the only one likely to succeed was clear to both sides. His authority among the prisoners was his biggest advantage.

Ta'mari asked for a week to check out the lists. With the help of some of his lieutenants from the prisoners' committee he was able, finally, to establish the real identities of the prisoners. To his great surprise, he discovered that some of the people on Jibril's list had never been caught by the Israelis. According to their comrades in Ansar, who provided him with the details, including, sometimes, even exact addresses, many of them were living in various places in Lebanon and Syria, some of them only a few blocks from Jibril's headquarters.

At the end of the week he had completed the job. He discovered which of Jibril's men were in Ansar under assumed names, but before he submitted his findings he insisted that Israel promise not to start interrogating them now.

The Israelis agreed. Their first priority was to make it possible for the

Red Cross to visit the two Israelis in Jibril's hands and this outweighed any other consideration. It was the Israelis' first concession but not, by any means, their last.

Dr. Amery set out for Damascus to meet with Jibril. From Damascus he went directly to Israel with a letter from Jibril authorizing him to talk with his people in Ansar and register them. He was given permission to enter Ansar for that purpose by the chief Israeli negotiator, Aryeh Marinsky.

Dr. Amery made the visit to Ansar together with Lova Eliav. They met with Ta'mari and with the rest of the committee and Amery was invited to enter the pen where Jibril's people had gathered. He received a royal welcome: the prisoners carried him around on their shoulders, cheering all the time. When he left he had Ta'mari's updated list in his possession.

A few months later, in an interview with the Israeli TV correspondent Uri Goldstein, Dr. Amery confirmed this: "A lot of the Jibril people that Israel claimed it didn't have were walking around Ansar under assumed names. I took the list with me to Damascus. Jibril wasn't there but I showed it to his deputy, Talal Naja, and to some others. They were very happy to discover people on the list that they knew. Now, they told me, the Red Cross would be allowed to visit Yosef Groff and Nissim Salem."

But Jibril went back on his word. The Red Cross was not allowed to visit the two men. This time, however, his intransigence got on the nerves not only of the Israelis but of the prisoners in Ansar.

Marinsky met with Ta'mari and members of the committee and informed them in no uncertain terms: "Jibril is the one who is holding up your release. If you want to get out of here, there is only one way to do it: put pressure on Jibril."

At that point Ta'mari made a very unorthodox suggestion. "We have an officer from Jibril's organization here with the rank of captain. He is very familiar with the situation here at Ansar. Get him released and send him to talk to Jibril. Maybe he'll succeed in convincing him that thousands of Palestinians and Lebanese are suffering because of him." Ta'mari made no secret of his contempt for Jibril's behavior.

Marinsky agreed. The IDF released the officer and even gave Ta'mari permission to send a letter with him to Jibril. The letter made its point very clearly: Feelings against Jibril are running high in the camp. If he continues to block the agreement, his men here may be in danger from the other prisoners.

At that point, all of Jibril's men were separated from the other prisoners and kept in their own pen.

When the rebellion in the PLO broke out, with pitched battles between Arafat and his opponents, among them Jibril, the Israelis feared that he would never let anyone see Groff and Salem. Marinsky returned to Ansar and met again with the prisoners' committee: "You guys are still sitting here while that bastard is living a life of ease in the best hotels of Europe. He doesn't give a damn if you are released because all we're asking from him is some small sign of life from the two Israelis."

Ta'mari had by now gauged the seriousness of the Israeli team's intentions. He also knew that news of Jibril's cruel stubbornness had reached the ears of the wives and mothers of the Ansar prisoners living in southern Lebanon. This had been done by the Israeli Military Administration at Marinsky's behest. Hostility to Jibril's men was getting more intense as the days passed. It was lucky that they were being kept separate. It saved Ta'mari and the committee a lot of trouble.

The first ray of light appeared in the spring of 1983, when the talks between Israel and the PLO moved to Geneva.

By this time Marinsky was very ill and had been replaced by another lawyer and former minister of justice, Shmuel Tamir. Before the new delegation left for Geneva, Ta'mari was taken to Tel Aviv for a meeting with Tamir. The meeting had been approved by the prisoners' committee. Ta'mari was permitted to change clothes for the occasion and he put on one of the pairs of corduroy pants that Dina had brought him. The pants earned a nickname among the prisoners of Ansar: *Bantaion Geneva* [Geneva pants]. Now, every time Ta'mari left Ansar wearing his corduroys, it was clear that he was attending a meeting connected with the negotiations.

When the two delegations met in Geneva, through the mediation of the Austrians and the Red Cross, there were members of Jibril's organization among the PLO negotiators. They were all housed at the PLO legation in Geneva. The head of the Palestinian delegation was an old friend of Ta'mari's, Muhammad Ramlawi.

For its opening gambit, Israel proposed releasing two thousand Ansar prisoners. The PLO's reply was offensive: In exchange you'll get one soldier and two corpses. The Israelis decided that even when engaged in hard bargaining, there had to be a minimum of decorum. The PLO, in their opinion, had transgressed the boundaries of good taste. The Israelis packed up and returned home.

Ta'mari refused to believe that the failure was the Palestinians' fault. Colonel Shatz invited him to use the radio in his car. "Turn it to whatever station you want—BBC, Monte Carlo." Ta'mari heard the news on Monte Carlo: the PLO was accusing Israel of being responsible for the breakdown of the talks. He heard the Israeli side of the story from Shmuel Tamir, a few days later.

Ta'mari was interested in having his comrades in Geneva fully conscious of what he and the Ansar prisoners thought, and in order to do this he asked permission to talk to the PLO delegation in Geneva. Tamir agreed. Ta'mari contacted Geneva from the telephone in Shatz's room. He got Ramlawi on the phone.

Ta'mari explained to his old friend just how precarious the situation in Ansar was: people were ready to explode—some were on the verge of hysteria and others already hysterical; the place was a pressure cooker without any valves. Israel, he told his friend, was beginning to plan for another winter, and all the frustrations and anger of the prisoners were going to be directed not only at the Israelis this time but also at the PLO leadership. He asked Ramlawi to give a message for him to Arafat: that the thousands of prisoners in Ansar had the feeling that the PLO was holding up the progress of the talks, dragging things out unnecessarily, and bargaining too hard. "Tell the Khityar [old man—Arafat's nickname] to think for a minute about the thousands of people here who are suffering and about the families waiting for them to come home."

The negotiations remained in a deep freeze.

During that period, something really hair-raising took place at Ansar. Ta'mari attributed it to the despair that had gripped most of the prisoners.

Among the people there were three Egyptians who had been in Sidon when the war broke out. They were rounded up by the Israelis and since they had no identification and could provide no reasonable explanation for their presence there, they were locked up with the rest. The three claimed that since there was peace between Israel and Egypt and since they had no connection with the terrorist groups, there was no reason to keep them at Ansar. Israel replied that if Egypt requested their release, they would be released. Their names were submitted to the Israeli-Egyptian Joint Military

Commission. After three months, the Egyptians replied—in the negative. The men remained at Ansar.

The Egyptians raised their claims from time to time. All the Israelis could do was to promise them that they would be handed over to the Egyptians the minute they were prepared to accept them.

When the negotiations got under way, the three relaxed: they were sure that they would soon be released. But when they heard that the talks had broken down, they grew desperate. They decided to go on a hunger strike. It soon became apparent that nobody gave a damn whether or not they starved themselves to death. At that point they resolved on more drastic action—something that would really shock everyone.

Without taking any sanitary precautions, not to speak of anesthesia, they sewed each other's lips together with fine wire.

Ta'mari was outraged, and not only because of the barbarism of the act. "They did something which went against everything we held sacred. They were nothing but three lousy crooks who made us all look like primitive animals. And everything that we had tried to do in Ansar was intended to prove just the opposite. We couldn't allow three gangsters to determine the kind of image we would have." Ta'mari had always been sensitive to the prisoners' image, even when the situation was desperate.

The next day the three were forcibly taken to the infirmary where an Israeli doctor took the stitches out. The Egyptians repeated their stunt a week later and the doctor was forced to take the stitches out once again. But, he notified them, it was the last time.

The Israelis were well aware of the terrible strains on the prisoners and tried to take steps—wherever possible—to make things easier. Every Friday, for example, all the Israeli guards left the pens and the internal gates were opened. The prisoners were allowed to mix freely for two hours. "Have a good time," Shatz told them. "Go and have tea with your friends. Only the minute you hear the whistle, I want everybody back where he belongs."

Shatz made it his business to use up all the Red Cross funds available for the personal needs of the prisoners. They were given more coffee, more sweets, more cigarettes, soft drinks (after they had been taken out of their glass bottles and transferred to plastic containers). Every pen elected a distribution committee to make sure things were fairly apportioned. When the camp was finally evacuated, large quantities of Turkish delight were left behind.

But while the prisoners were eating candy and trying to get through each day, Arafat was being forced into defensive positions in Tripoli. His people were shelled without letup and they began to retreat from one base after another. Ta'mari sent a letter to Arafat at that time, which read: "The release of the Ansar prisoners right now will not only provide us with a great propaganda victory—it will enable us to send you a steady stream of reinforcements to Tripoli!"

In Israel the fate of the six soldiers held in Tripoli became a major concern. The danger that they might be caught in the shelling moved Israel to reopen the negotiations, mediated by the Red Cross and the Austrians as before.

This time, agreement was reached. All the Ansar prisoners would be released in exchange for the six Israelis. Arafat approved the agreement from his base in Tripoli, but he wanted at least a gesture from Israel: the release of a hundred Palestinian terrorists who had been sentenced by Israeli courts.

Israel refused. The request for a gesture suddenly turned into an irrevocable condition. So, after agreement had been reached, the negotiations were again broken off. The Red Cross, which believed that both sides were being unnecessarily pigheaded, decided to take unilateral action.

Jean Hoflieger, one of the top Red Cross officers, flew from Geneva to Damascus and then—casting all caution to the winds—set out for Tripoli. He met with Arafat and then went to Ansar. Ta'mari requested him to tell Arafat not to be obdurate. "Tell him," he said, "that the people here have reached the end of their tether."

Hoflieger got Arafat to reduce his demands. Arafat was ready to settle for sixty-three additional prisoners and he handpicked them himself. Twenty-six were persons sentenced by Israeli courts for murder in terrorist attacks. Another thirty-seven had been caught on the high seas.

Israel was forced to accept.

The negotiating team returned to Geneva, this time to work out the technical details for the exchange.

All of the Ansar prisoners with families in southern Lebanon would be released at special centers in southern Lebanon. Anyone not wishing to remain in Lebanon would be flown to Algeria. It was up to Ta'mari and the committee to sort out the two categories. After two days the division was clear: one thousand prisoners would leave for Algeria, the rest, four thousand in number, were remaining in Lebanon.

Forty-eight hours before the exchange a large contingent of Red Cross representatives appeared at Ansar. Each prisoner was given a dark blue sweat suit and shiny white sneakers.

On the evening of November 22, 1983, Yehuda Shatz made his last visit to the tent of the Unified Command. When he reached the fence he called Ta'mari over. As Ta'mari approached, Shatz threw something over the fence: "Catch," he cried. Ta'mari caught the object as it flew at him. It was a heavy ring of keys. "Open all the gates," Shatz called out, "to all the pens."

A couple of Hercules troop carriers from the Israeli Air Force stood on the small landing strip adjacent to Ansar. A few hundred buses were ranged around the camp.

The planes were loaded first. The prisoners marched up in orderly fashion and called out their names and numbers to the Red Cross representatives. After being checked off the list, each prisoner was tied hand and foot with plastic handcuffs. Ta'mari, good as his word, was the last to leave the camp. As he stood with his shackled feet on the boarding steps of the Hercules, Shatz came over to say goodbye.

"Here," he said, handing something to Ta'mari. "Take this as a memento."

It was the giant key to the main gate of Ansar.

Toward midnight, the planes landed at Ben-Gurion Airport. There three Air France Boeing 747s awaited them.

According to the agreement, the Boeings were not to leave Israel until word reached Lod from Tripoli that the Fatah had brought the six Israelis to the port there. Meanwhile the prisoners had their handcuffs removed and began to ascend the stairs into the planes. The motors began to hum. But word had not yet come through.

The tension in the air was palpable. The Red Cross people at Lod were in radio contact with their office in Tel Aviv, which had Geneva on the line. In Geneva, the office had another line open with Damascus, and Damascus was in wireless contact with the Fatah unit in Tripoli.

Five minutes passed. Then ten, fifteen, half an hour. The motors were still humming on the runway. Only after fifty nerve-racking minutes did the message come through. It was relayed from the docks of Tripoli to the capital of Syria, and from there to Geneva, Tel Aviv, and finally Lod: the six had arrived.

The first plane took off.

A second message came through: a boat with the six Israelis had reached the French ship lying at anchor seven miles off the coast of Lebanon.

The second plane took off for Algeria.

A third message was received from the French ship: "The six Israelis have been moved to a gunboat of the Israeli Navy."

With that news, Ta'mari was ready to leave. All the others were already on the plane. As he walked to the steps of the remaining Boeing, three superior officers of the IDF stepped up to shake his hand. Ta'mari recognized only one of them, the head of the Military Police.

Behind them, at the very last moment, appeared Uri Goldstein of Israeli TV, which had been documenting the POW negotiations for the past year. Suddenly Ta'mari was faced with a microphone and cameras. The area was lit up. The noise of the plane was deafening and he was hoarse from all the work of the last few days. But he made the effort, for the last time:

"I believe and always have believed in coexistence between Jews and Arabs. I believe that the future is bright. Perhaps not the near future. Perhaps not in our lifetime. Yet I still believe, perhaps naïvely, in the future. But I believe in it without reservation. The day will come and people in this region will live together and face dangers together. Together, Jews and Arabs, we will say: 'Never again!'

"I am standing on the verge of freedom and I don't want to be illogical, in the positive or negative sense of the word. I hope that our experience, mine and my comrades, will prove to be a constructive one. I hope that my profound anger which wells up in me will be a constructive anger. I am angry that human beings are unable to live together despite the fact that they have so much in common.

"During all the time that I spent here, I shook hands with many Jews. After all, all of us are human beings. I cannot forget that in the darkest moments of my life, a Jewish hand was stretched out to me. On the other hand, there were people whose behavior was exceedingly un-Jewish. To be Jewish—is a value which one can gain or lose. Sometimes I feel that we, the Palestinians, are gaining that which you, the Jews, are losing."

He immediately corrected himself: ". . . which *some* of you Jews are losing."

Ta'mari turned and ascended the steps. In a minute he was lost to sight.

His five hundred days in Israel were over.

Late that night I returned home from Ansar. I had broadcast a report on the evening news magazine about the departure of the prisoners and the now empty camp. I had not seen Ta'mari.

On November 23, by six in the evening, the gigantic tent camp was no more. Blankets had been thrown over the barbed wire fences. Discarded clothes lay around in heaps. There were piles of garbage all over the place.

Israeli TV projected pictures of the six boys who had returned home, over and over again: Danny Gilboa being carried on the shoulders of cheering friends, and then the others, one by one.

Six Israeli mothers were overcome with joy.

Amalia and I were thinking of another woman.

Dina was on her way to Algeria to welcome her husband.

15

"Welcome, hero of Ansar."

On the afternoon of November 23, 1983, at intervals of thirty minutes, the three Air France jumbo jets landed at the international airport in Algiers. They had made a short stopover in Cairo at the request of the Algerian government: the Algerians would not countenance a direct, nonstop flight between Israel and Algeria, even under the auspices of the Red Cross.

The airport resembled a veritable fairgrounds. On hand to greet the prisoners were thousands upon thousands of people, families of the prisoners, mostly women and children. Police barriers had to be erected to keep the crowds from overrunning the central area where the official welcome was planned.

As the passengers descended, they were given a musical welcome by the fife and drum corps of the Ashbal, Ta'mari's pet project. Some of the prisoners burst into tears; others simply bent their knees and kissed Algerian soil.

As Ta'mari alighted, he searched the crowds for a glimpse of Dina but she wasn't there. He was embraced instead by Abu Ayyad, who was on hand with a host of Arab dignitaries for the occasion. The president of Algeria, Shazli Ben-Jadid, was prominent among them because of his great mane of white hair. Nayif Hawatmeh was there, as were other members of the PLO and the Algerian government. Most of the senior leadership of the

PLO, however, was not present: they were busy somewhere else—fighting each other in Tripoli.

Dina's plane from Geneva had been delayed and she was late arriving. It was ironic that, after so many thousands of air miles on behalf of the prisoners during Ta'mari's period in captivity, she should miss the great moment.

The Algerian government had prepared a royal reception for the prisoners. Lined up in three columns, the eleven hundred men were reviewed by Ben-Jadid, Abu Ayyad, and Salah Ta'mari. Ta'mari formally presented the prisoners' committee and Ansar's Unified Command to the president. He also made a point of introducing Dr. Emad.

After a number of fiery speeches about the sacred duty of the Arab nation to fight the eternal Zionist enemy and some references to the heroism and suffering of the Ansar prisoners and a pledge for revenge, the prisoners were loaded into buses and trucks and taken to a military camp. It was located near the town of Tabesa, not far from the Tunisian border, and already occupied by about a thousand Palestinian fighters who had been evacuated from Beirut the year before.

Ta'mari and members of the committee remained in Algiers for another day for interviews with the media. The first press conference was held at the airport itself. There Salah Ta'mari was interviewed by radio and television crews from all over the world.

In Tel Aviv, we were waiting impatiently for the news. I was at the radio studios, running up and down the stairs to look at the news from the various agencies coming in over the teleprinter. At the offices of *Yediot Aharonot* Amalia was doing the same. We hadn't planned it that way. It was just that we were both anxious to see what Ta'mari would say there after everything he had said here. It was in a way a moment of truth, a test, perhaps, for our relationship.

As could have been expected, only some of his remarks were subsequently reported, the so-called meaty political parts. The "potatoes," his personal comments, his particular slant, were, for the most, glossed over.

On page two of *Yediot Aharonot* a fairly full report appeared under the headline "Former Commander of the Ansar Prisoners Declares: 'I Dream of Coexistence.' " In the body of the article it was reported that he said that in addition to his belief in coexistence and his hope for a common life in a democratic Palestine of Jews and Arabs, he would continue to "fight together with his comrades against the cruelty and expansionist aims of the decision makers in Israel." The press reported that Ta'mari emphasized his distinction between the people of Israel and the heads of the political establishment.

The news agencies could not identify people such as Meir Rosenfeld or Drs. Shlomo and Portnoy, the two Israelis who had worked in the infirmaries in Ansar. Ta'mari's expression of gratitude to these people—with which he opened his remarks at his press conference in Algeria—were not quoted. He also sent special thanks "to a number of Israelis who tried to help him and displayed great humanity. I will not mention them by name," he added, "since I am not sure that they would want me to. I don't know whether it would hurt them."

The Israeli press gave prominence to his remarks on the "crimes perpetrated by Israel during the war in Lebanon." He recalled how the Israeli guards had stamped numbers on the prisoners' hands and added that a people who had suffered the holocaust was obliged to be more sensitive to human values. He called upon Jewish world opinion "to investigate the crimes committed by Israel during the war. If it should be proven that what I have said here is not true, I will be prepared to apologize publicly to the State of Israel."

At that press conference, Ta'mari claimed that certain of the Ansar prisoners had "disappeared" on the way to the airport, and were never released. Their absence had been discovered only in flight between Tel Aviv and Algeria. He appealed to the Red Cross to investigate.

This particular claim, denied at the time by Israel, was verified a few months later, after the second prisoner exchange with Ahmad Jibril had taken place. It emerged that sixty members of Jibril's organization from Ansar, who were supposed to be released with the others, had, in fact, been secreted away to another prison and kept as bargaining cards. In the end, these men were released as part of another deal in which 1,150 terrorists were returned to Jibril in exchange for Nissim Salem, Yosef Groff, and Hezi Shai, the third Israeli prisoner subsequently discovered to be in Jibril's hands.

In Algeria, Ta'mari demonstrated that he had not come from or landed in a political desert. He announced his full support for Arafat and added that while all the political currents in the PLO had been represented in Ansar, everyone believed in preserving the unity of the movement.

Some of the released prisoners were quick to show that their support for Arafat was their top priority: shortly after their arrival in Algeria they were again on their way—to join the fight in Tripoli against the rebels.

Five days after Ta'mari reached Algeria, we received regards from him. A friend of Ta'mari and Dina living in Rome called to tell us that Ta'mari had asked her to say that "he hadn't forgotten us and never would."

During those first days, we often wondered—although we never actually put it into words—when, if ever, we would be hearing from Dina again. The few people who knew about our ties had tried to rid us of our "illusions." What reason could she possibly have to maintain contact with us now that her husband had returned home? Israel was no longer relevant to her life. She had already thanked us sufficiently in a variety of ways. Salah was on his way to a new and unknown phase in his life. The attitude of some of his comrades to his Israeli chapter had to be a double-edged sword. There were, indeed, plenty of reasons to assume that the "Dina chapter" in our lives had come to a close.

Until the phone rang a few days later.

It was the third night of Hanukkah. We had just lit the candles when the phone rang. It was a friend calling—a friend named Dina. She wanted to know how things were with us and to tell us the news on her side. With her natural warmth and her direct manner, she told us about her new "troubles": "Salah is busy twenty-four hours a day. I thought we might take a short vacation somewhere in Europe, but no. He has a thousand and one things to take care of. He has to be in Tabesa with his people. 'They need me there,' he tells me. So what can I do?"

Life with Salah Ta'mari might be exciting for Dina. It was never easy.

Ta'mari remained in Tabesa about four months. The man who had been chairman of the Committee for the Defense of Prisoners' Rights in Ansar was now the chairman of the PLO Committee for the Defense of the Palestinians' Rights, a new body set up in the camp in Algeria.

Hundreds of Palestinians remained in Algeria. Some of them stayed because they had nowhere to go. Others stayed because they lacked the necessary papers for crossing international borders. True they were all free, but they were still living in a camp, behind barbed wire and under the watchful eye of Algerian soldiers. As in other Arab countries which had absorbed Palestinian evacuees from Beirut, the authorities in Algeria were wary of the disquieting effect the Palestinians had and the danger they might constitute to the stability of the regime. The Palestinians were free to move around the camp as much as they liked but they required special permission from the Algerian army to leave and the permission had to be coordinated with the camp authorities. It was almost natural for Ta'mari to become the chief coordinator among the various bodies.

He had other functions as well. "Every single individual had his own special problem," he later told us. "He had to find his family, or help them get passports or identity cards, or look for medical aid. Whatever the problem, serious or trivial, I was the address. Actually they were used to the idea that I was a kind of public service and I couldn't break them of the habit all at once. I had to stay with them until things became more or less settled."

But the truth is that as much as they needed him he needed them. He had been the unchallenged leader of thousands of people for over a year. It wasn't easy to give up that position overnight. Who could know if the future would ever grant him such a position in the Fatah again? After all, at the height of his career in Ansar, he had been the unquestioned leader of ten thousand men. There had never been one single organization within the PLO with so many people.

In any case, problems that had been familiar to him in Ansar cropped up again in Tabesa. There were, for example, the divisions in the movement reflecting the battle in Tripoli, except here they were exacerbated since leaders of the different organizations were able to visit the camp and explain their positions to the men.

"When there were serious clashes in Ansar," Ta'mari recalled, "I could always divert the attention of the men. Someone would throw a rock at one of the Israeli guards and soon everyone was united against the common enemy." In Tabesa there was no one to throw rocks at and the clashes that broke out required his personal and immediate intervention.

Most of the PLO people in Algeria since the evacuation from Beirut were there with their families. Now families were joining the ex-prisoners from Ansar and Ta'mari soon discovered that there were thousands of children wandering around the camp with nothing to do. He asked the veteran Palestinians why they had never set up a kindergarten. "We never thought about it," came the answer. Furthermore, they claimed, there was no place for one.

Ta'mari went to work. He requested that half the area of the officers' club be vacated. The officers were willing: "They thought I wanted a place to set up a central command. I sent to town for toys, a television set, and other equipment. Among the families of the camp inmates I found two professional kindergarten teachers. In a few days the kindergarten in Tabesa was functioning."

At the end of December 1983, Yassir Arafat left Tripoli. He had a surprise in store for a lot of people: he stopped off in Egypt and embraced Hosni Mubarak, the Egyptian president.

The extremists in the PLO—and there were such in Tabesa—were of the opinion that as long as Egypt hadn't annulled its peace treaty with Israel, Arafat had no business going to Egypt. The step was considered an act of betrayal. Ta'mari had long before foreseen the possibility of such a move— he had even mentioned it to me at our very first interview—and he came out in support of Arafat. "To continue the embargo on Egypt," he claimed, "was not going to force Egypt to cancel its peace treaty with Israel. The easiest thing in the world was to join the 'rejectionists' who said 'no' to everything. But negatives don't get you anywhere. We had to free ourselves of all the blinders we wore. That's exactly what Arafat was trying to do."

Ta'mari tried to explain his position to the extremists. In his opinion, Arafat's trip to Cairo "would weaken the Camp David accords by bringing Mubarak closer to the Palestinian position." Later, Ta'mari found "proof" for his supposition in the intensification of anti-Israeli activity in Cairo and the growing dissatisfaction among various sectors of the Egyptian public— lawyers, journalists, actors, etc. He attributed the growth of anti-Israeli sentiment to Arafat's visit.

The Israeli-Egyptian peace treaty had always been a sore point with Ta'mari. During one of our conversations in Israel he had told me that he felt that Sadat's strategy had been, in effect, an abandonment of the Palestinians, and he never forgave the Egyptian president for it. "It seemed to me that Sadat's attitude to the idea of land or homeland was like a carpenter's attitude to a piece of wood: you can cut it up, divide it any way you like, level it off here or there." He admitted to me that the day of Sadat's visit to Jerusalem was one of the darkest days of his life.

For me the exact opposite was true, as I had told him at the time: "It was one of the most wonderful and exciting days of my life." I had added that I thought he was wrong: "Sadat succeeded in destroying the barrier of hatred and bringing about the first peace treaty between Israel and an Arab country. And don't forget that the treaty points to a possible solution of the Palestinian problem as well."

I couldn't know for sure whether Ta'mari's attitude toward Arafat's visit indicated some change in his attitude in general. It was clear, however, that Ta'mari had come to realize that the peace between Israel and Egypt was a hard fact and that there was little point in fighting against it.

Following his visit to Cairo, Arafat continued to northern Yemen and then to Algeria. After twenty months of separation, Ta'mari finally met his chief again in Tabesa. It was his first opportunity to give Arafat a full account of what had happened in Ansar. Ta'mari told Arafat that for the moment he wanted to remain in Tabesa with the prisoners until all their problems were solved. Arafat apparently agreed. A month later, however, Ta'mari joined Arafat for a round of visits in Africa, and then returned with him to the Fatah's new central headquarters in Tunis.

From Tunis, Ta'mari left for Amman. This was his first visit to Jordan since he and Dina had left in 1970, following the events of Black September. Now he was officially representing the Fatah, and had come to arrange legal documents for the ex-prisoners, documents which would enable them to leave Tabesa. Jordan was the only Arab country willing to provide Palestinians with passports.

In Amman, Ta'mari met his mother, brothers, and sisters for the first time since the death of his father two years before. They had moved to Amman from Kuwait just a few months before Ta'mari had surrendered to the Israelis.

In addition to sitting with a team of assistants in various government offices, Ta'mari began the first of a series of projects designed to disseminate the story of Ansar to the world. He gave a lengthy interview to the foremost Jordanian paper, *A-Dustour,* which appeared in four installments. One of the pictures that appeared alongside the interview was a shot of the burning tents. It had been taken by Colonel Shatz. The newspaper claimed that the photo was "exclusive" to *A-Dustour.*

In the interview, Ta'mari amplified what he termed "the daily struggles waged by the prisoners against the Israeli soldiers." He described the social structure in the camp, the frequent hoisting of PLO flags, and the way in which the sick dealt with their difficulties. He also revealed how the prisoners overcame their physical isolation; despite the strict censorship of mails, they managed to maintain contact with Arafat and Abu Jihad and other PLO leaders. The paper offers proof of this story with a photograph of a letter from Abu Jihad to Ta'mari at Ansar in which two thousand dollars was enclosed for "expenses."

Following the interview, Ta'mari closeted himself for a number of weeks with a writer from the Jordanian publishing house Dar el-Jalil, which specializes in books by Israeli authors or books about Israel. Together they produced two hundred fifty pages of information about Ansar. The book appeared soon after.

From Amman Ta'mari left for Europe and the United States for political missions on behalf of the PLO. His first stop was Oslo, where the Norwegian League for Human Rights had organized a conference for the benefit of the Palestinians. Ta'mari addressed the conference, which was attended, for the most part, by representatives of pro-Palestinian organizations in Europe. He spoke of the "great moral achievements of Ansar," emphasizing the "crimes of the Israeli government during the war in Lebanon." But he also spoke about "Israelis who helped me during my most difficult hours," and the humane attitudes of individuals such as Colonel Rosenfeld and the Israeli doctors.

In Washington, he was accompanied by Dina, and the couple granted an interview to the Egyptian correspondent of *Aakhir Sa'ah*, who reported, among other things: "Dina Abd el-Hamid and her husband, who has just returned from prison in Israel, are in Washington as guests of the annual conference of the National Association of American Arabs. They intend to begin collecting funds through the organization and others friendly to the Palestinians in the United States for the purpose of establishing, in Washington, a museum to be known as 'The Ansar Museum.' "

Ta'mari had first thought of the idea while still in Ansar. The museum would be only one part of a larger "Palestinian Heritage Museum." Establishing it in the capital of the United States would serve, he believed, two purposes: it would spread the word of the "heroic struggle of the Palestinians" among the large Palestinian diaspora in the States, as well as among the American public at large. In that way it would also reach the eyes and ears of the Jews and Israelis among them. Ta'mari was well aware of the sharp criticism being hurled against Israel in the wake of the war in Lebanon, even by its supporters. This was the wave he would ride.

While still in Ansar he had requested everyone to try and preserve everything connected with the camp—documents, bulletins, handicrafts— and in Algeria he had collected as much as he could from the former prisoners. Photographs of some of the artwork done in the camp had been taken by a London photographer. Ta'mari had other pictures from Ansar, given to him as a gift by Colonel Shatz, who had documented life at Ansar with his own camera. Finally, some prisoners had purchased cameras from Israelis at the camp and used them until their film ran out.

The museum has not as yet come into existence, and not because of any lack of enthusiasm or activity on its behalf. According to Ta'mari and Dina, they still lack sufficient funds for the completion of the project. Furthermore, and this may be the more relevant obstacle, they have not yet received all necessary authorization from the Americans. A pro-PLO Palestinian museum in Washington may not yet be on the State Department's list of priorities.

Ta'mari's activities in the United States at the time were conducted in line with the PLO's newly emerging positions: an Arafat-Hussein dialogue joined to rapprochement between the PLO and Egypt was designed to produce a PLO more palatable to the Americans. This was now the PLO's tactical and political aim. After the war in Lebanon, the leadership had come to the conclusion that only the United States had the necessary power to force Israel into making significant concessions—significant for the PLO, that is. As a result, the PLO had to change its image in the eyes of the Americans.

The United States mass media, in Ta'mari's view, was controlled entirely by Israel and the American Jewish public. As a result, "my views and those of my comrades were never given a fair hearing. All information about the Middle East dispensed to the American public comes in an Israeli wrapping. We want the Americans to know what is really happening in the occupied territories, what it is we want there and what we really represent."

Ta'mari likes to use Israeli models when planning for the Palestinians and he doesn't even bother to disguise his sources. He dreams of a strong Palestinian lobby on Capitol Hill (like AIPAC, the American-Israel Public Affairs Committee), and the mobilization of the Palestinian diaspora in the States. He meets with congressmen who support the Palestinian cause and with the heads of the Palestinian community there.

Ta'mari's attitude toward the United States, however, is not simple. As far as he is concerned, America is the source of all evil. Nonetheless, without influencing public opinion there, no progress can be made for a solution to the Palestinian problem.

"In order to preserve their own interests," he says, "Americans use Arab money and Jewish blood. True, they pay Israel a couple of billion dollars every year. But that's still cheaper than what it would cost them to send their own armed forces to the Middle East. Israel does their dirty work for

211

them. In exchange, Israel gets paid from money that the Americans get from the rich Arab countries. They buy oil, even from Libya, and make billions in gigantic development projects and industrial complexes in the rich but backward Arab countries."

America's unqualified support of Israel, according to Ta'mari, "is embarrassing to their friends. That's why countries which are even more anticommunist than the Americans, like Saudi Arabia, find it difficult to defend American policy."

His complex attitude toward America bothered him later when he was mentioned as a candidate for the joint Jordanian-Palestinian delegation in proposed talks with the American administration.

From Washington Ta'mari was to return to Amman. The PLO leadership was continuing its dialogue with Hussein, a dialogue that had begun while Ta'mari was still in prison.

Dina returned to her home in Cairo.

She had frequently invited us to visit with her there. From the very first we had often spoken of the possibility of meeting—all four of us—at another time, in another place, away from all the pressures of work and politics, when Salah would no longer be a prisoner and we, even if only by extension, no longer his captors.

About six months after the prisoner exchange, Dina again invited us to visit her in Cairo. Ta'mari, still in Washington, called and promised that on his way back to Amman he would stop off in Cairo to say hello. By the time Amalia and I left for the Egyptian capital, we already knew that Salah would not be able to make it this time. Dina had called to apologize for him.

Her chauffeur, Fawzi, picked us up at the hotel and took us to the house in the Mo'adi quarter. We knew this well-heeled section of town from our stay in Cairo as members of the Israeli embassy. What we hadn't paid attention to before was the name of the street, which now impressed us doubly: Princess Dina Street.

The door was opened by a handsome Nubian servant, wearing a gold-embroidered silk *galabiyyeh* and the traditional white tarbush. "Welcome," he greeted us. "Please come in. The house is yours. I am Gaber."

"Hello, Gaber," I answered. I had spoken to him on the phone many times when Dina was not at home. He had never failed to pass my messages on to her with absolute accuracy.

Gaber led us into the spacious living room. You could see that the house had once been grandiose; even now it was still impressive, although you could sense the absence of a permanent mistress. The room was filled with *objets d'art*, antique furniture, Persian rugs, tapestries, and glass cabinets, but it didn't have a lived-in quality. It resembled a museum more than a home. This was the room, I imagined, in which Hussein had asked for Dina's hand almost thirty years ago.

Gaber served us cold drinks and told us that Dina would be down shortly. We had enough time to examine the room. There were lots of photographs on the walls and on the various tables and cabinets, some of them in silver frames decorated with the royal Jordanian coat of arms. There was a picture of Alia as a child shaking hands with President Nasser, another of Faisal II, king of Iraq, who was assassinated in 1958. There were pictures of Dina's grandfather, Sharif Abd el-Aziz, and another forebear, Sharif Hussein of Mecca. There was a picture of Ta'mari, clean-shaven and all dressed up. We almost didn't recognize him.

In the center of the room, on a table, was a representation of the Mosque of al-Aqsa and the Dome of the Rock in Jerusalem, done entirely in ivory and mother-of-pearl. We knew that Dina's father was buried on the Temple Mount in Jerusalem, not far from the grave of Sharif Hussein of Mecca.

Dina finally joined us. She had come down from the second floor in a small wooden elevator, the kind you can still find in the old mansions of Europe. We embraced and kissed and Dina again apologized to us for the fact that Salah couldn't make it. She also apologized for not coming to the airport to meet us. Later, at dinner, which was sumptuous, she apologized that the menu was so sparse. . . .

At this point Amalia couldn't contain herself and said: "Now you sound just like my Jewish mother. . . ."

We spent the weekend in Dina's company and never ran out of conversation. We spoke of her visit in Israel, what she did the whole time Ta'mari was in prison; we spoke of the negotiations for the POW exchange, of the Israeli soldiers who had returned home. But more than anything else, we spoke of Ta'mari—Ta'mari before and Ta'mari after, before his release and after. Despite the fact that he had been out now for more than eight months, Dina had not yet had enough time with him to catch up on everything that had happened to him in Ansar. Things were still moving too fast.

The day after our arrival we were shown around the gardens of the house, which also bore traces of former grandeur and prolonged neglect.

The tennis court was in disrepair, croaking toads inhabited the empty fish pond, and the giant hothouses had been rented out. Dina pointed to a wolfbane and remarked: "You have a plant just like it in your garden."

We returned to the subject of her visit to Israel. "The thing of which I was most afraid," she recalled, "was that the trip would be publicized at the wrong time. Not that I expected to keep it secret forever. I just didn't want it publicized at the wrong time by the wrong people.

"Actually," she added, after some thought, "I don't think I've really digested the trip fully. Someday I'll have to sit down and reconstruct it for myself in writing."

We had lunch in the large dining room on the long dinner table, the three of us looking very small at one end, with crystal chandeliers above, and Gaber standing by to attend to our every wish.

The next day, with Fawzi at the wheel of a Mercedes, Dina took us on a tour of Cairo, during which we revisited places we'd frequented during our year at the Israeli embassy there. We also went to have a look at the house we had lived in, in the Zamalek quarter of the city, on the banks of the Nile. There we had a touching meeting with the old bawwab (gatekeeper), and even Dina was visibly moved.

In the evening we returned to the house in Me'adi and before we left Dina gave us a gigantic box. "It's a gift from me to Reyout," she said.

Inside was the dollhouse that once had belonged to Princess Alia.

On November 20, 1984, on the phone from London, Dina and Ta'mari told us they were on their way to Amman to take part in the meeting of the Palestine National Council, the seventeenth since 1969. The PNC was the PLO "parliament" and this session was crucial for Arafat's leadership: it was taking place in the shadow of the split.

Ta'mari had missed only one PNC meeting since 1969, while he was in Ansar. It took place in Algeria and Dina had taken part as an observer.

On the evening of November 24, the television in our living room was tuned to Jordan. The sessions of the PNC were being broadcast live from the Cultural Palace in Amman. We knew that the PNC conference would be considered legitimate only if more than fifty percent of the 379 members attended. Up to the very last minute, it was not clear to Arafat and his people if, indeed, the necessary 190 members were among the three thousand people in the hall.

The chairman of the meeting, Salim Zanoun, called out the names of the delegates and each rose in turn to confirm his presence. When there was no answer Zanoun would declare: "Absent." Arafat's deputies were busy checking off names and counting. The tension was unbearable.

In the auditorium—and in our living room—more than a hundred names had been called out before we heard the name we were waiting for: Salah Ta'mari.

Somewhere at the back of the jam-packed hall, in one of the last rows, Ta'mari stood up, called out "Present," and sat down. It was the first time we had seen him since he had been in our house. What happened next was a bonus for us: within seconds the entire audience was on its feet in a standing ovation. The chairman took his cue from the audience and departed from protocol: "Welcome, hero of Ansar," and the TV cameras zoomed in on Ta'mari. Then they focused on the front row—on Yassir Arafat, standing next to the official host, King Hussein. Both of them were on their feet applauding.

In the final count, Arafat had more than enough delegates present to make the session legitimate. The five days of the council proved that he had won the day, regardless of the resolutions adopted. Hussein challenged the council to adopt a resolution calling for political cooperation between the PLO and Jordan, based on the principle of "peace in exchange for territory" and the UN resolutions 242 and 338. These resolutions call for Israel's withdrawal from the territories occupied in 1967 while recognizing its right to exist within secure borders.

The PLO did not take up the challenge. Many of the speakers rejected the king's proposal outright. Others, like Farouk Kadoumi, the PLO's "foreign minister," emphasized that the PLO was obliged now—"after losing Beirut and Lebanon, the command posts most vital to the revolution"—to explore all of the political possibilities while continuing the armed struggle.

Ta'mari also spoke at the council. He supported Kadoumi's line but put it in his own words: "The loss of Beirut and southern Lebanon are a terrible blow to the PLO. We have now become like *the wandering Jews.*"

Contacts between the PLO and the government of Jordan continued, however, and led to the Hussein-Arafat agreement, signed in February 1985. Ta'mari spent most of his time in Amman.

It was Dina who informed me that in April 1985 Ta'mari would be in Cairo for a few days. She had succeeded in convincing him to take a few days off to rest. "It'll be an opportunity for you two to meet," she told me.

Two weeks later I was on my way in the bus that went from Tel Aviv to

Cairo daily. I arrived in the evening and called Dina from the bus station in the center of town.

"I'm dead tired," I told her. "Let's meet tomorrow."

When I arrived at the house in Mo'adi the next day, Ta'mari opened the door for me. I almost didn't recognize him. His beard was gone. His forehead was getting wrinkled and his temples were streaked with gray. He had gained weight. His former litheness was gone. He was wearing a black and white striped shirt, tailored gabardine pants, and polished black shoes. We overcame our natural emotion at the meeting with mutual backslapping, and then walked into the garden to talk. It was three years since the Israeli radio correspondent for Arab affairs had interviewed the newly surrendered Palestinian terrorist and patronizingly offered him a cigarette.

Now, in the garden in Cairo, almost without thinking I pulled out a pack of cigarettes and automatically offered him one. And then, suddenly, I remembered.

"Just by chance I've got a pack of Marlboros," I said.

"I've given up smoking," he said to my surprise. "It's been two months already. Here's my substitute." He pulled out a pack of gum. "It's got nicotine in it but not much."

Gaber appeared with a tray of coffee and Ta'mari poured me a cup.

"I have to wait now and see you drink it first," I said, "just to make sure I'm not being poisoned. I knew then exactly what you were afraid of."

Salah smiled but he was soon serious again. "I want you to know," he said, "that before I left I went to Arafat and told him that I was going to see you in Cairo. He gave me his approval and blessing."

"And if he hadn't? . . ."

"Then I wouldn't have come, I guess."

I tried to decipher the message. I understood it to mean that Arafat was interested in continuing the dialogue with Israelis.

"So how've you been?" I asked. It was clear that Dina had purposely left us to ourselves.

He sighed. "I'm like a man in a race. I'm running all the time, trying to reach some finishing line. Then, maybe, I'll be able to return to normal. Meanwhile, I still have to catch my breath."

Then he said, very frankly: "You know, Aharon, I'm restless. I'm a lone wolf. I'm like a shooting star looking for its orbit. I suppose that most of us human beings are really afraid to take our lives in our own hands. There were four occasions when I was sure that my life was coming to an end—in

June 1967, in September 1970, in June 1982, and again the day I left
Ansar."

He had said "the day I left Ansar" and not "the day I came to Ansar." I
understood that after Ansar much of the flavor had gone out of his life. I
was to hear this from him again and again. He was always talking about
Ansar, returning to it, reliving it for himself and for anyone else ready to
listen. At the end of every conversation, he would return to Ansar. Most
"normal" prisoners try to forget their days in prison as soon as possible. For
Salah, Ansar constituted some sort of achievement, a high point in his life,
the beginning and the end of everything.

Ansar symbolized his whole world compressed into microdimensions:
the conflict, the confrontation with the enemy, the unity of the Palestinians, their struggle—and even the possibility of coexistence with the
enemy. From then on, in my opinion, his life would be played out in
the shadow of Ansar. The movement was not particularly receptive to the
Ansar experience. Its lessons, he was told, would be preserved by those
who experienced them. They had no meaning for the PLO as a whole.

Ansar 1982-1983 had been "the best years of his life."

Ta'mari took the gum out of his mouth, rolled it between two fingers,
and then flicked it into the ashtray. I was more relaxed. Despite his elegant
appearance, he was still the old Ta'mari. He took a fresh piece from the
pack and examined it absentmindedly before putting it into his mouth.

Still absorbed in his own thoughts, he surfaced to say: "Somehow, I can't
really get involved in what's happening. I can't play the game according to
someone else's rules. People want me to be one-sided and one-dimensional.
They think that anybody with a certain cause has to take the same position
all the time. But I, at least, like to think of myself as liberal, knowledgeable, and even broad-minded."

He paused a minute and then went on: "In the last analysis, Aharon, I
am left with my own agony. I have the feeling that I don't fit in anywhere. I
fight with everybody. Wherever I've been in the last year, people ask me if
I'm debating or struggling with them. I tell them I don't want to debate. It's
a waste of time. I want to struggle."

I tried to find out from Ta'mari what was going on in the PLO leadership.
He had just been in Tunis and in Amman, in the thick of the negotiations
for a Palestinian-Jordanian delegation which would hold talks with the
Americans.

217

Ta'mari made it clear that, despite his recent pragmatic moves, Arafat had no intention of giving up the military struggle for exclusively political action. And, indeed, Arafat made his intentions public not long after, in the wake of the *Achille Lauro* hijacking in November 1985: the Fatah was still against hijacking but it would continue its military struggle against Israeli military targets in the occupied territories and in Israel proper.

I reminded Ta'mari of the first talk we had when he spoke of "switching channels," when he had come to the conclusion that the armed struggle had reached a dead end.

He purposely ignored the intent of my question and answered instead: "The Arabs have a problem with themselves: their thinking is one-dimensional. If I talk about political struggle, I'm called a traitor and accused of abandoning armed struggle. If I talk about armed struggle, I'm supposed to join the extremists all the way down the line. But the truth is that all forms of struggle have to go on at one and the same time, hand in hand, and there'll always be people who are convinced of the efficacy of violence."

His remarks sounded absurd to me and self-contradictory, and I asked him if he really expected Israel or any other enlightened country to negotiate with them while they continued their murderous assaults on innocent people. "That's the core of the problem," I told him. "Don't you understand that the only way to get started on a political solution is for you to stop using terrorist methods?"

"If it depended only on me," he answered, "I would make life for you in Israel hell on earth—but differently from what you imagine. Not with bombs and fire and death. A different kind of hell that would destroy you from within, as Israelis. I would achieve more that way than with ten armored divisions.

"I would organize an orchestra of ten thousand children who would march up and down the occupied territories, playing on their fifes and drums. They would play every day, all day long, the whole week. They wouldn't do anything else. How would you people react? How would you react to children who have no homes, who have no homeland, who demand the most elementary of their rights by playing their fifes and drums? They would play until you couldn't stand it anymore. Your eardrums would burst and maybe even your hearts would break."

Here it was easy to see the difference between Ta'mari the fighter and

Ta'mari the dreamer. He continued. "Would you be able to stand by and watch Kahane break up a demonstration of children singing and playing? No. You and good people like you wouldn't let him do it. And I met lots of people like you while I was in prison. How long would it take before you were throwing stones at Meir Kahane to stop him? Your people would stop him, not the Palestinians. I would go even further"—and here he was carried away by his enthusiasm—"I would appeal to Palestinians everywhere in the world—in Chicago, New York, Bethlehem, Jerusalem, Algeria, Libya—to go out on the streets at the same time and sing. Everybody would be singing the same song at the same time. The world wouldn't be able to ignore all those millions of people then, would it?"

His impassioned "speech" was not a histrionic performance for my benefit. He was not even trying to persuade me of something. He was a prisoner of his own agony, of his own complicated inner world, of his own particular truth. And it was his truth, regardless of the contradictions.

His voice broke down. "I realize I'm talking to a blank wall. I feel like an artisan without any tools. But just you wait. I'll find a way. One day, these ideas will put on flesh and blood."

With a few pauses for lunch and the occasional cup of coffee, we passed the whole day in conversation. Twilight fell. The ancient palms in the garden moved in the evening breeze. The toads were croaking, and a kind of heavy sadness overcame us.

"While I was over there," he said, meaning in Israel and in Ansar, "I learned a lesson I already knew, that coexistence is absolutely necessary and absolutely inevitable. After everything I saw, I really believe that the Jews have the right to feel secure. You have the right to guard and preserve your great heritage, your culture, your identity, and your children. But no one there was able to convince me about historical rights or biblical rights or God-given rights. Maybe I'm naïve. I believe that we'll achieve coexistence in the future. Maybe in a hundred years, maybe in two hundred years. But from now until that time, the color red will dominate. Why? Because the road to coexistence is long and tragic. It seems to me that we all bear the seeds of tragedy within us.

"Neither pragmatism nor moderation has any relevance," he went on. "I want to return to Bethlehem. Am I an extremist in your eyes because I want to go home? Will I become a moderate if I agree only to go halfway home?"

"The problem isn't your desire to go home," I answered, "but the inhuman methods you employ to get there. And because of your methods, no one is even ready to talk to you about the problem."

He had an answer. "As far as methods go, it's not a question of moderates and extremists. It's a question of the type of challenge and the type of response. You can't demand of extremists to stop what they're doing as long as the extremists on your side do exactly what they please. I have a sneaking suspicion that even if someone in the PLO gets up tomorrow and says that we're stopping the armed struggle, it won't work. Every occupation is by nature violent. There'll always be some kid who will throw a stone—and stone-throwing is a form of armed struggle, of violence. It's also a form of response."

Ta'mari was weighing things in his mind the whole time. He was tortured. He had questions he couldn't answer. I also had questions, no less difficult, which he was hard put to answer. Even at the close of our long conversation, which went on into the night, we were no closer to agreement. There was still a great abyss that separated us.

Our one success, meanwhile, was that we managed to keep from falling into it.

Three months later I was still wondering about him—about his personal crisis, his ideological crisis, his place in the Fatah—when I was given some sort of answer from headlines in the papers.

The PLO had presented a list of candidates to take part in the proposed talks among the Palestinians, Jordan, the United States, and, indirectly, Israel. The Palestinians together with the Jordanians would comprise a joint delegation. Talks were to start with Richard Murphy, assistant secretary of state for the Middle East. The list of names was presented to Hussein by Arafat and then submitted by Jordan to the United States and Israel. It included seven names.

Salah Ta'mari's was one of them.

Shimon Peres, the prime minister of Israel, declared, in July 1985, that the list presented to Israel by the United States was unacceptable: "Israel is prepared to talk only to Palestinians from the territories." In other words, Israel rejected all but two of the seven people—Hanna Siniora and Faiz Abu Rahma, both residents of the occupied territories. The United States followed suit. Hussein was informed that Murphy would refuse to meet with any of the others.

Ta'mari's inclusion in the list did nothing to advance negotiations. On the other hand, it certainly increased the risks to his life. Dissident extremist groups issued a pointed threat: "The Palestinian representatives in the 'surrender delegation' will pay a high price for their treachery." The murder of Fahad Kawassma in Amman not long before was a pledge of their seriousness. Kawassma, the deposed mayor of Hebron, had maintained contact with members of the Israeli peace camp.

My own opinion was that Ta'mari's inclusion in the delegation was a sign that his position in the Fatah was even stronger than before. However, the idea of a joint delegation fell through and Ta'mari disappeared from the headlines.

Toward the end of the summer of 1985, Dina and Ta'mari came to London to meet us. We had started writing this book. They spent long hours and weeks with us, contributing their share to the telling of our common story.

Amalia's Epilogue

A flock of gray and white pigeons fluttered around the black chimney on the roof of the neighboring house. Ta'mari was in the kitchen, washing empty ashtrays. The cigarette butts, matches, and wrappings from nicotine-flavored chewing gum had filled the small garbage can to over-flowing—silent witnesses to the hours of conversation, reconstruction, checking and double-checking of facts, arguments over details, and the amassing of heretofore unrecorded biographical data.

The floor of the kitchen was covered with wall-to-wall carpeting, a bit frayed at the edges. There was a kitchen stool to one side, next to a green telephone. Above the telephone hung a board stuck with reminders and telephone numbers. Ours was there in its place, on a yellowing piece of paper. Dina had sat on that stool when she called Aharon to play him the voices of the Israeli prisoners held by the PLO.

The typical London drizzle outside gave us a feeling of being even warmer inside. The children had eaten McDonald's hamburgers and chocolate and the wrappers were on the sideboard near the sink. It appeared that even Jordanian princelings, and not only Israeli sabras, enjoyed American junk food.

Salah suddenly turned from the sink to Dina. "You forgot to scatter crumbs for the pigeons," he said, teasing her. "I told you they'd move to another house. Look, they're all over there already."

I walked over to Ta'mari and looked out.

"I'm going to make lunch," he said to me. "Now you'll finally see that I know how to cook, not only talk."

"Do you need any help?" I asked, although I already knew the answer.

"I don't need any help," he said defensively.

"Of course not. If you said you did, what would happen to your pride?" I was needling him. "We're *only* in the kitchen, Salah. It's *only* lunch."

"It's not *only* anything," he answered. "It's *everything*, Amalia." Then he added: "You look very pretty today."

"I'm very sad today," I said. He didn't say anything. "And I know that you're sad too. But that's all right. You don't have to admit it."

It was our last day in London. Tomorrow we would be on our way home, back to Israel. He, too, would be on his way. His bags were already packed. So were Dina's, but they were off in different directions.

We had spent almost three weeks together in that house, like castaways on a desert island, completely cut off from the rest of the world. We had had three weeks of coming together and going our separate ways, three weeks of beginnings and endings, of traveling long distances and standing in one place. With the utmost sensitivity to one another, we had tried to reach into long-forgotten and deeply buried periods of the past. But we were always aware that there was a line we couldn't—and shouldn't—cross. None of us wanted to say anything that might topple the complex structure of relations we had so delicately constructed.

We were, after all, enemies, in a very real sense. And yet we were close friends whose antennae were finely attuned to each other's nuances of speech and tone of voice and angle of glance. In those three weeks everything had penetrated deeply into our consciousnesses: Salah's low voice, Dina's maternal warmth, my fear of making faux pas in English, Aharon's interminable checking of the tape to make sure that nothing was lost or erased.

The house had three stories. Thick rugs muffled the sound of footsteps on the stairs, and anyone who went out seemed simply to disappear, just as anyone who came in appeared as if from nowhere. Salah—who did most of the talking—sat the whole time in an easy chair that looked out onto the street. A car with Lebanese plates had been parked nearby one morning. Then it disappeared and after a few days returned. We didn't like the car, but our fears of the first few days, of being secretly trailed or spied on, had vanished. Nonetheless, whenever we went to eat at the Italian restaurant down the street, Salah sat in the corner with his back to the wall.

That last evening we decided to go to the movies. Dina claimed she hadn't seen a good movie for years. We suggested *The Little Drummer Girl*, with Diane Keaton and Klaus Kinsky, which was playing in Leicester Square.

"I'm not interested," declared Salah. "Who can bear to see that garbage? Besides, I've got a great book to read."

The book was Milan Kundera's *The Unbearable Lightness of Being*. I had given it to him.

Dina didn't give up. "Watch me convince him to go," she whispered to Aharon. "Patience."

I suddenly noticed that the pigeons had returned to the kitchen porch. Somebody had taken the trouble to scatter breadcrumbs. I wondered who.

Dina finally convinced Salah to go because he announced that he would go to the movies on one condition: "On the way back I want to play the pinball machines."

"We'll see about that when the time comes," was Dina's rejoinder.

By the time the movie ended it was already dark. The fact that an officer of the Fatah, the former queen of Jordan, and two Israelis had just sat together in row twelve of a London cinema watching a movie about the savage conflict between Israelis and Palestinians was of interest to no one in particular. It was part of another script, of a movie not yet filmed. We went into Swiss Centre for coffee. It was the only café still open.

Salah ordered a hamburger and malted milk. His vegetarian days from Ansar were over. "This time, too," he said, angry and disappointed, "the Palestinian was depicted as an insufferable and despicable lout. I should have known that it wouldn't be any different."

"Your friend John le Carré," I put in, "wasn't particularly flattering to the Israelis either."

"Maybe," he answered. "But here too it's only the Palestinian who is capable of blowing up people by remote control and then, two minutes later, getting into bed with a woman. Only the Palestinian."

It was too late to play the machines when we left and we walked in the dark to the car. Our impending separation hung over us and Dina and I walked in silence. Salah and Aharon were close behind. I could hear Salah saying: "Tell me, Aharon, why am I doing this? Why am I walking with you like this in the middle of the street, in the middle of the night, perhaps endangering my entire future?"

His voice was complaisant and soft. He was asking a question that concerned him very deeply, that disturbed him, that seemed to be crucial to his self-understanding.

He answered his own question, in his own way. Maybe because it was our last evening together. Maybe because he thought there might not be another opportunity. Maybe because it was dark and the darkness made it easier to say things that were hard to say in the light of day.

"I'll tell you what I'm doing here. What you're doing here. What we're all doing here. We are creating a fringe, a small but sane fringe. In the history of all national conflicts there were fringes like this—except in ours. Each of us does his best to demonize the other, to depict the other as more obstinate, baser, more dangerous.

"So meanwhile," he went on, his hands deep in his pockets, "we're here by ourselves, but I'm sure that others will eventually join us, dozens and then hundreds. When the children of those you killed and the children of those we killed all grow up and run the world, everything will be different. I know my ideas are unsuited to these times, that we just don't fit in. Believe me, these are the lousiest times in history."

Back in Israel we began to "readjust." A few days after we arrived, three Israelis were killed by the Fatah in cold blood on the deck of a yacht anchored in Larnaca. Two days later, Israeli planes bombed terrorist bases in Tunis. Salah was on his way to Tunis at the time to meet his brother-in-law and cousin, Nur Ali. Salah missed his plane. Nur Ali, the deputy head of operations in the PLO and an officer in the Fatah, was killed.

In September 1985, Israel's Knesset passed an amendment to the law on terror, forbidding Israelis from meeting with members of the PLO. The penalty for violating the law is three years in prison.

Reyout and Or began the school year at a new kindergarten. On the first day, the teacher asked the children to draw a picture for a friend. Or asked us to help him write something at the top of the drawing.

"What should we write?" we asked him.

"Write: 'Shalom, Hussein. When are *you* coming to our new kindergarten?' "